W9-BLL-976

ABIGAIL E. WEEKS MEMORIAL LIBRARY
UNION COLLEGE
BARBOURVILLE, KENTUCKY

THE HEART TO ARTEMIS

Other Works by Bryher

BRYHER

THE
HEART
TO
ARTEMIS

A Writer's Memoirs

A Helen and Kurt Wolff Book
Harcourt, Brace & World, Inc., New York

ABIGAIL E. WEEKS MEMORIAL LIBRARY
UNION COLLEGE
BARBOURVILLE, KENTUCKY

823.91
B916

To the memory of my master, Stéphane Mallarmé

© 1962 by Norman Holmes Pearson
All rights reserved. No part of this book may be
reproduced in any form or by any mechanical means,
including mimeograph and tape recorder, without
permission in writing from the publisher.
first edition
Library of Congress Catalog Card Number: 62-13519
Printed in the United States of America

THE HEART TO ARTEMIS

 *One*

When I was born in September, 1894, Dorothy Richardson's Miriam was a secretary. Mallarmé had just retired and was no longer teaching English to French schoolboys. The death duties that were to obliterate most of our feudal estates had been introduced in that year's budget while the *Fram* was drifting through the polar ice and would-be explorers dreamed about Bokhara, a fabulous city that was then more difficult of access than Tibet. I opened my eyes upon the end of not only the nineteenth century but of a second Puritan age. An epoch passed away while I was learning to speak and walk. Its influence remains as the start of memory and as a measuring rod for progress that even Edwardian survivors lack.

There were no motorcars, no taxis and no aeroplanes. The garden flowers were different; speech followed a more complex and leisurely pattern, the houses were usually cold. The real background to these formative years, however, was the sound of hooves; the metallic thunder of the big animals drawing the carriages called landaus, the lighter trip-trop of the hansom cabs. On land, apart from a few trains, horses comprised the whole of transportation. I only realized how largely they formed a part of my earliest consciousness when I woke up in Lahore over fifty years later to listen to the passing tongas and wonder why the clatter seemed so familiar and comforting in that otherwise strange land? It took me some minutes to discover that it was because I was back in the world of the horse.

I was born at Margate, in Kent, but we returned to London when I was three months old and I have never been back to that town. On my father's side, I was of mixed Yorkshire and German descent. The earliest ancestor that I have been able to trace was a Johann Jürgen Ellermann, an ex-dragoon who married a Maria Dorothea Kelzen in 1726 and settled down at Hitzacker in Lower Saxony. They were Lutherans. According to a family tradition, they possessed a mill on an island in the Elbe and after it was swept away in a flood, a generation later, they went first to Hamburg and afterwards to Hull. Why they chose the lesser adventure of England instead of the greater one of America has always been a puzzle to me. My grandfather grew up in the north and became a corn merchant. He was appointed German consul at Hull and married a Yorkshire girl, Anne Elizabeth Reeves. There were three children, first two daughters, Ida Annie, born in 1856, and Emily Mary, born in 1858, and then a son, my father John Reeves, who was born at Brough, near Hull, on May 15, 1862.

I have often wondered if my father was teased about his parents at school because he would never speak of Germany and I only heard about these ancestors after I had grown up. Being a historian, I then wanted to trace them but the political events in Germany in the early nineteen thirties stopped my research. It was not until this autobiography was begun that I reached Hitzacker the summer of 1960 and my discovery of the ruins of the old mill that my ancestors had left more than a century before belongs to a later chapter of these memoirs. I knew nothing about the Elbe when I was young. Perhaps my love of water and flat landscapes is some proof, however, of the influence of heredity? I often heard my mother say in a puzzled voice, "Why does the child always want to go to the marshes and never to the Downs?" I know that I thought rushes growing in a slowly moving stream were the most beautiful sight in the world and sometimes, to please me, my father would draw such landscapes on a piece of paper with a bird, perhaps, rising from the reeds.

On my mother's side I was Middle English, not actually from Warwickshire but not so far, I like to think, from Shakespeare's Stratford. She had the most beautiful skin that I have ever seen, the forget-me-not blue eyes of the Angles, their same feeling for plants and mistrust of everything that did not come out of the earth. She did not like the sea but she loved the wind. I suspect that she must have had a Celt among her ancestors but cannot confirm this as a fact. She was full of temperament together with a sense of art that, in her case, was translated into love. So my inheritance was the north with the strands of plowing and the sea inextricably mingled. It never occurred to me until I was fifteen that I could be anything but a sailor and I have always been glad to feel the merchant tradition rooted in me and the slow, stubborn blood of the Lowland nations.

It is fitting that my first memory should be a historical one. On the evening of June 22, 1897, my parents took me out to the steps in front of our house and lifted me up to see the illuminations. I had never known night except from a window. The sky surprised me, it seemed so large. Lights flashed, I was not sure if they were candles or stars. It was the Diamond Jubilee of Queen Victoria and I was two years and nine months old. The lamps were gold, the night was black and it was so long past my usual bedtime that I was convinced that I had suddenly grown up.

I have only confused memories otherwise of the London of the period. Horse-drawn omnibuses rattled down wide, gray streets. Occasionally the jingling stopped suddenly because straw had been spread across the road and then we knew that somebody in an adjacent house was ill. The gas was lighted solemnly every evening and there were no bathrooms. Water was heated in the kitchen and carried upstairs in mahogany-colored cans. I remember the smell of soapy flannel when Ruth, the nursemaid, washed my face while I sat in a brown enamel tub in front of a big fire. It was very wicked to splash. Everything was large and solid, the chairs, like houses, were never to be moved and there was seldom enough crawling space between the heavy table legs and an immense chest of drawers.

I was told that in babyhood a fox terrier shared my pram and that I learned to walk when left alone on a rug in the garden near a bed of ripe strawberries. These incidents remain legends. I cannot remember them although a faint picture remains of pride in tottering round a room on short, fat legs without holding on to the chairs. I do remember my favorite toy, a clockwork elephant that my father had brought back from some journey and that walked with a buzz and stiff, tiny steps right across the carpet.

Clothes were a nightmare. I wore a thick vest, a bodice, woolen

5

knickers, one flannel and one white petticoat, long black stockings, high black button boots and a serge dress. Over this, I had a white pinafore indoors and when I went out a triangular piece of cloth round my neck to keep the air from my throat, I had a large hat, sometimes with a feather on it, it either blew off or the elastic cut into my chin, a heavy coat, gloves, and sometimes a muff. It was the customary attire of all little girls of that period, many even wore a third petticoat, and except that the materials were thinner, the same in summer as in winter. Is it surprising that after wearing such polar equipment continuously I shudder when I think of that time? I never went bareheaded or barefooted and could not run without heavy garments whipping about my knees. No wonder that the Victorians worshiped Nature! How mysterious the elements must have seemed to them when they had never felt sun or rain except through heavy layers of tweed. As for my hair! It was strained back into a pigtail that caught in bushes or fell forward into the ink; worse still, it was done up in rags called "bobs" every evening and brushed round a hoop stick in the morning to make it curl which it never did. Somehow at least one tight hair always got caught in those bobs; besides they stuck into one's neck or tickled one's ears. To this day I feel intense pity for any child I see with long hair, and no single act in my life ever gave me greater pleasure than having my hair cut short in 1920.

My first recollection of summer is of watching my mother walk across the balcony with a shiny, green watering can in her hands, sprinkling the then so fashionable red geraniums in our window boxes. The wet leaves and the black loam had an acrid scent that was slightly tinged with dust but quite free from petrol fumes. Perhaps this watering was a rare event or I recall it so vividly because I have always responded to warmth but shrivel into a hibernating dormouse in the cold.

There were trips to the Zoo with its frightening revolving gate. "Keep your hands still or you will get your fingers pinched." Sometimes the ticket collector nodded; then I entered proudly on my father's shoulder. None of the animals frightened me but the afternoons were short and how could I choose between waiting in front of the gay, noisy monkeys whom I was said to resemble or trotting to the pond where a hippo rolled and snorted in the water without its keeper ever saying "don't splash"?

There was also drama. I was often lifted over the railing in the elephant house to stand in the narrow passage opposite the cages. It was almost my teatime one visit when the keeper arrived with a round of crisp, brown biscuits. My father took the first one and handed it to the biggest elephant there. How wonderful it was to see the trunk find, then grasp and lift the morsel to an almost invisible mouth! Its feet alone were halfway to my shoulders; a tassel tip of tail swung to and fro. The second, mother elephant got her portion, we came to the baby at the end of the line. There was a single biscuit left in my father's hand. I watched, hoping that he would give it to me. I could have borne being asked to share but to lose all was unendurable. I could not have been more than three because I did not know how to protest. I had no words. All I could do was to yell loudly and violently, to my parents' surprise. They called it overexcitement, I know now that it was jealousy. I supposed that my father preferred the baby elephant to myself.

I am certain that children experience human passions with uninhibited force. The only difference is that, unlike adults, they bend to the storm and do not reason with it. A residue remains to influence their subsequent development but the tempest dies down rapidly and it is this quality of *apparent* forgetfulness that has led generations to deny that their charges could be subject to mature emotions. They are; only like myself on that occasion, they cannot explain, they lack the vocabulary.

The Zoo, of course, was an exceptional treat but every morning I was taken for a walk in Kensington Gardens. (We lived somewhere in Bayswater but I have been unable to trace the road.) Why did Ruth have to bustle in, ordering me to put my toys away just as I had upset the button bag, a favorite plaything, or arranged my animals in rows? "Try to be good like the little prince," she would say, buttoning up my coat, "he never fidgets." Still, as we crossed the big road into the park she would tell me stories about the Queen's cream ponies or about her own (was it Hampshire?) village. How old was she? Eighteen perhaps and still a little homesick. "When the hay was cut," she would begin if I were particularly restless, "all of us children climbed on top of the last wagon, you have no idea how slippery it was."

"And you had how many horses?" I would ask faithfully because this was my favorite tale.

"Two and they pulled us right up to the big barn."

"And there was a table inside . . ."

"With pies on it and cakes and loaves of bread and tea and we ate until there wasn't a crumb left on the board."

I had seen such barns when we were in the country and I could imagine the pies; unlike most children I liked meat better than candy, and loaves with a broad, brown base and a softer bit on top that reminded me of a farmer's wife with a flapping apron. It was near and natural, part of a village life that could have changed but little since Elizabethan times, with the years divided by seasons and ruled by crops. I have wondered since how much my wish to feel the reality of the past was originally wakened by these simple but ancient stories.

I remember surprisingly little about the park itself. I had already decided that it was not amusing to be virtuous, one must not shout, one must not play with fire or water, above all, one must never "answer back." The trees and green chairs were not to be fingered as I passed them but there was one place where I could dig, half secretly, and make mud pies. I was shaping a lump of earth one morning and wishing that it was good to eat when Ruth snatched me by the hand and rushed me to the edge of the road. An old lady in black was driving past us in a carriage. Was she coming from Kensington or had she been to look at the Memorial? "Wave to the Queen," Ruth said excitedly, "wave, look, she is smiling at you." I did not wave, I did not smile, according to Ruth I sulked. How much more important a mud pie seemed at that moment than a royal coach that was not even drawn by the cream ponies! All the same it was an incident that I never forgot.

A short time afterwards my father bought a small house in Worthing, so of that early London no impressions remain other than the geranium-scented afternoons, an elephant's cake, the first view of night, the last glimpse of a Queen.

Worthing in 1898 was a sleepy little town where many of the roads still ended in meadows. I imagine that my family chose the place because it was near enough to London for my father to join us every weekend. He came down on Friday from a mysterious place where he must never be disturbed called "the office" and took the first train back on the Monday morning. We were a small household by Victorian standards so that mercifully I was often left alone to play by myself. Ruth helped in the house, my mother made most of my clothes. The garden was tiny but there was much to explore in it, I could run my fingers along the "frizzly moss" at the top of a low wall, we had a fox terrier called Vick. These were the years that turned me into a thinker before the pressures of an ignorant society planted in me this or the other fear. It has seemed to me since that I have never again been so completely a whole. I knew what I wanted, I judged people clearly. I was not afraid.

We used to pick primroses in Goring Woods and blackberries along the neighboring hedges. "Long stalks, remember," and "Don't squash" were among the first orders to echo in my ears. The word "common" as applied to grazing has always fascinated me yet I fear that this may be due to its association with the long oval of Broadwater Green that was then famous for a sweetshop where they sold black and white peppermint humbugs, the only candy that I liked.

We drove on hot summer days to the foot of the Downs and then climbed on foot up a narrow path to Chanctonbury Ring. My father looked for mushrooms and my mother once found a round, polished stone that we thought was a bullet but I suspect now was a sling stone. The way back led through a village where each garden was a plot of fragrance. The quality of the plants may be better today but our midsummers are no longer scented; June then was clove pinks, July mignonette. Erect we miss them less but at crawling time what substitute is there for their graces? The nearer that we are to the earth the more its odors mean to us, it is not only the spring sap of the primroses that comes back to me but leather reins and seaweed as well as the hotter smell of cut grass.

A child's first books, if they stir the imagination, may alter its life. Perhaps the sea air stimulated development but on the day that I was three years and nine months old I was given a copy of *The Swiss Family Robinson* because "in three months you will be four, darling," and from that moment I became conscious of the world.

I could not yet read the book myself but Ruth had no peace, she had to go over it again and again, it was the essence of truth to me. Yes, this was the quality that set it apart, mine had been a puzzling landscape until Pastor Robinson arrived. The mental capacity of children is always underrated, I wanted facts, not fables; how were bridges built, what was a raft, why did a porcupine have quills? There was no television in 1898 and very slight difference between my nursery and the one where Madame de Montolieu retold Wyss's story to an invalid grandson in that Elba summer of 1814. The narrative of the shipwrecked family became part of the common experience of childhood. I imagined that I saw flamingoes when Ruth took me along the marshes for a treat, trefoil that I gathered in the meadows turned into "potato flowers," one day I might have a dog like Turk. There were many scoldings because I was always turning the big Victorian workbasket upside down to serve as Mrs. Robinson's bag. What could the red, withered scales of sorrel be other than coffee or the empty chestnut husks than coconuts? Perhaps I was born with a longing for adventure instead of a heart? I have never wanted to remain anywhere permanently, no matter how beautiful the landscape. My roots go deep but their ground is the English tradition and not a particular earth. It may also be the influence of that Kentish sea whose sound I heard before I knew its name.

My joy in the book was so intense that I wanted to keep it forever. In case it was lost I desired to be able "to make it up" again. How were words printed and who put pages between covers? I could not yet write the alphabet but I could imagine stories even if these were not original but about myself in the guise of Ernest or Jack. Fritz was too old and too perfect. "When I grow up," I insisted to everybody, "I am going to be a sailor."

I was sitting under the scrapbook-red cloth of the nursery table one winter morning, pretending that it was Rock Castle and that I need not hear Ruth if she called me. It was warmer than rowing on an upturned chair—the tub-boat—towards the cupboard that was land because the wind was whistling under the windowpanes, and the garden was white with sleet. The door opened, the draft blew the tablecloth over my face, "Where is she?" it was my father's voice, "Put her coat on as quickly as you can, there's a wreck."

A wreck! Just as in the book! So, in spite of the grownups, "But it's just a story, darling," adventures were true. They did not have to call me twice, I pushed my arms correctly into the right sleeves, they buttoned up my raincoat collar. I gasped as we got outside, the hurricane had made a funnel of the street and in spite of holding tightly to my father's hand, it almost knocked me down. My mackintosh hood had a strange, rubbery smell, our neighbors passed us as they hurried up the road and I was soon so breathless that I wished that I were back under the nursery table long before we reached the front.

Half Worthing was already standing along the beach. It was strewn with gold. Oranges rolled across the pebbles, the breakers tossed them up like ingots or floated them ashore in a surge of weed and spars. Women joined hands, their bonnets tied firmly under their chins, to try to reach a breakwater where the fruit piled up in heaps. Several of them had baskets, a boy ran past us with his cap full to the brim and driftwood under his arm. More oranges bobbed in on the crest of waves exactly like escaped balloons. Water broke over us and flooded the gardens. "The salt will kill the shrubs," a man bellowed and I wondered why. My great delight was to be taken out to sea in summer on my father's shoulder, he was a noted swimmer, and they had always told me that the salt would do me good.

"Look! Over there! Look!" Men in cork jackets and high rubber boots were trying to launch the lifeboat. They shoved, the sides stuck to the shingle, men joined them and heaved. The crew pushed and sprang, they were riding the waves like a picture in another of my books, then they seemed to disappear in the trough of the waves. "Portuguese." I caught the murmur around us, it was, my father explained to me, a country south of England. We stared into the distance but there was no sign of the ship, strangers spoke to each other (this was most surprising in Victorian England), it got very cold. I did not grumble when the time came to go home. I knew now what wreckage looked like and what a storm could do to the girders of a pier. They told me afterwards that the Portuguese sailors had been picked up by a coaster but I immediately suspected that this was said to reassure me.

A short time ago I went through Worthing on my way to see friends living in the neighborhood. I had not been back for over fifty years. I found the Queen's Road, but a small block of flats had been built on the site of the house where we had lived and the garden where I had played. There were fewer changes otherwise than I expected. The driver of the car was a Worthing man and, by one of those extraordinary coincidences, remembered being taken as far as the beach when a toddler to see the wreckage and pick up oranges. It was the color against the violence of the sea, I imagine, that made such an impression upon us children; perhaps it was also our first experience of the forces of nature threatening our limited but familiar world.

The first time that we revisited London I was lifted into the train and put on a cushion in the corner where my short legs only just reached the rim of the seat. There were big flat buttons in the upholstery; naturally I tried to pull them out and was scolded for being fidgety. It was October so I must have been just over four years old. We rambled slowly through a landscape of bare bramble hedges and smoky blue sky that has always seemed to me part of the essence of England. Sometimes a big cart horse, in those days they were usually called Dobbin, ceased grazing, shook a shaggy mane and looked up at us. We stopped eventually at a junction in front of two big posters. There was a bottle of spilt ink on one of them and an old man on the other, he seemed to be a chimney sweep, holding out a cake of Pear's soap. "We are just halfway," my mother said encouragingly, lifting me back into my place. The train began to move, seemed to hesitate. At that moment I became conscious of *time*. Why, I thought, the instant just past has gone. I breathed, that particular breath would never recur again. I tried breathing more and more quickly. It did not help. I could not keep pace with time. I knew that I was alive but that I would die (though this was simply a word to me) and that merely sitting still used up moments and moments of life. I was not afraid but immensely interested. Dr. Sachs, the psychoanalyst, said later that it was early to have had such an experience but people are usually more concerned with "how" a child ought to develop than with "when" and few of us are allowed to be natural. We are all born with a rhythm of our own, it may be slow but nothing is ever more dangerous than to interfere with it.

We stayed in London with a friend of my mother. She was an elderly Devonshire lady with cheeks like wild roses and white hair under a lace cap. Her house was so old that it seemed to have lost interest in people. It was less ghostly than aloof as though too many thoughts had fretted themselves to nothingness against its high walls. The curtains, the furniture and the banisters that ran the length of the narrow staircase seemed an identical mahogany brown. Sometimes we could not see across the road for fog. It was somewhere in Bayswater, then a fashionable part of London, but I cannot recall the name of the street nor can I remember our mornings there, though we must have gone often to the park, in memory we seem to have lived in a perpetual afternoon. My father had gone away on some mysterious journey but my mother was happy to be in London again among people she knew. She was isolated at Worthing where we had few acquaintances. It was far less easy in Edwardian times to make new ties than it is now. People lived on reefs of their own making, even if they reached them by bus or carriage rather than by ship, and barely knew their neighbors' names. It was the same with all social groups. Our cook was stricter than my family about making new friends.

The old lady spent most of the day sitting in an immense armchair. Her daughter was a widow with nine children of her own; most of them were grown-up but Gerald, the youngest boy, was not much older than myself. She liked to tell me stories and I loved listening to them if they were about Gerald who went alone to school, had laces in his boots instead of buttons and a clanging iron hoop. I was just as pleased if they were about the family collie, Roy. Only too often, however, as I was settling myself on my hassock, I heard the, to me, grim words, "Once upon a time." I felt that I was being tricked when people told me fairy stories. I wanted to know how many planks were needed to build a boat in precise numbers and not general terms. I certainly did not want to hear about fabulous beans. My father had explained to me how fast and far a man could walk so why expect me to believe in "seven-league boots"? The outside world was such an exciting place that what I craved for was information about the things that I could touch and smell and see. Once I had my facts, I could make up my own stories and I think that has been the way with me all my life. I had to sit politely and listen, however, whether I liked what I heard or not. I knew only too well what happened if children were rude. They were smacked and sent to bed.

Most children are realists. A Victorian hobby was the making of scrapbooks and a few months later Ruth was cutting up some pieces of red material to make a cover for an album. "Here," she said, handing me some cloth and meaning to be kind, "take this and pretend you are Red Riding Hood." I flung the stuff on the ground, stamped on it and kicked her. "I want to be myself," I screamed, my vocabulary as usual being unequal to my feelings. It was not egotism; it was simply that I felt perhaps more than most the wonder of the world and dreaded having it taken from me.

One autumn day my father returned. He brought me an Indian standing on a small piece of scented wood with *Quebec* on its base. A few days later we returned to Worthing, our own garden and the sea.

I was just five when I was given a new and exciting picture book. Unfortunately I then had a disagreement with Ruth that ended again in my kicking her. Retribution was swift, "After being so naughty, nobody will read to you." I decided not to howl but took my present with me to a favorite hassock in the shelter of the drawing-room sofa. I opened the book at the picture of two girls and a small boy sitting round a tea table in a garden. There were a dog and cat in front of them and verses about them on the opposite page. I had had some alphabet blocks with the usual symbols of "A is for Apple" and "Z is for Zebra" but I had never learned to put syllables together. Full of fury, I sat and struggled. Dog and tea were easy but there were some longer words that were baffling and difficult. "What can she be up to?" I heard, "She is so very quiet." It was such a wet afternoon that for a wonder I had not been dragged out for a walk. Teatime came, I wasn't even hungry, "Come along, darling, whatever are you doing?"

"I am reading my book," I replied proudly.

There were the usual incredulous smiles so I read the poem out to them, slowly, stammering a little over one or two long words but without making any mistakes. I can still hear my mother's astonished words, "She has taught herself to read."

Alas, we are so concerned with morals when it comes to children that we fail to recognize how much motive power there is behind anger and stubbornness. Few remember that to learn to read and write is one of the great victories in life. I would never allow anyone to read to me again but I devoured every scrap of print that I could find from my father's novels to the timetable. It did not matter to me what it was so long as it was a book although I always rejected fairy tales, "They are not true." The Victorian age denied us so much that I wanted reality, not magic. I soon acquired an immense speed, reading like my father not in words but paragraphs. It gave Authority a weapon over me because from that moment onwards a favorite punishment was the threat, "Your books will be taken away from you," but I cannot be grateful enough that they never attempted to censor what I read and one way or another I collected quite a library.

I am inclined to think now that much of the best writing of late Victorian times went into children's literature. It is a myth to suppose that the nineteenth-century child felt particularly secure, the stories were mostly in the Zola tradition and stressed suffering, poverty and the evils of drink. I had one extraordinary volume largely taken up with an account of a small boy's struggles not to compete with his drunken father in emptying tankards of porter. A Bible teacher saved him, of course. There were also grim accounts of disaster through a father's death leaving the family without funds when dogs and possessions had to be sold and the children scattered as "poor relations" among harsh and unforgiving aunts. Such a fate was usually ascribed to the indulgence of the parents. They had given the family a pony or a trip to the seaside instead of saving every penny against a possible "rainy day." The cloud that seemed to hang over all of us in a far more sinister way than any horror of giants or dragons has been brilliantly described by Dorothy Richardson in the opening pages of *Pointed Roofs*. Her account of the disruption of a family through the father's failure in business differs only by the maturity of its writing from one of the major themes of our childhood fiction. It was essentially religious in character; what we had today might be gone tomorrow. I was never afraid of animals or the dark but I always began to tremble when I heard that trade was bad.

Virtue might be rewarded on the final page but it was a point of honor to endure countless tribulations first. Fortunately it was the righteous who died. The sinners were left to go on battling against temptation. Death was presented factually and boldly, my mother protested mildly when Ruth gave me *Little Dot, or the Grave-digger's Daughter* one Christmas but I read it all the same. It was a remarkable tale. The heroine gathered daisies to strew on graves and taught her boy playfellow to pray. One character after the other was carried to the churchyard until "after a cruel winter" Dot, herself, died and only the old gravedigger was left to scatter the appropriate daisies on her tomb. Whenever I hear now of conferences to determine the vocabulary to be used in books for children and of the care taken not to upset their delicate imaginations, I can understand why they prefer their horror comics to literature. Our age treated us properly. The world was a harsh place and the sooner we learned the difference between good and evil the better. Ludicrous as some of the stories were, they spoke of realities and this was healthy.

There were gay stories like *Bunchy, or When I Was a Little Girl* by lost, anonymous authors who recorded their own simple experiences. I read a lot of bad poetry in an *Empire Reader* that I enjoyed without understanding what it was all about. I supposed Barbara Frietchie for example to be an English heroine. *Chatterbox* followed a little later. The tale I liked best was about a boy and girl escaping from a house during the French Revolution. Years afterwards, I discovered that it was by G. A. Henty. It must have been the first story by him to fall into my hands.

We had our problem novelist, Mrs. Molesworth, the Virginia Woolf of the nursery. She wrote on envy, jealousy and hatred as well as of the things that we wanted but she also understood our fundamental problems, the difficulty of obeying arbitrary rules or of making father, mother, teacher or nurse comprehend why we were frightened or why we wanted things when our words were few in number and abstractions were shadows. She dominated also because of her style. If she wrote of bread and jam, you saw it on the table and were hungry or you looked up at the familiar nursery walls after a smacking and knew that the heroine's feelings on a similar occasion were your own.

I could scarcely have been six when my father gave me *Peter Simple* to read. Why Captain Marryat should ever have been considered nursery fare I cannot imagine but his stern and often bitter tales were on most of the children's bookshelves of the period. I have a copy of *Jacob Faithful* given me by my mother on July 20, 1901, when I was six. The first chapter contains the starkest description of two deaths through drunkenness that I have read anywhere during my adult life. I have never forgotten Peter's struggles with his sea chest on joining his ship nor Jack raking over the shingle to find a piece of rope to sell but otherwise Marryat really was "too old" for me. It was excellent, however, to have so realistic a basis for one's literary beginnings; how innocuous Zola and the *Plague Pamphlets* seemed afterwards.

Happy and epic as my childhood was, I wonder that I recall so clearly the gray of that Victorian world. Yet in one of my earliest conscious moments I wondered if adventure had died just before I was born. It may have been the landladies who alarmed me, those yellow-faced women who let rooms to us for holidays. So often there was no husband, "He went off, ma'am, and left me with four children," or he was ill, "No, he's never been the same since he took cold on his lungs," and there were glimpses of babies in shawls in the basement to confirm Ruth's stories. Most of the infants she had known seemed to have died. Was it the stiff dresses that little girls wore or the burden of my own long curls? I know that I was convinced that if I wanted to be happy when I grew up I had to become a cabin boy and run away from the inexplicable taboos of Victorian life. We were ruled by gods that were neither Athene, Poseidon nor the Nine Muses but thou shalt sit down to lunch every day at the same hour, thou shalt not go out without gloves.

It has become fashionable recently to extol the nineteenth century with its quaint and charming womanliness. Nothing proves so completely the loss of an entire generation in the First World War. It was not an album of family portraits of people living in security and ease. Up to the eighties children were imprisoned for a variety of minor offenses, the educational methods were usually barbarous, unmarried women without incomes were treated like slaves. Those of us who were born even at the end of the period do not idealize it. How could we ever wish to see such conditions return?

The Easter of being five, spring got into my blood and I started running away. Contrary to what most psychologists believe I never wanted security but always longed to be "on my own." We were spending the holidays at Bognor and I was playing in the garden. Suddenly I knew that neither toys nor tenderness could make up for not having the chance that I wanted with my whole mind and strength. I had to explore the world myself. I felt that I should suffocate if I stayed any longer on a quiet lawn. I flung down my playthings and darted out of the gate.

I ran along the sea wall, feeling alone and free. I wanted to linger near some drying nets but it was dangerous to stop too close to the house. If I could reach the little steamer, a quarter of a mile away, I could scramble aboard and hide; they could not send me home again once we were afloat and there would be no more voices saying, "Don't worry your head about such things. You are too young, darling, to understand."

It was late afternoon before I was recaptured by two old fishermen who talked to me while Authority stole up in the rear. I was not smacked but the return after such a taste of freedom was a humiliating disappointment. It was torture to be cooped up inside a house. I ran away twice more in as many weeks and something died in me every time that I was brought home. I had to obey and bolt whenever the call came; it was like falling in love without its timidities and hesitations, yet I knew then as I know now that I was not running away from fear but rushing towards life, full of an almost mature desire for experience and danger.

There were two glorious hours when I got as dirty as I wanted, paddling along the edge of the sea. I almost spoke to a group of small, noisy boys who were pelting each other with seaweed but decided correctly that I should not know how to play their games. I watched them and looked for pebbles, the blue ones with white markings that were like marbles and glistened when they were wet. Alas, on that occasion hunger drove me home. Ruth was in charge and calmer than my mother would have been, she had decided that I would return at teatime and contented herself by watching for me from the window.

Some scientists think that truancy is a survival of migration. It may well be so, I have always loved change. It was also the age. There was no outlet for energy, particularly for girls although I was luckier actually than the next generation. Nobody then had thought up child care! The nursery routine was casual. Ruth spent most of the morning dusting or making beds while my mother was busy shopping. There were no telephones and no vacuum cleaners. I played by myself most of the time and ate exactly the same meals as my parents; because they enjoyed their food and there were no taboos I had the digestion of an ostrich. I was happy at home apart from the law that is still a basic part of adult theory. I suffered until I was twenty from well-meaning but conscious efforts to retard my development; intelligent children, they said, had to be "kept back." Why? It cost me years of difficulty afterwards to repair what need never have happened. If a prisoner is left in a windowless dungeon, he loses the power of sight. Exactly the same thing happened to my brain. Growing up was a denuding of the intellect, it was not progression. I can forgive now some of the educational mistakes that were made (it is difficult to train a child), but not the social customs that deprived me of the rich development that might have been my portion. People have said that I am erudite; this is not true if I am matched against specialists but whatever I know I have learned the hard way, alone. At least the isolation preserved me from influences; the important thing is clarity, the ability "to flow" and sometimes to adjust. Yet how much natural intelligence is wasted, generation after generation, because of the imposition of blindly traditional laws?

Eventually my father found a temporary cure. If I would promise not to cry if a ball hit me "and they can sting" he would take me with him to watch the local football matches. This was a challenge that I accepted joyfully and to this day there is a special magic about Saturday afternoons. It was usually too cold to sit on the stands so I trotted up and down beside my father, stamped my feet as he did to keep warm, and under his instruction soon mastered the finer points of the game. How exciting it was! Of course I would not cry, boys never cried, but it was a deliciously frightening moment when the enormous ball hurtled towards us. Once my father caught it and flung it back to the players. It was a proletarian introduction to sport because I watched our butcher's boy toss an orange-striped sweater to my father to hang over a bench, I joined in the applause when the milkman's son kicked a goal. I never saw a first-class match but once. My father thought them too mechanical, he liked the small-town atmosphere of our local team, perhaps it reminded him of his own schoolboy games?

Nobody then had heard of football pools. It was just a friendly, probably not very skillful, game. According to my mother it was brutal but I loved the speed, the shifting patterns and the shouts. No matter how cold it was I pleaded to stay till the last moment. Then if I had been good during the week we went to a shop and I was allowed to choose a book.

My father had retained a boyish streak of gaiety and gave me a paper-bound copy of *Jack Harkaway's Schooldays,* the nearest that I ever came, I suppose, to a penny dreadful. I found it extremely valuable, it taught me to balance a jug of water on top of the door if Ruth had been particularly trying and to stuff my drawers with a towel for the smacking that was bound to follow. I am afraid that in infancy I linked most colorful events with my father. It was only later that I realized how much I had in me of my mother's temperament. It was she who first took me for a motor ride and who said after her first flight when she was well over seventy, "Oh, how easy this is! I should like to fly around the world." As a child, however, I completely disappointed her. She could have been a famous dressmaker and I think she would have enjoyed having such an establishment but her whole life was devoted to my father. She embroidered beautifully and was noted for her skill in dressing dolls, copying old pictures in minute detail, and then giving the group to a charity sale to benefit some hospital. I would only play with animals, hated clothes and was the roughest urchin of our neighborhood. The ideal Victorian child was a frail creature whereas I was as tough as a hippopotamus and as mischievous as an ape. The first time that I was taken to a toyshop to pick out what I wanted, I chose a book and a toy sword. Eventually my mother surrendered and gave me a wonderful fort with both a drawbridge and a secret passage. The only disadvantage was that to use the passage I had to turn the fort upside down. I am not ashamed that I was so belligerent when young. It is better to be a leader of lead soldiers than to repress the wish and explode into something far more dangerous aged twenty. How much more peaceful the world might be if there were fewer checks upon development imposed in childhood! I do not mean license, there must be discipline but to save ourselves trouble we do not let children work through the various stages of development at their own time and there is too much imposition of socially acceptable ideas upon a growing mind.

I have no clear memory of the arrival of a new century but plenty of the Boer War. My parents were not pacifists but both disliked war and would not have it discussed in my presence. All this only increased my curiosity and I built up a distorted picture of South Africa from posters, newspaper headlines and words overheard by chance. What did I imagine war was like? I supposed that soldiers slept in tents, got as dirty as they liked, yelled and shot their rifles. Every penny that I could collect went on a toy army and "caps," bright pink rounds of paper that banged when fired from an inch-high cannon. My mother told me in vain about children who had blown off their finger tips or singed their eyelids; she even appealed to my affections to spare her nerves. I should normally have listened to her but the glory of the noise, the smell of burnt paper, were too exciting to be relinquished.

I added new words like veldt and kopje (only I did not know how to pronounce them) to my vocabulary. I watched the local volunteers leave, not in scarlet but in khaki, for Southampton. Then on a winter morning I noticed that the greengrocer's wife was crying as she weighed the potatoes. I stood there level with a sliding bin of lemons, other people came into the shop and they too wiped their eyes with their handkerchiefs. Something sinister and most mysterious had happened. "Her son has been killed," my mother explained as we walked away, "he was shot through the head." In spite of my books I still had no real consciousness of death. Oh, I tried to explain, it was a story that had ended the wrong way but perhaps it could be rewritten? "No," my mother shook her head, it was something that none of us could change, the boy was buried in Africa. In a shadowy way for which I had no words I supposed that there would be no time if one were dead.

The seasons passed. I remember chiefly the food, roast beef with a light Yorkshire pudding that was dipped in real gravy, hot toast spread with dripping in front of the nursery fire on a winter day, farmhouse butter and tiny farthing buns. I preferred bacon to chocolate and loved suet puddings. There was little fruit and in general few vegetables although, due to my father's French upbringing, some were served at home. I remember being given a tomato as a special treat one birthday, they were extremely rare. Alas, the excellence of English traditional dishes disappeared with the First World War. The mass production of crops is economically necessary but they will never have the flavor of different varieties grown to suit particular soils. Unless I was reading or out of doors, I rocked on a steed with a red saddle and reins that for once was in the shape of a donkey, not a horse. It stood in front of a tall, folding bed that shut up during the day and could be let down at night. I often wondered what would happen if it closed up silently while the occupant was asleep. There were the sea and the stories that I made up about myself as a Robinson explorer and between them that shadowy world of "must and must not" so unlike the graces of the gods.

These were the years when my father was probably at the top of his powers. He had many interests but he had taken to shipping "like a duck to water" as somebody once wrote of him and he was still in the North Atlantic trade. The problems must have been tremendous and yet every weekend he took me for walks along the sea front and towards its (for a five-year-old) so distant pier while he taught me the countries of Europe and their capitals. He loved traveling as much as I do now myself. Years later I saw his application for a passport. In answer to a question "Do you often travel abroad?" he had replied "As much as possible, it broadens the intelligence."

At dusk between tea and bedtime I arranged the animals two by two across the carpet and into my wooden Noah's Ark while my mother or father, no matter how busy they might be, told me stories. There was a sad one about a sentinel at Pompeii. He had watched the lava coming towards him but he had never left his post. Yes, my mother had seen Vesuvius and the picture of a dog much bigger than Vick, made in tiny stones on a pavement at the entrance to a house. An avalanche had carried my father away in the Alps, he had been almost suffocated by the soft, tumbling snow. Sometimes he went to places called America and Canada or he showed me sketches that he had made of landscapes during his visit to India. Such things rather than nursery rhymes were the folk tales of my infancy and a time was coming, perhaps quite soon, that would be the mythical first day of "going abroad." I had only to learn to sit still in a train, to be more obedient and to say some French words. I stuck two lions on the ladder leading to the ark and wondered.

All my life I have suffered from "geographical emotions." Places are almost as real to me as people. At eight o'clock one May evening my mother's voice woke me up. "We are going to the Paris Exhibition tomorrow if you are good." It was 1900 and I was five years and eight months old.

The hour on the ship, my first, blurs into other voyages. There were to be so many of those hot summer crossings in my childhood. I expect that I took my father's hand and followed him to watch the baggage being lowered into the hold. Everything was heavy or where possible solid and I have wondered since whether it was the constant shifting of such tremendous weights that first gave men the courage to build skyscrapers. Certainly a historian could reconstruct the age from its luggage. Trunks had hooped lids bound with straps and buckles. Square hatboxes were new. I seem to remember that they were considered a little "fast." Light cases must have been synonymous with a lack of morals because nothing less ponderous than pigskin studded with brass nails was ever carried.

There were always oilskins thrown over a line of deck chairs and apprehensive faces under wide, uncomfortable hats. "So long as you close your eyes, my dear, the motion is hardly perceptible," we would hear while I watched the seamen enviously because the thing that I wanted most was a boy's sailor suit. "I go below and lie on my back until the stewardess tells me we are inside the harbor." Such phrases were as much a part of the trip as the heavily fringed rugs and bright yellow bags.

22

At Dieppe the train surprised me, the steps were so high. It was hard to climb them, even with the guard pulling at my arms. To my astonishment, quite big boys raced along the platform in blue blouses and socks. I had been promoted to long tan stockings for the journey, only babies in England had their legs uncovered. Fisherwomen held up baskets of fish or, shouting against the wind that refrilled their white bonnets, offered us dolls dressed in bright banded petticoats and wooden sabots exactly like themselves.

The white pattern of the seat covers is so early a recollection that I seem always to have known it. They were very clean in contrast to the dusty floor but rough to the hands. I remember that the compartment was full with three people on each side and that I made a tremendous effort to be still and not ask too often, "Shall we soon be in Paris?" All the same, it was an eternity, those four hours.

Discipline might be suspended in private but in public I was supposed to be seen and not heard. I might not run about, there was no question of nibbling a biscuit between meals. Thus in a train I had nothing to do but look out of the window, read or make up stories.

My children's paper that day was full of animals dressed as boys. Jacko, the monkey, with a scarf flying out from his neck, was pelting an elephant with snowballs. I stared at the drawings hoping that I might get into the world on the other side of the pictures because then the danger of my "worrying about the time" would be over but that afternoon I was too excited for any magic to work. I could not say that I had been to Paris until I had set foot in the city and I was afraid that if I were disobedient, my parents would turn round and take me home.

At five I knew nothing of history. I had seen people shake their heads and whisper the word "Dreyfus" but I did not know what that name meant nor that fifty thousand English had marched in protest to Hyde Park. I had heard others say, however, that they would not venture to the Exhibition on account of the hostile feelings of the French about the Boer War.

My first impression of Paris is of walking down a street from the station and seeing Americans wearing tiny flags in their buttonholes lest they be mistaken for the English and molested. In my then frame of mind I was hopeful for a fight. I remember perfectly well that I clenched my fists, shouted the words of a patriotic song of the moment that I must have learned from my nurse and waited eagerly for a Frenchman to reply. It never occurred to me that I could not knock him down. I was plump and small, of less than average height, so it must have been an incredibly comic spectacle but pride and a magical belief that being English I was certain to win blinded me to reality. I neither thought of leaving an attack to my father nor that my truculent behavior might bring retribution upon my parents.

Aggression is a part of nature and a special need of childhood, it was the hours of inactivity that made me clench my fists, and how much of history is not due to such simple psychological reactions? We have the knowledge now to understand but how often do we use it?

Curiously enough, I could have played more easily with French than with English children. My father had been partly brought up at Caen in Normandy and I think that this must have been the happiest time of his life. Certainly my training at home was more French in character than English. Wherever my father went, he took me with him. If he discussed politics with elderly gentlemen whose black beards came to the bottom of their waistcoats, it was not only expected that I should listen but I was occasionally allowed to express an opinion, naturally echoed from my father's views. My political education began in Paris because we lunched most days at a restaurant near the Madeleine that was popular with ministers. I soon discovered that government was an exciting game, it resembled the animals in my picture book defending their snow fort. There was a party working for the good of the country; everything that they suggested was right. Then there was a second, possibly secret group that was plotting to come to power and if this happened it would be, almost certainly, the end of the world.

I listened greedily. France was a republic. I was not quite sure what this meant but I knew that England was a kingdom because it was ruled by a Queen, an old lady in black for whose sake I had been snatched from my mud pies. Anybody might govern France, the boy riding his bicycle or (as I thought then!) the woman selling balloons. The royalist system was safer, my father explained. Safer! Then I knew that I was a republican. Liberty, equality, fraternity, to be free, equal and friendly, these were the signs of adventure and being a boy whereas to be royalist was to be old, careful and as prudent as a governess. "I believe in the Republic," I announced and the old gentlemen (I wonder now which ministers they were) patted my head.

The entrance and the symbol of the Exhibition was an immense arch. It was the magnified twin of a hair ornament of the period, a two-pronged comb over which the convolvulus of many decorations ramped in flowery dots. Everything at that time had to curl; there ought to be some special term to describe the horror a blank space evoked in 1900. I have often wondered how English lawns survived. It must have hurt their owners to see them bare of hillocks and curves; the formal borders of yellow calceolarias, blue lobelias and the pink geraniums that were beginning to be considered more discreet than their scarlet fellows were a riot of geometry gone mad.

There was a long wait before we could buy our tickets, then we walked through the archway into an avenue lined with white pavilions. My first impression was of gravel. It was deceptively like sand and seemed to be endless. We turned into a building (was it to the right of the entrance?), it contained Krupp's exhibit of long, burnished guns.

My mother hurried me out. My father explained that it was wrong to spend money and labor upon tools of war. I ought to record my own dismay but nothing in the Exhibition interested me so much. I wanted to touch the shining barrels of the cannon, it was, at that age, the normal reaction of any child towards the models, say, in a science museum and little different from my feelings about the toys in the next gallery that we visited. This contained a "set piece," a corner of the Champs Élysées arranged with dolls dressed in the costumes of the day. A soldier flirted with a nurse, she was very lively in her wide skirt with bright, flowing ribbons, a little girl was running after a hoop (I decided critically that she was grasping her stick in the wrong manner), and small boys, again in short socks, were playing an unfamiliar game. How odd! Just look at the soldier's red trousers! All the English knew that khaki was better than scarlet because it blurred into the landscape. And that baby in front of them, howling wildly, with tears streaming down its face! Were the tears paint, I asked, but my mother shook her head and explained that they were made from some transparent type of glue. The pebbles, the park bench and the trees were familiar enough but remembering Kensington Gardens and that I had been in London as well as Paris, I felt secretly superior to the woman beside me, holding a long skirt up in her left hand. I hoped that she

25

ABIGAIL E. WEEKS MEMORIAL LIBRARY
UNION COLLEGE
BARBOURVILLE, KENTUCKY

did not think that I liked toys. I really had no desire to play with the figures but only to know how they were made.

In room after room, gilded ropes kept the crowds from pressing too closely against the furniture; the walls were hung with tapestries, there were curtains as stiff and solid as marble. Every object was carved and suitable in size only for a giant or else a dwarf. Mermaids slipped out of mother-of-pearl water lilies to clasp with breakable fingers the handles of tall vases. The legs of a small table were distorted into strange shapes while the interior of a great glass cabinet became a shell of glittering surfaces, enamel, garnet, coral or amber that reproduced in miniature insects and orchids, reptiles, parroquets, or the strangest of aquatic plants.

There is really no link between 1900 and the present day. It was an incredibly restricted time. An invitation to tea was a sacred obligation; in the rare event that a bill could not be paid directly to the shopkeeper in cash, a check was immediately sent to him with a precisely worded letter on hand-woven paper. It was easier to alter the laws of the land than to miss a dinner party to which an invitation had been accepted. The decree that conventionality was itself godliness left no room for vision. Many of the ordinary sensations of atmosphere were unknown because the air had to reach us through mufflers and veils. It was not fashion but the taboo against exposure of the skin. Our symbol of freedom was Nature, we were the last descendants of Rousseau (though we were unable to read his books) and as movement was difficult because even a man's clothes hampered his agility, we tried to become a unity with the landscape. Some of the people about me literally lived on views. The storm and the savage became emblems of mystery with walks and drives through the countryside the only permissible form of self-expression. No wonder that so many masochistic heroines of the period as an ultimate in self-torture took to their beds.

So perhaps the age, as it felt itself dying, flowered into this immense jungle of tiny and useless possessions? Surely modern art was born at the Paris Exhibition? After walking all day between jeweled thimble cases and Fragonard pictures reproduced on bead bags so tiny that they could not even hold a handkerchief, thousands of people must have longed for blank walls and straight lines.

My self-confidence, however, was not to last the day. It was late in the afternoon before we started back to our hotel. A monster darted out of one of the still unfinished passages of the Exhibition, a huge white face with great, vermilion lips bent as if to bite me, two white tentacles dotted with scarlet pompons moved to pick me up. I do not think that I had seen a clown before. In utmost terror, I opened my mouth and howled.

Even a clown could not spoil my pleasure in the moving railway but I had a second fright inside the picture gallery. I ran in unsuspectingly to face a large and realistic painting of the Crucifixion. It was not a bit like the illustrations in my Sunday book, *The Peep of Day,* but a mass of blood, contortion and terror. How could a child of five possibly understand such matters? So I began to cry if I were taken into the pavilions. How did I know what other mysterious doom might be waiting inside? Besides it was dull, the showcases were high above my head. We soon arrived in best English fashion at a compromise. My parents hired a wheeled chair pushed by a bearded, elderly Frenchman. Of course I did not sit in it, I was far too active but I explored every inch of the grounds in his charge while my parents examined acres of furniture.

He spoke no English but I found out somehow that he had a family. I loved trying to talk to him. My father had begun to teach me French before we had crossed the Channel and I read my little red lesson book for pleasure. At first I had to learn so many words daily, then my father promised me a new English book for every French story that I read and narrated correctly to him afterwards. I was seven before I managed a whole book by myself. It was the inevitable *Malheurs de Sophie.* A second language was one of the richest gifts that my father ever gave me. Think of the wealth in my head! Apart from Mallarmé, I have always preferred the freedom of English poetry but French fiction is more mature. I owe my first steps in psychology to it; it sharpened my reasoning powers. Oddly enough, it had also a moral value. After I left home in 1920 when the task of my generation was to break the unhealthy taboos of the nineteenth century, I seldom made the mistake of repeating them by plunging into their opposites. There was always Flaubert at my elbow and later Stendhal to remind me to look at the meaning behind the act rather than at the deed itself. I thought and dreamed in French for a large portion of my childhood but it was, alas, before the days of phonetics and as the rules of pronunciation were never properly explained to me, my accent remains Churchillian, my inflections incurably British, to this day.

We used to drive through the Bois on those May afternoons, usually in an open victoria. The traffic was bewildering, it seemed faster than in London and, for me, on the wrong side of the road; I do not remember seeing any motorcars although on a later visit the first taxi that I noticed was French. Its driver sat in a goatskin coat high above the engine and aroused much admiration.

There were no patient horses pulling huge water carts like the ones we saw at home, men watered the streets instead with hoses. The problem of dust was a real one; it rose in clouds unless the roads were damp because this was long before the days of tar. I supposed the Tour Eiffel to be a giant roundabout somehow connected with the Exhibition.

I liked these drives, there were Arab horsemen to watch with long cloaks falling over their beautiful horses. The nurses looked gay with colored ribbons that would have made such excellent kite streamers, floating from their white caps. They held their charges firmly by the hand. Most of the little girls wore fawn or pale blue coats; this surprised me because colors were frowned upon in England, we were dressed in white or navy blue. The always more fortunate boys built castles in a gravel pit. "It's dangerous, darling, you might catch something if you played there." The hooves flashed, the wheels turned so swiftly along the avenues that I wondered how we could ever cross to the other side and the scenes reappeared, years afterwards, in the drawings of Toulouse-Lautrec.

Who knows? Could I have seen a writer who was to teach me so much about my craft walking along the Bois with her little black bulldog? If so, I should have noticed only Toby Chien. 1900 saw the publication of Colette's first book, and I wish that I could say that I remembered her because the two writers of the generation that preceded me who most truthfully expressed the atmosphere of my childhood were Colette and Dorothy Richardson, one from each side of the Channel. I caught, I think, the last influences of their age. Like them, I have always been passionately interested in concrete things, in "what is" rather than in metaphysical speculation. (In this, the wheel has turned again as we approach Robbe-Grillet and his school.) Each period has its own characteristics and what I feared and hated in the nineteenth century were its irrational conventions. Alas, as I have written elsewhere, to be sensitive to an environment as an artist has to be is also a disadvantage. The future generation, busy with its own conflicts, will live on our victories and be contemptuous of our defeats. People speak of a present commercialization of sex; this is true but shallow. Sex is not dominant as it was in the Victorian age when it was repressed so completely that unconsciously every act, every code of manners, was colored by it. Colette will be read for her style, Dorothy Richardson for her share in the evolution of the novel but a few years after we who survive are dead, who will recognize their courage and their honesty? Both were true revolutionaries, fighting not for dogmas of any color but for the elementary rights of an inarticulate body of women who were treated like slaves until the end of the First World War.

Colette was twenty-seven in 1900, I was five. Almost fifty years later I wrote to explain what her books had meant to me, less as a writer than a historian. She replied; I am told that this was rare in her old age and through Adrienne Monnier we were to have met, but before this could happen she died. Perhaps it was as well. Knowing her command of language, I should have been shy face to face with her, speaking my British-sounding French.

I have recognized moments of my foreign childhood since in several books. There are exterior scenes from *Si le grain ne meurt* that are as evocative as old photographs although I was mercifully spared Gide's scruples. One Paris, however, would have seemed completely strange to me. The Champs Élysées of Marcel Proust was near in time but so remote from my experience that the place belonged (as it did) to a totally different city.

I have had the same feeling when reading the contemporary English memoirs that have recently appeared. Many of them describe a world of great estates, retainers and traditions of which I never even heard when I was a child. We belonged to the solid, Protestant "middle" and we stuck to its training. There was no loosening of any customs for us when King Edward came to the throne. Our household was less extravagant than thrifty and the emphasis was on character rather than caste. I once saw a socialist report upon my father. It listed his business activities but then added, "There is no sign that he has ever tried to use wealth or power for his personal advantage."

My first visit to France blurs into a second that we made the following summer. There were giant hoardings where the plaster buildings had been and a general air of indifference and dust. On one eventful afternoon, however, we were resting upstairs in the hotel on a particularly hot afternoon. I had been given a copy of a child's version of *Robinson Crusoe* to keep me quiet. It was such a disappointment after the excitement of the title that I threw it down in anger. The hero had scruples about going to sea! He was not a child but had the tiresome views of any grownup about danger and a most uninteresting desert island. There were none of Pastor Robinson's lovely explanations about how to grow fruit trees and evaporate salt, no tame ostrich and no dog like Turk. My personal experience with a parrot had also been unfortunate. One had taken the trouble to push its beak through the cage and nip me although, and this was what had hurt me most, I had been careful not to tease it. Alas, I had no other book so I went to the window to watch the passers-by.

The square was always crowded. How could so many horses get into it at the same time? Big drays full of barrels blocked the impatient carriages. A boy dodged between them with one of those long unfamiliar sticks of bread under his arm, the round stiff bowlers of the men shone in the heat, occasionally a woman crossed the road, in a hat as wide as a door, holding up a handful of skirt. What a dull world it was, nothing ever happened, oh, when should I be able to be a cabin boy and climb up a mast?

Suddenly in the middle of this so ordinary afternoon, people began to run. They came in dozens from the side streets, carriages stopped, men cheered. It was the first time that I had heard the collective roar of a crowd. Immediately opposite but so far away that I could not see his features distinctly, an old man came to the front of a balcony. My father rushed into the room, "Kruger is speaking," he said and we lined up in front of the long window.

I supposed that these people had come to take him prisoner but as soon as he held up his hand the square was silent. He began to speak, they started to applaud.

I was extremely puzzled. Kruger was our enemy. In spite of my family's refusal to speak of the Boer War in front of me, I was intensely curious about the struggle. (Is nationalism a phase of immaturity? If so, a child has time to develop but it is a long and dangerous process when it comes to countries.) Suppose I left the room unperceived and reached the hall, could I escape before the concierge stopped me? If I were able to wriggle through the crowds I would seize him myself. I did not stop to think of the problems involved in taking Kruger across a friendly land to Dover but I did feel that in gratitude England should make me a sailor.

We looked down upon a mass of heads. I decided regretfully that I should have no chance of crossing the square in time and opened my mouth to yell derisive remarks in English. At that moment Kruger finished his speech, he left the balcony and the square rocked with cheers. "Why is he free?" I said, "Where are the soldiers?" At six it was so difficult to understand that France and South Africa were not at war.

I should have been even more astonished had I known that Kruger would live at Clarens for several years, half a mile away from where I was to spend most of my life and where his house is now a museum.

Other things were equally strange. A day or two later I saw a line of young men with colored cockades marching down the street between two lines of soldiers. Even to my eyes they looked unhappy. "It's the conscripts," people said, the term was new to me and I asked its meaning. "If you were a French boy, you would have to go into the army whether you liked it or not," my father explained, to my indignation. If you forced a man to be a soldier it took away the freedom of choice that was the crown of being grown-up and why did they put *Liberté* on the inscriptions if it meant nothing? Truly my elders were peculiar!

It was only on my third visit, when I was seven, that I came to know the Champs Élysées possessively and with the full rights of any Parisian child.

It happened on a gloomy day. I had spent the morning looking at dull pictures in the Louvre. I was also very hungry because I could not eat French food. Perhaps a far-off ancestor had been an Eskimo? Perhaps there was something lacking in my constitution? I was able to bear the hottest sun but an east wind made me seasick and I was a continual source of embarrassment to my mother because if people offered me chocolates I refused them scornfully but it was unsafe to leave a bottle of olive or even cod-liver oil within my reach. I disliked sauces and unfamiliar flavors. I wanted bacon for breakfast and roast beef for lunch. I longed for my nursery tea of bread and butter spread with golden syrup. I hated brioches and French pastry. Yes, the Café Voisin where we often used to eat was wasted on me, I was utterly and vociferously English in my tastes. My parents had ordered a carriage that particular afternoon, it meant another two hours of sitting still. At that moment, my German governess interceded for me, could she not take me to the Champs Élysées for a treat? Paris was not London and, to my surprise, my family agreed. Half an hour later I was sharing the reputed French freedom from convention. I was sitting in the coachman's seat of a small goat cart and *I was driving it myself.*

We were halfway along the path that ran parallel with the road when a carriage stopped at the curb and I heard my name. Oh well, I had not really expected anything so wonderful to last but my parents waved, told me to enjoy myself and drove on. What was a sin in England (because you might catch measles, darling) was not wicked in Paris. I smiled when I heard phrases later about "Continental morality." I knew all about the double standard, had I not experienced it myself, aged seven?

Now for the first time I saw Paris from my own level of vision. Leaves had fallen on the paths, I took off my gloves to hold the reins more firmly and was not ordered to put them on again. The figures that looked at the cart admiringly were both my own age and size. The trip ended when we reached some crossroads. We sat down on a bench in front of a Punch and Judy show instead of going back. The excited children about me whispered or shouted but I was still unable to understand all the French words and it was too much like being told not to fidget in a carriage. "It's not real," I complained, suspicious of the puppets and their sometimes visible strings. I had no use for make-believe, mine was an active world. Wisely, my governess led me away but the painted box, Dog Toby in his frilled collar and the man who came out in his shirt sleeves and walked up and down the lines holding out a cap marked one end of my new geographical chart. The other was a stall among the trees. Its owner was cooking what appeared to be pancakes on a miniature stove. A boy stood in front of him with half a one in his mouth, other children played ball or ran up and down, pretending to be trains. "They are called *galettes*," my governess explained. I supposed that the word was part of a lesson but as she had been so kind to me I would learn it to please her. We did not move, there was another whisk of batter into the pan and a moment later I was handed two of them on a plate.

I did not know what to do. Nobody had ever given me anything to eat in the open air before. My governess smiled encouragingly. I bit the *galette* excitedly, it was hot, papery, and flavored with some mild spice. It was not an English bun but this was freedom and I would teach myself to like them. All the same, I wondered whatever could have happened. The universe seemed to have turned completely upside down.

The climax of that day was yet to come. There was a roundabout beyond another line of trees. An old woman in a striped skirt sat on a throne on one side of it and as the painted horses passed her by, black, brown or chestnut with white spots, she slid rings down a metal bar for their riders to catch.

The horses stopped, the ring emptied. I was lifted onto a saddle, my steed had a bunch of feathers fastened above its head, and bright, painted reins. They gave me a stick with a hook that was doubly satisfying because it resembled the iron hoop that I had never been allowed to own. I could hold on to the pole that kept the animals in position but I was too big, was I not, to be strapped? The woman walked round collecting dues, was it ten, was it twenty centimes? The machinery and the music started together, slowly at first, then faster and faster while we leaned forward to snatch our rings and our sticks jingled with their sliding circles. A baby cried, it had a belt on too, oh, how I despised it! I was a warrior, astride a horse at last, I lunged ferociously, the rings got tighter because there was some mechanism whereby they were looser for the younger children but tighter for us, until as we came to an unexpected stop I had tied with a bigger boy as the winner. Solemnly we were offered sticks of pink, white and orange candy done up in frilled paper. A remnant of English nursery training persisted and I was about to shake my head when my governess reminded me to say, *"Merci, Madame."* In a daze of surprise I followed her towards the Tuileries sucking the first lollipop of my life, earned as well in open combat. No wonder that after such an afternoon to be in France seemed more "grown-up" than living in England. The Champs Élysées was admirable for my seven-year-old mind. It is interesting to recall that I was introduced to it by a German.

I cannot remember that anybody laughed at me, asked me if I were not too tiny to sit at so large a table or whether I would not rather be at home playing with toys in all my visits to France. Such incidents were far too common in Sussex where there was a much sharper division between the drawing room and the nursery. A French family traveled together as a matter of course and my father having been educated there, I am sure that he thought of me as another smaller adult. Waiters and chambermaids treated me, in common with other French children, as a responsible member of society. It was understood that I would not run about a restaurant, upset sauces or shout and because this was taken for granted, I behaved reasonably and quietly throughout the leisurely meals. Later on, I had not the courage to force a younger generation to repeat the training but for myself I am grateful. It spared me much of the exterior worries of growing up. I was not afraid of dining out because I was used to it.

The Champs Élysées belonged to 1902. My first trip in 1900 ended at the station among a crowd of men in blue blouses and leather belts whom I had already learned to call *facteurs* and not porters. Much in my later life was to depend upon this experience. Now I was initiate, the sea was my birthright but Paris had given me some knowledge of the "Continent." Destiny was to lead me in a different direction and to another country but it was in France that I first learned to be a European.

One bitterly cold January evening people began to talk above my head in whispers. I was always curious, the wreck had proved to me that it was not only in stories that disasters happened and I listened cautiously while pretending to play. Suddenly Ruth came into the drawing room with her bonnet perched upon her thick, coiled hair, my outdoor clothes over her arm and her special "we have no time for nonsense" expression on her face. She bundled me into my coat and gaiters and I followed her into the road where the lamplighter had already lit a row of gas lamps. We never went out at dusk when it was about to be bedtime and I was puzzled. What was the crowd doing round the little post office in the next street? Ruth picked me up and pushed her way towards a handwritten notice stuck up in the window. "There is no change in the Queen's condition," somebody said and a woman began to sob. It must have been about the hour of the Queen's actual death but communications were slow in those days and I doubt if many in Worthing heard the news that night. What would happen if the Queen died, I wanted to know, as we walked slowly home? Ruth said everybody would be very sad.

"Look, Miggy," my father said at breakfast the next morning, holding up a newspaper with a big black border, "you won't often see this again however long you live." Miggy, shortened from Midget, was his usual name for me. I stared at the impressive headlines and wondered what was to follow. It was frightening and exciting at the same time. Ruth, of course, talked about Queen Victoria's funeral for days. She told me how the horses had had to be unharnessed and sailors set instead to draw the hearse, with many "mark my words, the world is going to change," though it seemed to be going on exactly as it had before. I had still never seen a motorcar nor heard a telephone. There were always women walking up and down a green patch near us after they had been to the shops; it was believed that the grass absorbed the dust from the hems of their trailing skirts. Apart from the new reign a general topic of conversation was about the quarantine newly imposed upon dogs brought in from abroad. How I hated a government that could separate a family from its pets and such a prejudice acquired in childhood seldom disappears.

I was frightened of one thing only, it was measles. If I wanted to sit on a breakwater, shout at another child or buy a penny ball at the corner shop where they sold sweets and toys it was always forbidden "because you might catch something, darling." It was both a mysterious plague and a punishment for enjoying one's self; it meant imprisonment in an extremely dull bed, worse still, "if you get a rash your books would have to be burned." I was a short, round puppylike creature of inexhaustible energy, I do not remember feeling tired once during childhood and to be put into my cot even half an hour sooner than usual seemed unendurable. Yet here was an irrational plague able to strike at will the humble and the mighty, no sacrifices placated it, its origin was unknown.

"Please may she come and play with me?" A small head was poked through the privet hedge one summer day but diplomatically the figure addressed my parents. I looked up, it must be the little girl from next door, a family had taken the house for the summer. There was a whispered consultation, instead of the intruder being told to leave, I was taken into the house, put into a clean pinafore and then, to my intense surprise, left with the stranger.

Everything seemed upside down with the reversal of the customary rules but thanks to my books, the standard code of play was reasonably familiar. I could not understand all that my companion said (she used a lot of slang that she had picked up from her brothers) but I found out that her name was Sylvia, and that though she was two months younger, both of us were six. Why hadn't I spoken to her earlier? She had been making faces at me for a week.

There were others in her family but they were all older. One brother was ten. He was very rough. Did I know what it was like to have my arm twisted? She didn't howl but she knew I would. Indignantly I demanded an immediate trial but there was no brother about. It was the first time that I had been alone in an unfamiliar house and I looked curiously about me, the nursery was littered with stamps and tools as well as toys. It seemed curious to talk to someone of my own size but I was readily adaptable. Sylvia knew much more than I did about the things of the world but she could not say her alphabet. I asked her at once to show me her books but they were babyish things, full of pictures, of a type that I had outgrown before I was five.

We played together for about two months, usually rather roughly. Ruth complained, of course, that Sylvia wrecked my manners and in an ecstasy of joy I watched my mother scold her when she dipped a finger into the treacle jar and then licked it. Once she shouted "Beast," this was very daring, at our cook. Our worst escapade was dropping my white muslin dresses into a tub of water just as they had come back, nicely starched, from the laundry. We also had a glorious fight.

I had been given a small tricycle, ancestor of the modern scooter. Authority had forbidden it on the sea front but I was allowed to ride it up and down our quiet road. Sylvia naturally wanted it so we bargained that as she was the guest she should ride it first as far as the beach and I would ride it back. Ruth was on holiday, her substitute was thinking of other things. My companion set off gaily, I trotted beside her. All went well until at the appointed moment she refused to dismount. She even called out mockingly that having got the tricycle she was going to keep it. I was prepared to share but not to cede, I snatched the handle bar, she slapped me. I hit her as hard as I could, she had to jump off in order to slog me back. The butcher's boy stopped and shouted encouragement, quite a crowd collected. Sylvia tried a number of her brother's tricks but through sheer luck although she was bigger than I was, I managed to knock her over. It was a moment of pure and exquisite pleasure that I have always remembered. Unfortunately my mother arrived at that precise moment. We were both smacked, led off howling, and the tricycle was confiscated for a week. Considering the circumstances, I felt this to be unjust.

Sylvia could have had half of anything that I owned but she had little imagination in play and her idea of a good game was to snatch. Look for your misanthrope among the middle members of a big family; contrary to what people say, an only child has inestimable advantages and is the one to be interested in people in later life. The others get disillusioned in the nursery. There are psychological reasons; a single child has time to develop and unless we can go through a fiercely individualistic stage we never truly understand co-operation. Teachers prefer the regimented pupils, they are afraid of any departure from the familiar, but do such children make the best citizens?

It is hard for us to realize in middle life how strong the primary emotions of childhood are. We temporize and smile in some delusion that this is being mature. Fifty-eight years afterwards I went past the corner where I had won my first fight and it was as if it had happened yesterday. The stones and landscape were the same except that they had built a house on the lot where the ladies had trailed their skirts on the uncut grass. The fact that I had fought in defense of my rights seemed infinitely more important than the anguish and terror of two wars. Those seemed far away. It was the smell of the seaweed, the being willing to share but having a consciousness of right and wrong that emerged in a clarity of feeling I had not felt for decades. I am certain from personal experience that life is simply the working out in practice of our first seven years.

I cannot remember being lonely in my childhood, I did not know what the word meant. I hardly missed Sylvia when the summer ended and her family returned to London, there were so many other exciting things to do. My official introduction to history came through nursery lessons and *Little Arthur's History of England*. I preferred my desert islands but the stories fascinated me, particularly the ones about Alfred winning a book through learning to read and, for some strange reason, King John losing his jewels in the Wash. Many years later, I discovered that its author had written a vivid fragment about her own childhood. It is printed in a biography of her, *Maria, Lady Callcott*, by Rosamund Brunel Gotch. It is amazing that she should have survived the experiences that she describes to become a sane and tolerant woman in an intolerant age and she should not be forgotten. Her father was a naval captain and her mother the daughter of an American Loyalist who had returned to England. Maria herself belongs to that intrepid band of Englishwomen who have gone exploring throughout our history. She sailed both to India and Chile, where she knew Cochrane, she taught in Brazil and traveled in Italy and France. Her life reflects the currents of the time, she was roughly contemporary with the *Swiss Family Robinson,* and she is much nearer to modern thought in her opinions than the Victorians who followed her. Some of her travel books are more for students of the period than for the general reader but her account of her schooldays is one of the most interesting accounts of a child's struggle for survival that I have ever read.

There was so complete a wall between being six and three quarters and being seven that I forgot for a long time what infancy had been like. Babies think in patches with long intervals between them but suddenly existence became continuous. It was helped by a major change. Toys and books were packed and sent to a shadowy place called "storage." The house was to be sold, Vick had died, I should pick no more primroses in the Goring woods. We went instead to London in the middle of September on our way to spend several years abroad.

Two

If the years between birth and seven formed the skeleton, the subsequent time until I was fifteen furnished flesh and blood. It was so great a change as to make stories of rebirth entirely credible later on. Nothing can equal a sense of foreign lands acquired in childhood; if this were a common experience it might do much to prevent war. It must be early; it should come at the precise instant when body and mind are both ready for exploration. The least profitable time is at adolescence when the schools advise it for their own convenience, because that is the moment when the stability of a familiar environment is required. A second language or unfamiliar customs then only impose an unnecessary strain. No, the right time to travel is between the ages of six and thirteen and I was fortunate to go abroad at a moment when I was most sensitive to fresh impressions.

Our new life began with a short visit to London. It was such a warm October that I was allowed to sit on the balcony with an illustrated book that I had been given for my birthday, *Tales from Shakespeare* retold for children by E. Nesbit. I knew the stories by heart within a week although, like an Elizabethan prentice, I did not always like the more famous ones. I had little use for Hamlet, with a magnificent excuse to fight he wasted pages trying to get out of it. I preferred Pericles especially when he found the salt-stained armor on the beach. *A Midsummer Night's Dream* disappointed me, the important character was Oberon's boy and there was not a line at the end to explain what eventually happened to him. *The Tempest* began well but the exciting part, the voyage in the open boat, was over in a couple of lines. Why did they treat Caliban so harshly and who forced Prospero to give up his books in a Mrs. Molesworth surrender to the nursery principle that too much reading was selfish? No, among them all, the play that I liked best was *Cymbeline*. It passed all the tests of an adventure story, there was a cave, a battle, and plenty of movement in the palace garden. I imagined this to be a place with box hedges and gay, brown, scented wallflowers growing out of stone walls such as I had seen at Pevensey Castle. The princes were like Robinson boys and I would have followed the Roman general wherever he had bidden me. Why there was so much fuss about Iachimo in the coffer I could not understand but grownups were strange, and it was no odder than playing in the garden without a sunbonnet but having to wear one if we went into the fields.

I looked down that day into a melancholy Bayswater square full of old trees. The russet-spotted leaves had not yet been raked into heaps. It was desolate and quiet. Suddenly to my surprise the bleak railings turned into gently moving reeds, there was water flowing over the gravel path and Imogen herself was standing with her back to me among the rushes. It seemed perfectly natural. I was making up my mind to speak to her when my mother called me. I turned to answer her and when I looked down at the garden again the figure had vanished. Hallucination in childhood is common enough. It is only interesting that I should have seen a Celtic Imogen whose name even then seemed the color of a dark leaf rather than Arden's Rosalind.

I am glad that I knew of Shakespeare so early although it was a simple approach. The classics are for childhood and old age, middle life belongs to contemporary experience.

> 'Tis far off,
> And rather like a dream than an assurance
> That my remembrance warrants,

as Miranda said. The stories sank to a sea level of consciousness. I often do not read a play for years but whenever I return to it the associations of childhood stick to the names like burrs, I smell the buttons of white asters that filled the autumn garden at the turn of the century and the bitter scent of the slowly burning leaves.

Shortly afterwards my first governess arrived, a stern and elderly Hanoverian lady who had just returned from India where she had been teaching a detestable child called Willie. He was everything that I was not, obedient, affectionate, and if he were sometimes naughty it was to be able to confess afterwards that he had unwillingly distressed her. There was the afternoon that he had eaten a mango. It was not "willful disobedience," the poor boy had forgotten that he must not touch that fruit. I could not understand the temptation because I had never tasted mangoes; if I had, I should stop talking to her about strawberries and cream. She had heard him sobbing that night and they had spent two happy hours weeping together. It would be much better—she looked at me grimly—if I would try to follow Willie's example.

Fräulein (I never knew her name) did not like walking but a brisk trot in the afternoon was half of Authority's idea of goodness. She compromised by taking me to the Indian section of the Victoria and Albert Museum and telling me stories of ayahs, cobras and plagues. She did not appear, alas, to have had any real acquaintance with elephants. In a London where ladies wore black or dove-gray clothes, she appeared, aged sixty, in long white dresses touching the floor with either an amber necklace and a yellow sash or, on Sundays, pink with coral. It was too much for the cabmen who caught glimpses of the colors under her coat, my mother's friends were startled but politely silent. I liked her eccentricity but not her discipline because she insisted that only Prussians understood virtue, "If you were a German child you would have to get up at six every morning, wash in cold water and waste no time poring over silly books." She also had a habit of looking up at breakfast and murmuring for no apparent reason, "I am a lady by birth" until my mother was forced to remark in desperation that if this were true, she would not have to tell us about it so often. Lessons went fairly easily because I really wanted to know more French and double my reading possibilities but I felt no affection for her, she could not control me and on several occasions my mother had to be fetched to administer a well-deserved scolding.

Our next move was to Hastings before setting off for a winter abroad. The first thing that I noticed on the front was an object on wheels shaped like a coachman's box, standing between boards that said "Five Shillings a Trip." My sense of adventure must come to me from my mother. After my father had sternly forbidden any experiments, she put me into my thickest coat and to my humiliation wound a thick, white shawl round my mouth. We slipped out after lunch while my father was reading his paper, my mother boarded the monster, I was lifted up beside her and she gave the driver a gold half sovereign. Other people joined us, we must have been about five passengers in all. At first nothing happened except some sputtering noises. Then there was a jerk, we almost fell off our seats, a horse reared, people stared. We drove smartly along the road and it was gratifying to notice a lot of ladies with their pugs, scurrying up side streets. "How fast are we going?" a gentleman asked.

"Twenty miles an hour."

People gasped! They shook their heads in disbelief. More horses stood on their hind legs, boys shouted unseemly remarks. We reached the end of the sea front and turned solemnly round, all too soon. It was unfortunate that my father, having finished his newspaper, had come to join us on our walk and met us proudly getting out of the car. He was extremely angry with my mother who said merely that she had liked it so much that she was ready to do it over again and at once. We had no premonition that within four years my father would be making excuses to me about there being no stable for a pony because we had to have a garage, this was a completely new word, for a similar motor-car of our own.

We spent part of every winter but one between 1901 and 1907 in Italy, going on from there twice to Egypt and once to Sicily. We missed only 1905 when we went to Spain and Algeria instead. In 1908 and 1909 we did not go so far afield but stayed in the South of France. The summers were spent in Switzerland with sandwiches of time in France and England. I counted my age by the countries that we visited, and the additions to my history books in the Stories of the Nations series.

The greatest gift parents can give their children is experience. It is far more valuable than either care or money. These years abroad deepened and shaped my whole life. They extended my perceptions because there was something new to learn daily but it came from my then level of consciousness, not out of theoretical advice or books. It is growth that is important; too much protection is as dangerous as none at all. How often the experienced soldier survives where the recruit is killed. I am particularly grateful that my parents brought me up free from routine (that came in adolescence when I was better equipped to resist it), and that I was toughened by much exercise. How otherwise should I have got through the subsequent changes and wars?

A short time ago I stood on the Pincio looking across Rome. It was a gray, wet morning in early May. I did not pretend to know the modern city, I had never lived there, but the flutes of tiles and steps, the domes and towers, the travertine and marble were so familiar deep under consciousness that they were part of my own skin, I could not remember when I had seen them first while the difficulties of our early travels were as vivid as if they had happened yesterday. In 1902 it was not a matter of a few hours in a clean and comfortable aeroplane between London Airport and Ciampino, the journey took from two to three days.

How can I make people understand what the trip was like fifty years ago? There were no motorcars, we traveled by steamer, train or horse-drawn carriage, sometimes we rode. There were no passports, I had my first one in 1919, nobody spoke English but French was a lingua franca everywhere in Europe and, if necessary, in remote districts, we drew pictures of what we needed. The trains were dusty and unheated, occasionally porters brought round "foot warmers," long metal cylinders filled with hot water, but my legs were too short to reach them so that I was wrapped in a rug. It was so dirty that we always kept some old and special railway clothes. There were no dining cars at first (I resented them when they arrived, it was much more fun to picnic in the compartment) and no baths nor running water taps in the hotels though enamel tubs were brought to us with cans of steaming water. All the same, I was kept clean, too scrubbed, I often thought, for comfort. There were many insects; bugs, fleas, lice and scorpions. I was drilled to pull my little pigtails forward whenever I sat down; we wore tiny muslin bags full of insect repellent sewn into our stockings and vests. (An English doctor who had been in India had told my mother of the trick and it worked.) Yet again this was an advantage in my later life, fleas never shocked me, I merely went to work with soap and powder. We take our water for granted. I learned that there was no greater crime than to drink it unboiled, if I were thirsty I had to wait patiently perhaps for a couple of hours until we could get tea or occasionally mineral water. (This was suspect because they had a habit of filling the bottles at the fountains.) We never touched salad or fruit except oranges and tangerines that could be peeled. It was before the banana age. Nor was there much heating. We sometimes had a stove or more often a brazier filled with glowing charcoal in the sitting room. It was stricter at the customs as a rule than it is now and every town had its *octroi* if we made an excursion. We did not know of the connection between malaria and mosquitoes but it was an English superstition that an attack might come from being out at sunset. We often arrived at a station in the middle of the night or set off at four in the morning. It was a life designed to shock the child care theorists to the core but oh, what an advantage it has been to me! I can vary my hours instantly to suit either side of the Atlantic, I do not mind where I sleep provided that the place is reasonably clean, the only thing that bothers me is a draft. Every nursery rule was broken during those years, I ate whatever my parents ate including gazelle and octopus, and never had a day's illness until I caught a slight attack of German measles from a maid on one of our visits to England.

The only thing that I resent is that I did not know what Clio was offering me. It *was* the eighteenth century, at least at Naples. Scholars read about it, I have lived in it but alas, although I remember the flavor, I forget the details. Life was tougher and death always near. There was more individuality and color, much more eccentricity, perhaps because the weaklings perished. People believed in their opinions, sometimes they had a "cause" for which they were willing to die but it was simple stuff, the theoretical hair-splitting of today was unknown. (I should have caught a hint of it had it been in the air.) I do not think that human nature has changed very much since prehistoric times but each age has its atmosphere that cannot be transmitted through books and it ought to be an object lesson to the artist. He has to be in advance of his time yet he must also recognize that though the essential elements of his work may survive, the mood, the light and shade will never have the meaning for a future audience that they had when he created them.

Yes, if a century had lost itself and I had woken up in 1802 adaptation would not have been difficult. I knew that there were streets down which it was dangerous to walk after nightfall, Italians talked as casually about brigands and blood feuds as we spoke of Guy Fawkes Day and fireworks. The roads were turbulent, sometimes there were fights but nobody dreamed of sheltering me from the news as children are isolated nowadays. Outbreaks of plague and armed soldiers on the trains were as natural as the small, sweet oranges or the enchanting emerald lizards.

I accepted these hardships with pride. It was an honor, as my parents said, to accompany them abroad instead of being shut up in a nursery. I also knew that it mattered more if I were naughty on the Continent than at home because I discredited not only myself but every other English child. And now what do I remember of the cities with their enchanting names that were already so familiar from my mother's stories?

A pole creaked, the rain beat steadily on the black hood, we could hear the waves slapping against the side of the cradle or what was the new word that they had used, gondola? I was wedged between the knees of my mother and father and we seemed to move, saying nothing, for hours. I tried everywhere to find a peephole but was told to sit still. It had been a long journey from England although we had broken it by spending a few days at Lugano. (I remember nothing of this visit to a place that was to be so important to me in later life except that it had rained there and I had been given my first paintbox.) Now I felt cramped and restless; I wanted my supper.

Suddenly there was a rush and a yell. I caught a glimpse of the Mediterranean night with its soft, almost bodily darkness. Then we shot into a harbor of wavy, brightly lit marble. A carved balustrade vanished into the sea but there was a roof overhead and people stood watching us from a gallery. A barelegged man leaned down from the flight of stairs, lifted me out and set me down beside a pile of red carpets stacked on the first-floor landing. The reflection from the lights, the tassels on the hood, bobbed up and down as they handed up the luggage. So this was Venice? The ground floor of the hotel was completely under the sea, it was a glorious adventure.

About every twenty-five years a particular combination of wind and tide floods the entire city up to the level of the first-story windows. The following morning we went round the Piazza of San Marco and up to the Cathedral by boat. "Remember this, Miggy," my father said, "it may never happen again in your lifetime." (It did in the late twenties and occasionally in recent times but then I was in England and merely saw the pictures, how familiar they were, in the illustrated papers.) There were few pigeons, they were clinging miserably to cornices. Only the names of the cafés were visible. Yet even at that age I was aware of an extraordinary beauty, of palaces rising from the Adriatic as if the architects had built them to be entered, not through doors but through porthole-shaped arches. Alas, that December the brightest marble lost its color and the wind blowing along the narrow canals gave us all coughs.

We went to High Mass at San Marco on Christmas Day and stood on planks with the other worshipers. My father lifted me up to see the Cardinal's red robes (he became Pope shortly afterwards) but the incense suffocated me and much as this may surprise some people, the candles and the chanting seemed remote and cold after the friendly Noah's Ark warmth of the little Protestant church to which I was taken at home. After the service the only way to leave was by boat.

Venice itself left me with a mixture of good and bad impressions. The Campanile was lovely, it was still the old one that fell down a short time afterwards. Fräulein led the way, I panted after her because it seemed a very long climb until we came out into the sunlight above a panorama of islands and water. It was one of my original landscapes, houses, bridges, and always somewhere a ship. It was much, much duller when as part of my lessons we had to go to picture galleries. I was too young for Titian or Carpaccio to arouse my imagination and I preferred feeding the pigeons. There were fewer of them in those days than there are now and it was quite a feat to lure them to the far end of the square. I learned some new words, however, like porphyry and lapis lazuli, and it was useful to know something about the Doges when I discovered Marco Polo, three years later.

Do I remember the Rialto or is the memory a reflection of later visits? I know that I trotted up and down cold, narrow streets in search of balls to hang upon the tree that had mysteriously arrived in our sitting room. I had never liked Christmas very much and the more Fräulein chattered about reindeer and the letters that Willie had written to Santa Claus, the more determined I became not to be tricked.

On Christmas Eve I pretended to be asleep. Several times a head peeped round the door. I kept my eyes shut, my ears alert. Finally somebody whispered, "She can't still be awake." I did not move, I tried not to breathe, finally the rustles ceased and a fat stocking was fastened to the foot of the bed. Enjoying the moment thoroughly I sat upright and said firmly, "I knew you were Santa Claus."

I was not smacked (I deserved to be!) but I was told sternly that if I did not go to sleep at once, that very minute, the stocking would be taken away. Of course I was infuriating but why force make-believe upon a child when the facts of nature are so much more exciting? I was perfectly willing for grownups to revert to play provided that they did not try to deceive me. Let them tell me stories on the free and open basis that these were merely tales and I would listen to them happily but it was undignified to be asked to accept an old gentleman bustling down the chimney.

Another exploit was getting lost. I upset an inkpot during lessons and Fräulein, muttering, "The little devil, what can I do with such a child?" snatched her own sponge to mop it up. My mother took her into a chemist's shop to replace it and left me outside with my father. It was a real apothecary's booth. There were decanters of amber and violet liquids in the window, a glimpse of white porcelain jars and a smell of orris. I decided to follow my mother and investigate. It was dusk and neither of us had noticed that there were two doors. I pushed open the wrong one and found myself facing a barber. A lot of men with soapy faces looked up in surprise. The barber in his long white coat came over and asked me in Italian what I wanted. I shook my head, he repeated the question in English.

I was looking for my mother who was buying a sponge. Of course that was next door, come, he would take me there. To add to the confusion the shops were between two streets and by the time that we arrived, my mother had left by an opposite entrance. There was no sign now of parents anywhere. I was not to be frightened, the barber said, he had children too, my mother would come for me very soon and in the meantime I could watch him at work. I assured him indignantly that I was never, never frightened, I told him the name of the hotel where we were staying and added firmly that I could find the way back by myself. What a glorious opportunity it offered to explore Venice alone! I could hang over the parapets and study the canals without Fräulein tugging at me and saying, "You'll get a sore throat lingering by that stagnant rubbish." I might even get aboard a ship without anybody seeing me. The word "lost" has two meanings, one is to be alone but the other is to escape and it was the second that appealed to me. At that moment my family arrived, stupidly frightened. My father was being reproached for "not being able to mind the child a minute." I was even more annoyed when the barber patted me on the head and called me a *bambina,* I knew that word, it meant "baby."

My governess took to her bed. "A lady by birth" could not cope with such a little monster of wickedness. She remained there to my huge delight until we left for England two days later.

It was another winter and we were in Rome, this time without a governess. Did I know what an event this was, my family asked? Sometimes people spent a lifetime's savings to come to the "eternal city" and here I was, only eight, with the treasures of the world open in front of me. "And now, darling, you have been poring over Baedeker for days, what would you like to see first?"

"The Colosseum," I squealed, "because of the gladiators."

There was a horrified silence. My father explained that *everybody* went at once to St. Peter's. So off we drove in a bitterly cold December wind while I reflected sulkily upon the oddity of parents. I knew that I had to wait for anything that I wanted but was it fair to offer me a choice and then snatch it away? The columns and the marble made no impression on me. The towering statues in their rigid, stone robes seemed cold and unfriendly. I dragged behind with only one thought in my head, how soon would my parents tire of staring at all those chapels and take me back to the hotel?

How different it was the next morning! The wind had dropped, the sun was out and I tore into the arena, Baedeker in hand. "The lions," I shouted, "look, the lions, they came up there!" Some silly tourist asked me if I wasn't sorry for the Christians. I dived into lovely underground passages, I tried out seats all round the amphitheater, I even hid a chip of marble in my pocket when nobody was looking although I knew that this was a sin. Why wouldn't people answer my questions? How old would I have to be before becoming a gladiator? Was a shield very heavy? Were the prongs of the trident pointed and was the net the same as the one used now to catch butterflies? "She knows more about it than the guide," an old gentleman remarked. Yet at the time I had not even read Henty, there was only the one page in Baedeker but it was outdoors, I could run about, it belonged to my age.

Many years later I had a vivid dream. I felt that I was being given the chance to step back in time to see one episode from the past. I ought to have asked to listen to Sappho or to watch Hannibal leading his elephants over the Alps. I demanded instead a good seat at the Games and promptly, of course, woke up.

We stayed that December at a hotel in the center of Rome. I happened to return there a few years ago and the flowers, the gilt chairs and the sense of some discreet drama being acted out in a room along one of its innumerable corridors appeared to have survived half a century of change. All that I missed was a stolid figure on short legs, in the blue coat and narrow tippet of fur that had been the uniform of 1902, scribbling in rough, uneven letters "Rufus was a Roman boy, he was a gladiator," along a much thumbed page in an exercise book. What is the relationship between a person of such infinite confidence, such wary hardness and myself? One is so much younger at sixty. This is surely one of the mysteries of Time that is almost interplanetary?

It was there in the restaurant under perhaps the same frescoes of the seasons that I was allowed to sit up for dinner for the first time. A long table near by was set with silver and flowers and the headwaiter told us that some diplomats were expected. I watched them take their places with great interest, the men wore black instead of the mulberry-colored silk that I had seen in Titian's banquets but the bare throats and arms of the women blazed with jewels. I glanced up gaily at their faces and froze in terror. It was as if I were looking at malice and greed as they might have appeared in some medieval morality before an unworldly audience. I felt in a flash what would happen to me if I fell into their power, if I were one of those barelegged urchins, for example, who hoping for a few soldi ran after the carriages to open the door, or some old woman in her hovel who was behind with the rent. "Something has shocked the child," my mother said, was it that the ladies had no sleeves, that was called evening dress. It would not have mattered to me if they had worn no clothes at all. "They are not alive," I stammered because I had no vocabulary to explain what I felt. Perhaps it was an illusion and I maligned my neighbors but I have seldom had so overmastering a sense of evil in my life.

I watched women washing clothes in the yellow Tiber water and picked up chestnut husks at Frascati. I stood enthralled in front of a sculptor at the Villa Borghese, he was copying a statue in a dark clay that I mistook for bronze. At Pisa, I remember only the Leaning Tower and an icy wind. I had never heard of Robert Browning but I recognized our Florence in his poems a few years afterwards. The streets could not have changed since the eighteen sixties, they were full of stalls and carts, sometimes even of goats. There were plenty of old ladies lodging in bitterly cold pensions or lofty palazzo rooms, to escape, as they thought, from an English winter. Some painted water colors, others read guidebooks. They marched in black buttoned boots from church to church, admiring canvases that are now unfashionable, uneasily conscious that the painters (like Filippo Lippi) had not always led virtuous lives but assuring each other that "it's a man's art that matters, dear, not his life" whilst staring at a panel of some kneeling patriarch half obliterated under smoky varnish in a corner of the ceiling. They shouted violently at peasants who struck their mules (I have read since that a concern for the welfare of animals was the only political outlet then permitted to a lady), they founded tearooms. For all their good will, I doubt if they understood Italy yet perhaps we should not laugh at them, stumping along with their twin torches of Italian beauty and English stolidity. Comprehension is not always necessary nor, in general, should a foreigner try to reform another country, yet sometimes the stranger in his "very serviceable suit of black" perceives the essence of a past that has become merely a hindrance to the native.

We stared at Florence from the outside just as Mrs. Browning had watched it from her windows. "Look!" I tugged at the sleeve of my father's overcoat, there was a shepherd boy hardly older than myself, crossing the bridge with a kid over his shoulders. The squares were wide, the streets were narrow, they were almost as dangerous as the cars are today, with coachmen yelling, flourishing their whips and each trying to pass a rival's carriage. We flattened ourselves against the wall to get away from the donkeys and their fleas, we jumped back as the wheels of two barrows touched and the owners screamed like brigands at each other among the spilled lemons.

I almost made the headlines of the newspapers, however, trying to burn down the Uffizi. In 1903 there had been little change since Elizabethan times in the attitude towards children. I suppose that we must have inherited the former status of slaves, we were sometimes petted and often smacked; absolute obedience was the ideal though it was seldom achieved in practice and while we were forbidden to have opinions of our own we were expected to share adult interests beyond an eight-year-old's understanding. It was a Spartan discipline. Every morning I was taken to visit churches, galleries or museums. All paintings looked alike to me with fat cherubs, masses of cloud or old men praying in dingy, umber robes. I particularly disliked Michelangelo. His name was repeated so often that I sometimes wondered if it were another term for Italy. To look at pictures might be for "my future good," a phrase enough to wreck any self-respecting child's day, but what I wanted was to run along the Arno and to watch the puppies chasing their tails in the sunlight. It was dull, it was cold, I shut my eyes in desperation, screamed, "I won't look, I *won't* look," and walked backwards into a pan of charcoal, the accepted method in those days of heating both hovels and palaces.

Embers flew all over the wooden floor, the custodian, cursing and half asleep, grabbed the brazier just as it was toppling over, several copyists sprang from their easels to stamp out sparks. People scolded me in half a dozen languages, they glared at my mother and insinuated that a *bambina* should be left outside with a nurse. "We thought we could trust you," my parents said reproachfully as they hurried me into another room. For once the reproof had no sting. "I won't look," I yelped, "I won't look however much you scold me. I *hate* museums." Finally we compromised; if I would walk round with open eyes, holding my father's hand, they would give me the book that I wanted so badly that very afternoon.

I had seen a horror comic with the most wonderful cover in a shop window of the Via Tornabuoni. A man was lying on the ground with a spear through his chest while two warriors stood above him, slashing at each other with swords. According to an inscription underneath it was "the fight for the body of Patroclus." Who was Patroclus? Why had he been killed? Authority objected of course; "You won't really like it, you know" but a bargain was a bargain and I insisted. Oh, what hours of toil over horrible Greek verbs I might have spared myself later had I allowed myself to be overruled. The book was *The Boy's Iliad* by Walter Copeland Perry and it led me back to museums and not away from them.

I began the *Iliad* in the train and now I can never see the Tuscan hills without thinking of the boyhood of Achilles. Chiron fed him on the hearts of lions. My mother, consulted, thought that these might be tough. I wished that I could have watched the foot race or followed Penthesilea (Perry had wisely included all the myths), I tried to imagine the outline of the camp on the shore, going back in my head and beginning again, if I felt that I had not got the details right. If I had been able to draw the scenes that I imagined, Troy would have been startlingly Elizabethan with Gozzoli touches. The walls were the sun-baked blocks of the hill towns that we passed, a sentinel's cloak was not army scarlet but the red of the anemones in the grass. My white canvas tents were wrong but I did not know of any others. What was a tripod and why was it so valuable as a prize? Were greaves anything like gaiters and were they fixed on with straps? How was a javelin thrown? What I needed was Lorimer's *Homer and the Monuments* but that book, alas, was not yet written. I heard the chariots turning on the sand as I dreamed, the sea wash thundered in my ears and my sleep was full of the beauty of the ships.

It is strange that after *The Swiss Family Robinson* the most profound impressions of my childhood came from Shakespeare and Homer. I still think Perry's retelling of the stories for the young is unsurpassed and I am particularly grateful that he used the Greek names for the gods. These gave me the clue to the objects that surrounded me. I lived through and with the myths as I suppose a later generation identified itself with what it saw in films. Besides, the appeal was direct and simple. The choice of Achilles was my own. Who wanted more than a brief life provided it were crammed with adventure? An hour of action was worth a lifetime of security.

I soon got *The Boy's Odyssey* but this was disappointing. The cruelty to Polyphemus shocked me, it was, after all, his cave and the slaughter of the suitors upset my nursery ethics. Exactly what had they done? Even now the dark and savage side of the ancient world seems to emerge more clearly in the wanderings than in the fight before Troy; in this, the poems are true to life because the years following a war are often more brutal than the calamity itself.

My friends tell me that Perry's versions are not simple enough for the modern child. To me, the theory that a limited vocabulary should be offered to an age group is more horrifying than any atomic threat. We have neither the right to stunt development nor to make it too easy; the overcoming of obstacles is one of the greatest joys in life.

Achilles had a rival, however, in the Perseus of Kingsley's *Heroes*. I think the flying in the story brought my fantasy wings although I did not know then that I was to love the air so much. Years afterwards, following analysis, the Gorgon became for me the symbol of truth. We can endure this only if it is reflected in a mirror or shield, if we have to face it directly we die. It is also part of another story, the eternal struggle of Mithras. The best and most daring among us cannot hope to catch more than a second's reflection, and that at long intervals, of absolute verity.

If Florence was the Brownings, Naples was the eighteenth century, as I have said, and I loved it more than the rest of Italy. The streets were a child's playground, they were noisy, dirty but how they blazed with color! The donkeys drew their carts down alleys so narrow that the wheels almost touched the walls. We brushed past vegetables arranged in pyramids, there were onions, leeks like green ribbons on a white dress and gay rosettes of radishes between balls of artichokes and hoops of lemons. A trader wailed mournfully, windows opened and bargaining began while baskets appeared and were let down on ropes from the top stories. Oh, what arguments there were! Sometimes a basket hurtled down a second time with a rejected bunch of carrots. People left their pans of fish or macaroni to join the fray, almost all the cooking was done in the open air, the donkey snatched a carrot top, coins jingled. I stood on tiptoe on the front seat of our carriage because now the crowd was blocking the road and we could not get through it. "Oh look!" I turned excitedly, I had seen the woman with the black hair falling untidily over her face and the big, open mouth before, "Isn't she just like the Gorgon on the mosaics?" She was going to throw something, yes, we dodged, and a lemon missed the dealer's hat by centimeters. Everybody yelled, the coachman cracked his whip, my father consulted his watch, what did they care for the time-consciousness of the north? The cart moved on a yard to repeat the same drama next door. Our driver turned somehow and drove to the lower road down a real flight of steps. They were broad, it is true, and there were only about a dozen of them.

Little girls looked up, waved as we passed and then went back to their proper occupation, catching lice in each other's hair. Children of my own age were at work (I still think that most of them were happier than if they had been at school) and, although they went barefoot and were thin, seemed gay. They often danced, not for tourists but because somebody had given them an orange. It was the same world that the Latin authors have described except that the gutters might have been cleaner and the cobbles kept in better repair under the emperors.

It was that day that we climbed Vesuvius, slipping two feet back in hot lava dust for every foot that we advanced. I held my father's hand and we looked at the crater, I half hoped that a sudden eruption would drive us down the slope as in *The Last Days of Pompeii*, a not very satisfactory book that I had just read in the ever useful Tauchnitz. I preferred Whyte-Melville's *The Gladiators*. Still, it was easy to imagine being trapped in the oozing lava as if it were a bog. We looked round for my mother but she was nowhere to be seen; there was only an angry crowd in the distance. She had been following some way behind us when a number of men had thrust her into a carrying chair, despite her vigorous protests. Halfway to the summit they had set her down to demand their pay. My mother had grasped her sunshade firmly and had told them that she had no money. They would have to wait until they reached my father. Vesuvius had a bad reputation as to brigands although officially it was supposed to have been cleaned up. Apart from two other tourists we were alone and we were all a little uneasy. To be taken prisoner when people were flourishing their fists and shouting was not quite the same as reading an adventure book. My father refused to pay one lira till we had got back to the station and going down, in tremendous, scooping strides, was quicker than our ascent. It turned out all right in the end but judging from the noisy atmosphere around Pompeii today, the neighborhood has not changed much during the intervening years.

I reached Pompeii at last, the wine jars and the loaves were exactly as my mother had described them to me but on that special day, perhaps I had expected too much, I was deserted by Clio. I ran along the chariot ruts, the past was at my elbow but a blue sky, an insect buzzing around a pillar, held me firmly inside the present. What did "the mysteries" mean, I begged, not knowing that they were the fruit of much experience, only to be discovered alone. I touched the stones, I knew that it needed but a single incident or word and I should enter into antiquity instead of looking at the ruins but nothing happened. We can imagine another age but we cannot leave our own however much we try to transpose ourselves. The centuries pass, a little color remains but the true hopes and fears of our ancestors will always be just off focus in the way that we can remember childhood but can never re-experience its emotions.

Baia consoled me with its blue sea, short turf and the enameled lizards that I already associated with Apollo. It was a holiday place, we ate an omelette and fresh oranges at some primitive inn and I played on the slopes outside it afterwards among stones from old Roman villas. There was a cruel custom of sending dogs into the neighboring caves from which they staggered out, poisoned by the bad air. Most English tourists paid the men not to drive the animals inside but this, as we realized, only helped to prolong the custom. At another place, a small, half-naked boy ran down a passage with a raw egg in his hand to emerge with it apparently cooked. Actually, as my father explained to me, he changed his first egg for a boiled one at some corner. His trip was merely through a tunnel heated by hot air and was pleasant on a winter day because I pushed in myself as far as I was allowed.

Which was the cave that I visited alone with a guide? It was not at Baia itself but in that neighborhood. I went down long corridors towards the "underworld," a dark sheet of water, and emerged triumphantly but, to my mother's dismay, with black smears over my hat and coat. I think the pathway had been lit by torches.

We were in Naples once for New Year when all families able to afford them bought eels. I shall never forget our drive across the fish market. Urchins sprang onto the steps of our victoria, they thrust a snarling head and a slimy wriggling body almost onto my mother's lap. It was useless trying to leave, we were wedged into a solid mass of carriages, vendors and stalls. A beggar's rags were held together by a patch of scarlet, there was a dark clip of coral on a woman's shawl. We could not hear ourselves speak, the yells, the whip cracks and the ringing hooves were louder than thunder. Men who looked Turkish rather than Italian held up pails of mussels, two men bargained clamorously over a shallow dish of oysters. There were skates and cuttlefish, spines stuck together with mud and glazed oblongs that we could not recognize. The ground was slippery with oily skins, fish bones and scrunched shells. It stank, it was a madman's picture of hell, I was frightened that our horse would fall and excited at the same moment, while beyond the quays sailing ships from the beginning of time were anchored next to modern liners waiting to take emigrants to the States.

It was always a world of fish, as we can see from the surviving paintings, and I haunted the Aquarium. Again each window was a mosaic, only it was fluid and vertical, instead of being part of a pavement. Some of the fins had dots like grape pips, I recognized a mullet hiding in the corner, what was the name of that creature with long, lemon stripes across its back? My favorite place was in front of the sea horses, surely they had just been broken off a pediment? The rose and orange tassels of the sea anemones opened and shut, a coral full of miniature caves that was not at all like the necklaces that the traders dangled on their trays seemed to be the playground of a shoal of sprats and could that porous, sticky lump possibly be a nursery sponge? To tease my mother and test my own courage, I forced myself to watch an octopus edge sideways across the sand until the dark tentacles whipped suddenly about a rock. What would happen if the glass should break? It was enthralling but it was puzzling as well. How long was it possible to breathe under water? Could a fish think? After we came out into the sunlight we bought newspapers from a boy my own size who told us that he went to English classes at night school and wanted to go to London. I have always wondered whether he got his wish.

Yet Death walked openly through those crowded Neapolitan streets. A bell tolled or rather it was rung by hand, people began to scatter, we, ourselves, were swept inside a shop. The sound came nearer, a man started to pray, my mother ordered me sternly to hold my breath. Four men walked along the deserted street, carrying a bier. Their dirty white overalls almost touched the ground, their faces were hidden by their hoods. I had looked at so many pictures of such scenes in the galleries that I muttered "plague" and nodded with the rest. No, I was not frightened, it was not measles, it was just the pest. I had read about it in my history book. Really they must not be afraid.

I did not feel so confident when a beggar grabbed my arm as we were entering a church, a few days afterwards. He was kneeling on the ground, his deformed and noseless face was at the level of my eyes and supposing him from the Bible stories to be a leper, I jerked my shoulder away from him and howled.

We sometimes went to Capri for the day. I am glad that its landscape was a part of childhood but the place belongs to a later date in my story when I was there with Norman Douglas. All the same, I never walk up the hill through the aromatic rosemary bushes towards the villa of Tiberius without my father's lectures upon the superiority of the law courts in England to imperial despotism echoing through my mind. Naturally the English were more moral but it would be pleasant to have one's wishes immediately fulfilled without a judge or elder saying, "But you will be sorry afterwards," in a hurt, astonished voice.

I disliked the Blue Grotto intensely; a heavy fisherman sat down on me as we entered it and then, as now, Capri was full of guides. One man followed us onto the steamer protesting that he had lived in London and was almost an Englishman, had he not learned to drink tea in the English manner, half full of rum? It seemed cruel to tell him that we had never heard of this curious custom ourselves. "You must not laugh, Miggy," my father explained afterwards, "there is great poverty here and he wanted a job."

Why was Italy poor? It had the sun. Yes, my father agreed but there was much mismanagement and some of the officials were corrupt. I listened to his explanations with excitement, they were like the stories of the emperors, and it was an invaluable training, no matter how mixed up I got at the beginning, for my subsequent life.

My father also invented a game to pass the time when I had read and reread all our books, including his own. I was to imagine that I had to take a party of tourists round Italy. Learning depends upon interest. Sums were a nightmare to me but I had no trouble in working out the cost of tickets and sleepers, first or second class, in liras or pounds. I looked up trains and steamers, planned how I could show my group the most things in the least time. I do not know if some intimation of the air age was already stirring in my bones but I am one of those universally despised people who depend upon a first, sharp impression. I can really get more out of a hurried tour than by staying a leisurely month in a single city.

The greatest of our Italian expeditions was Paestum. Hardly any visitors risked such an expedition in 1903. Only the main temples had been uncovered, the swamps had not been drained and it was so full of malaria that it was only safe to be there during the middle of the day. There was no museum and no hotel but it was full instead of delicious rumors about brigands and, according to Baedeker, of a special breed of ancient, white oxen.

The first stage of our journey was by train to Salerno where we spent the night. I read about its university in the guidebook but was too young to realize that it was the place where something of Arab medicine and science was absorbed by the West during the early Middle Ages, although the name stayed in my consciousness; it had a flavor of its own like a small, wild grape. The following day we took the train once more to a station in the marshes and then drove to our destination in a fly-spotted, broken carriage. I saw the white oxen first with squeals of joy but the only human inhabitant was the custodian who was shaking with malaria.

We sat on the temple steps to eat our lunch and I was scolded for trying to catch a lizard, "It might be a snake." My father took photographs and in one of them I am standing beside a column, plump and happy, with the usual narrow fur tippet tied round my neck in spite of the heat. Paestum is far more interesting today. The museum is full of beautiful statues, the mosquitoes have been destroyed, the roads uncovered under the amazing walls but I shall never forget that first impression of loneliness and melancholy. It was like some wretched corner of a Troy half buried in sand.

The South. Something new happened every moment that I was there. How could I go through such experiences unmarked?

Three

Nobody ever gets over their first camel.

When we landed at Alexandria after a voyage from Naples in December, 1903, I had been extremely seasick for three days; most humiliating behavior for a would-be cabin boy. I refused lunch, I did not even want the large, Jaffa orange that somebody had given me, everything swayed from the motion of the ship. Suddenly from the window of the train that was taking us to Cairo, I saw a camel and its foal. They were strolling with great dignity along the road, the baby's flanks were a mass of curly wool and I remembered having read somewhere that they could scratch their ears with their hind legs. I recovered at once, I knew that I was going to enjoy myself and that whatever happened, nobody could take away the fact that I had seen a camel in its native land.

There is nothing left now of that Cairo of almost sixty years ago. Europeans were rare; there were a few judges at the law courts, some merchants and a handful of tourists come to winter in certain sunshine in spite of the cholera that had raged earlier that season and of which they were probably unaware. Otherwise it was a city of the Khalifate, crowded, noisy, magnificent with color. From waking until the moment when I was dragged protestingly to bed, I stood on the terrace and watched the crowds, except for those glorious moments when we mingled among them ourselves. The men wore robes, either of white or strange, soft colors, clove, the red of a nectarine if a ripe fruit were cut in half and less amber than the shade of the Persian tea that I saw them sipping from glasses whenever we went into the bazaars. The water carriers in the indigo cotton of the poorer people pushed between smart carriages. I was fascinated by their howl (did it mean water?) and by their bloated, goatskin bags. I almost fell over the parapet whenever the syces raced by, their short, scarlet waistcoats embroidered with gold gave an impression of butterflies. Europeans told us that these boys died young; it was the dust, the exertion of running in front of the swiftly moving dog carts and then having to wait after sunset in the sudden cold for their masters.

The city itself was a gigantic maze. Streets were here today, tomorrow even Ali, our dragoman and my firm friend, could not find them. The air was thick with scent, roses and jasmine, or with a heavy mixture of castor oil, straw and camel dung. To my delight, one of these grave animals, as her carriage squeezed by, tried to snatch a floppy leghorn hat from a frightened tourist's head. We often had to wait while strings of donkeys turned down alleys hardly wide enough for a dog, the bright green fodder of their loads bursting out of inadequate sacks. There were scribes with brass inkpots sitting majestically on stools outside the coffee booths in the manner of their predecessors during the days of imperial Rome. We drove along the narrow streets of the opium smokers, I did not find the odor of hashish unpleasant as most people do but the curled-up figures lying on scraps of carpet did not impress me as being happy. (Europeans may have good intentions but they are not always wise. They stopped the drug but doctors have told me since that far more harm was done physically by the substitutes that people found than by the occasional pipe that had been all that the majority of smokers could afford.) I preferred the storytellers. You could see that the audience was living inside the tale, it was one, Ali said, from *The Thousand Nights and a Night,* not only from the expression on their faces but from the slow way their sleeves moved as if in trance whenever they reached out to take a glass of sherbet or water with a ring of lemon in it from the polished trays that small boys, exactly my own height, carried round to the absorbed and staring figures.

It was still the world of the camel and the horse. I cannot remember seeing a motorcar either then or during a second visit the following winter. We spoke of caravans in no romantic way but as somebody now might book a ticket at an airport. How often we drove slowly down the Street of the Saddlers! It was a traveler's oasis, the place where he could buy anything from the soft, red, beautifully ornamented saddles used at ceremonies to the tough, leather bridles for the riding camels. That man with a black fur cap had ridden here with his goods from beyond Teheran. The trader there, Ali explained, no, not the man in white but the merchant who was talking to him in the brown striped burnous, he was from Damascus. There was a Negro with a great basket from Nubia or even Khartoum. This bazaar was both the goal of the journey and the point of return towards the home that many would never reach. We like to read of the tents of the Bedouin but let a man's donkey go lame, let him not have enough to pay his share of the tribute money and he would add his bones to the whitening heaps in the desert once the tribesmen and the jackals had finished their work. There were the additional perils of influenza, smallpox and plague in the crowded inns as well as the constant risk of robbery; an engine may not be so picturesque but people do not realize what they owe to the aeroplane and the car.

The shops that we visited were still Oriental palaces instead of the tourist stores full of goods from Birmingham that they became a few years afterwards. Everything was leisurely. We talked. Presently a single carpet was unrolled, its red as soft as when Persian hands had knotted the colors a century before. I was not interested in rugs, I preferred the man who was putting a puzzle together from cubes of ivory and blocks of ebony wood. He sat in a corner while a group of small boys round him polished bowls and whispered to each other in brief but eager grunts.

How kind the merchants were to me; perhaps it was because I asked them the Arabic name of every object that I could reach. They clapped their hands, a cushion was brought, it was much easier for me to sit cross-legged in front of them than on a chair and they taught me to bargain in the Eastern manner which was, as it should be, an art. We spoke an English patterned upon Arabic sentences and full of foreign words. First I must not want the article for which I bid. To desire it was to lose it. This was rather too difficult for a nine-year-old, so I compromised by choosing something for a friend! I picked up a little bowl and asked the price, the classic beginning. Hearing the sum, I laughed incredulously, a guinea, why, it wasn't worth two shillings. A servant brought in a tray full of tiny cups of thick coffee that must be sipped but never drunk. I fingered the bowl again as if by chance and offered the equivalent of three shillings in piasters. They taught me to feel with my mind across to their own, neither moving my face nor showing any interest until the touch of thought to thought was as actual as the turquoise hilt of the sword that I hoped my father would buy. It is a common trick in the East and easy to learn with the un-stiffened mind of the child.

After a time, the merchant would clap his hands again and a servant would bring in dishes of Turkish delight in all the colors of a dragoman's robe. I knew that I must take one piece only and make it last. Had I tried mint tea? I should have a glass some other afternoon. That matchlock there, it was from Afghanistan, how much did I think that it was worth? I touched the bowl idly, as a favor to me they would sell the little toy for ten shillings. I smiled, and they gave me silk to hold, so thick and white that it stood up by itself, or explained that carpets hung on walls, only ignorant Europeans spread them on the floor and imagine, trod on them, without even taking off their dirty shoes! I took another sip of coffee, stared at a prayer rug and waited. There was one special moment when, without its seeming to matter, my lips must offer the piaster more.

Sometimes I won, sometimes I lost. They scolded me, shaking their heads and not letting me have the bowl if I had been impatient or had let the right instant pass. Occasionally they praised me and added a present, telling my father that he ought to leave me with them for a time to learn their art. Oh, I thought, what a splendid idea! I was perfectly willing to remain because what was England but a tiresome place where I was usually cold, added sums up wrongly on a sticky slate or went for long, monotonous walks? Here I had words to taste that were as strange as any Turkish sweetmeat, Aleppo, Beirut, Isfahan. All the tongues of the Levant rang in my ears and I fell in love forever with Arabian calligraphy, with the beautiful letters shaped like crescent moons, scimitars or flat-bottomed boats. I should even like arithmetic if I had an abacus with colored beads like that scribe in the alcove. How much they gave and taught me, treating me as one of themselves, in that Cairo that was so near to Napoleon's Egypt, and so far, so very far, from today.

Something happens to a Western child partly brought up in the East. It is not a matter of languages, they are forgotten, alas, within weeks of a return to Europe although it is said that there are about a thousand main words and as many more derivatives of Arabian origin in English. It is rather that such children understand the people around them instinctively, with emotion instead of reason. They are not worried about sanitation or any Western ethics; the superstitions, stories, noises and colors belong to their own level of development and are accepted with joy. They have their privileges; these come neither from wealth nor caste but because *they are able to read and write* and are assimilated therefore into an adult world instead of into some arbitrary age group. The tale a sheikh muttered to his donkey boy, the gossip round the well, is theirs within a matter of moments and completely according to their choice they may, or may not, pass the information on to their parents. The chasm between East and West is greater today than it was in 1900 because, strange as it may appear, democracy widens the gap, it cannot close it. The West has reached a high degree of literacy. It refuses to understand that millions not only do not want education but are actually afraid of it. Eastern rulers are the twins of the barons of King Stephen's time. They exult in power, they delight in ostentation and boasting while their followers live under the yoke of a fanatical puritanism that often goads them into senseless massacres. Once the English grasped this difference but the Americans are so sure of the superiority of their own ethical system that they actually believe that if they could impose it upon Asia all discords would vanish! Of course there are intellectual and highly trained minorities but these are few. Development has to come from within the Orient itself and if we can help, it is by providing more sewers and fewer books. It is useless offering chunks of our alien civilization to the cruel, shifting, mighty and barbaric East.

We observers were few in number but we formed a special class within the human race (a subclass if you will), our age limits were between three and eleven, our purpose, to be messengers between two continents that had otherwise few points of contact. We were more than interpreters; two personalities, the native and the secret agent, mingled in our blood, we watched events around us but made reports entirely to ourselves. Perhaps our force came from motion? If in maturity we identify ourselves with some foreign land it is because of a variety of psychological factors. We children never had to choose. We skipped between our countries as if we were at play. Our judgments were sometimes faulty but we grasped, more often than not, facts that officials could not see because of their preconceived opinions. They had policies while we had love. This is possibly not so valuable as is sometimes supposed but it may last longer than oil.

My first religious experiences came in Egypt. I had been well grounded in Bible stories and the inevitable *Line upon Line* and was often taken to the Protestant church near our home. We had gone to some services, on special occasions, in the Italian cathedrals. Both had seemed remote, a part of the particular grown-up world to which I never wanted to belong where "you must do as you are told" was all that seemed to matter. Islam was different. I understood a mosque at once. Perhaps it is worth while trying to analyze the impact of Moslem thought upon a European child because its power is growing rapidly in Africa and I was at the uncomplicated level then of, say, the river tribesmen today. First of all, every man prayed for himself under an open sky. There were no pulpits, no sermons, no confusion. It was natural to ask for water in the desert, to give alms to the beggar and protect the stranger. Even Ramadan was not like a European fast. We were free to eat what we wanted as long as there was not light enough "to discern a white thread from a black" in the sky, afterwards what was it but a test of endurance? "Trust God and tie thy camel" were the words of a leader, adventurous and practical. Phrases have their original meaning for children; they are not yet soaked with cynicism or association. I thought that "In the Name of Allah, the Merciful, the Compassionate" was the most beautiful invocation that I had ever heard. (Yes, I am aware that the pedants prefer another translation but I cling to the phrase that I then knew.) There is no quality greater than compassion even if I chose it first because of a personal hope that if I were particularly naughty I should not be sent to bed without my supper. Above all, there was no insistence upon mildness or contemplation. Islam asked direct tasks from its simple followers and was rewarded with fanatical devotion.

Why were we allowed to attend a ceremony of the "dancing dervishes"? Some earlier travelers had reported seeing them but this was the last year, they told us afterwards, that non-Moslems were allowed to watch the genuine rite.

We were perhaps half a dozen Europeans, placed behind a rope at the side of a huge, dimly lit chamber. I did not need Ali's whisper to recognize a Descendant of the Prophet, I had seen his green turban. The leader chanted the Koran, his companions occasionally answered him. They had been praying and fasting for twenty-four hours. The dervishes stood in a circle in fluted robes, not unlike some elongated Albanian kilt. I thought of Ramadan and wished that I could keep the fast to prove myself as tenacious as an Arab. Quietly, as if the first white sail were fluttering from a mast, a dervish began to turn, so slowly that he hardly seemed to move. Another robe trembled, then a third until all were following in a grave circle. Something began to whirl in my own mind, I was not myself any longer, in a moment I might reach a state beyond my senses. It was in no way incomprehensible, I was on a journey and very, very happy but I was neither where my body was standing nor quite in the air.

Before the climax of the ceremony somebody took my hand and we, as unbelievers, stole quietly away.

My mother admired Sir Richard Burton and lent me the biography that had been written by his wife. One of my aunts had met him at dinner, "a very disagreeable man but handsome in an ugly sort of way" (precisely what an aunt would observe!), and it was natural that Burton should become the hero of my childhood. He had been brought up abroad just as I had been, he was a swordsman and I had begun to fence, he defied authority with joy and my greatest wish had been granted to him, really to pass at will from one nationality to the other. Had he not transcribed sixty words of monkey language and teased a solemn colleague with faked antiques? I plunged as deeply as I could into the Arab world through books, his *Medinah and Meccah* became a carefully studied manual of conduct while I dreamed of an Arab pony and sleeping out in a tent. I missed discovering Lady Hester Stanhope until I was grown-up but I grabbed my father's copies of the aloe-bitter novels of that great Englishman, Marmaduke Pickthall, although they really were above my head. I still remember some scenes from them vividly but in general I could not understand what they were about. It was only when I was older and read the strange story of his life that I appreciated his gifts. Why has he been forgotten, especially at this time when people are so interested in the East?

At ten I preferred *A Short History of the Saracens* by Ameer Ali. I soon knew the Khalifs, the differences between the Sunni and the Shi'a or the story of the Assassins almost by heart but of all things in the world it was a chapter on taxation that filled me with enthusiasm. I tormented my parents asking how much this or the other thing cost. They did not know that I contemplated taking over an island or an oasis and that I was worried about the expenses of soldiers and roads. Even today although I grumble about paying more than anyone around me, the mechanics of taxation and the science of "costing" fascinate me, in spite of a lack of technical knowledge. People say that I absorbed my interest in finance at home. This may have been true at the start but it also developed from my historical reading. The cost of moving an army excited me almost as much as its battles. I was, at the time, precisely ten years old.

The East is childhood or age; it is never the middle years of planning and anxiety. It can be unspeakably cruel. I knew a man whose friends had had the head of a relative tossed inside their door. Study the Arab tales; the unattainable jewel is neither wisdom nor beauty but something beyond their experience and that is, justice. And justice is also the passionate wish of the always Kafka-like child, adrift in an incomprehensible world. The Orient has had to flatter and bribe during the thousand years that it has taken the North to batter out its concepts of equality and freedom. They may not meet; yet there has always been a close relationship between England and the East. The form of a Mycenaean dagger was carved at Stonehenge. King Alfred received a gift of drugs from the Orient, the contact continued during the Crusades and from the end of the eighteenth century to 1939 it would have been difficult to find a town in Britain that had not sent some citizen out to India. Many never returned but those who came back brought new words and spices or, in another sphere, equally unfamiliar philosophical influences. We have so thoroughly assimilated those elements that they have become part of our birthright just as we have left the Orient with a memory of "English justice" and officials who were isolated from family feuds and could not be bribed with gifts.

I could not accept Islam after I was fifteen. After my mind developed I was horrified by its attitude to woman and its fanaticism. It advances literally by the sword (as now in certain parts of Africa) and a religion imposed by force can have no roots in faith. In 1903, however, it spoke to me as simply as to most of the Sufis; in trust, in compassion and as a defense against danger.

Religion in Egypt was not only Islam, it was also *The Book of the Dead*. This was the original adventure story, a voyage through danger into heaven. I took to this ancient faith like a duck to water. It never preached; it always explained. There were no terrifying pictures as in the Italian churches of wailing figures tumbling into hell. It was true that the Osiris story was grim but it was also remote. I did not think of Isis (years were to pass before I read of "the woman who was made a man by her father, Osiris") but Horus, the child, the hawk-headed, was both a warrior and a perfect Henty book hero. It was so simple; a boat sailed along the river just as our steamer puffed its way up the Nile. The would-be initiates faced tests; we had to find water, we might lose the path or, through pure weariness, drop our spears. If so, vultures and hyenas were waiting to pounce on us while we lay helplessly on the sand. To endure was the first triumph, then Thoth himself, his friendly ape beside him, would welcome us and lead us to the judgment hall. If we had murdered, looted or robbed the unfortunate, the crocodiles were waiting in their pool but if our hearts balanced (I loved the feather that to me *was* truthfulness and not a symbol of it) we should remember the passwords and run out to the lotus fields to play for ever and ever. Yes, the journey was the twin of life, free from snares and the incomprehensible subtleties surrounding me in the West. The only bit of it that I could not understand was the sacred beetle. I looked at scarabs and the live ones clinging to ledges in the mud walls and wondered. Life and age, death and renewal are shadowy to a child and I clung the more closely to Thoth, the ibis-headed scribe, and his wonderfully gentle ape.

When there are so many memories it is wise to concentrate upon a few. Many children have a good uncle in their lives, with me it was Dr. Boyce. He was no real relative, we met him riding near the pyramids, but he talked to me seriously without mention of any babyish topics and our friendship survived even his prescription of some odious potash lozenges when I got a sore throat from the dust. He came from Kent but was partly Irish and, with the dash of eccentricity common in the British Isles, he had worked almost without holidays for years as a specialist in children's diseases so that aged about fifty he could retire "and see the world." We often had no news of him for months and then he would call upon us suddenly, bringing me a Tibetan necklace that was subsequently stolen, to my sorrow because of its associations, and speaking of places with authority that I could not find on my schoolroom atlas. Eventually he took a post as private physician to a Russian nobleman to learn the language and prepare himself for a supreme trip. He wanted to go to Bokhara ("You must pronounce it Bo'hara," he corrected me when he told us), a city more rigidly behind an Iron Curtain then than it is today. He would have got there, I think, but he was due to start in the summer of 1914 and hurried back to England instead because of rumors of a possible war. The conditions that he had seen in Russia had shocked him profoundly and conservative as he was, he was sympathetic towards the revolution. In the autumn of 1914 he went out to a hospital in France and died from overwork a year or two after the Armistice. Almost the last time that I saw him was during the influenza epidemic of 1918. "Why didn't you get inoculated?" he said reproachfully, looking at my pile of handkerchiefs, and took me straight round to Dr. John Matthews who not only inoculated me for many years but became a lifelong friend and stimulated my interest in vaccines. In the desert, however, when we first met, Dr. Boyce flattered me by asking my opinion about Egypt; my parents liked him as much as I did and all that winter he joined us on most of our excursions.

Our first long trip was to ride across the desert to Sakkara. We left the pyramids behind us but as we trotted close to the Sphinx, Ali explained that it had once almost disappeared under the sand. We ambled forward over a wide plain and the light was so clear that everything seemed fluid. I resented being accompanied by a donkey boy whose indigo robe was belted up almost to his waist but Ali was firm, "It is the custom of the country and there must be somebody to water and feed your animal while you are having lunch or seeing the tombs." That first day we did not notice any gazelles but on a subsequent occasion some passed us in the distance; they were shy, as if somebody had drawn a few dark lines with a palm leaf against the horizon, and incredibly swift.

I wonder if my introduction to ancient Egyptian life on the walls of the tomb of Ti was not similar to the experience of another generation of children at the cinema? The pictures were in panels and full of action. An official walked across a field, men were reaping or feeding cranes, a boat shaped like a throwing stick was crowded with rowers. It was different from reading. I could see the movements, notice how a robe fell or the shape of a loaf of bread. Yet if I had not studied my two authorities, Baedeker and Henty, I reflected, I might have thought that the scribe was holding a stick instead of a reed pen or that the awning on the ship was a house. There were broken steps leading to an underground passage half choked with sand. The guide flashed his candle along it and my mother swore that she could see the track of snakes.

We ate our lunch under a green umbrella at the Rest House near the ancient Step Pyramid that rose mysteriously out of the sand. I did not want to go back to the hotel but if I ran away without a guide I might die of thirst before I came to the wells. We were alone, visitors usually found the ride too exhausting but we were used to exercise and went over in the early afternoon to the tombs of the sacred bulls. We walked through a stifling passage into a hall full of slabs of granite but I found it hard to understand why the animals had been worshiped. The guidebook wrote of mysteries but in its traditional manner did not explain what these were. I always seemed to be waiting angrily at the threshold of a door. It was too heavy for me to open but if I could have got the other side, surely there would have been a book or something to translate what seemed so obscure?

I shall never forget the end of that day. We rode to Bedrashen where we could take a train back to Cairo. An immense statue was stretched out under the palms. It was all that was left of Memphis, a lesson in the transience of empires and inexpressibly sad.

Cairo fifty years ago was the myth of a child's imagination. We went to Rhoda, a legendary island where Moses was said to have drifted ashore among the bulrushes that were still a part of the Nile and to the underground crypt where the Holy Family was supposed to have rested. Travelers' tales, yes, but as my mother said in front of the patient donkey tugging at a water wheel and the hut of sun-baked bricks, it was "exactly like the Bible." I visited an ostrich farm and remembered the Robinsons on their island as I watched a round orange descend a bird's long throat. They tried to sell us eggs decorated with signs and waved white feathers that made a noise like palm leaves when a boy swished them through the air. Hieropolis, the priests' city, had already become the summer quarters of Egyptian officials but at sunset nothing could take away the gold of its name.

Time was not unlimited and one night we took the train to Luxor to see Karnak and the Tombs of the Kings. My favorite excursion was to the Rest House, a square, whitewashed building where Cook's fed and soothed their tourists after a slippery descent down a barely existent path from the steep and crumbling hills. The groups from the steamers had to see "the sights" within so many hours but individual parties could explore the valley quietly, a tomb or two in a morning. After lunch I had to wait, trying hard not to scuff the sand against the metal legs of the chairs because that would disturb the ladies round me, dozing under their green-lined sunshades. The dragomans were asleep in another court, their hands folded above cinnamon robes while the minutes stretched like the worn elastic on my old hat until my parents took pity on me. A nod, and I was off with a donkey boy to the terraces of Deir el-Bahri that I had decided were the color of myrrh. In imagination I was already in Punt, in that land that had been found, forgotten and eventually rediscovered. Was it deep in Africa as some authorities said? Or was it the coast of Somaliland along the Red Sea? I wanted to stand alone and unhindered in front of the pictures, the Egyptians running down the gangplank like the sailors that I had seen in Naples, the beehive huts described in Baedeker, and the servitors carrying treasures up to the King. Nobody understood how important it was for me to remember every detail because they had not seen my exercise book; I was writing a story a whole nine pages long about a stowaway aged ten who went to Punt and came back with a pet monkey and a spice tree in a pot.

Was it destiny or merely a chance meeting? We were riding down the valley one hot morning when we stopped to talk to an Austrian archaeologist in a white sun helmet. He was examining a wall and I suppose that I must have questioned him because he took my hand and began to teach me hieroglyphics. M was an owl, I traced it after him on the rock with my fingers, here was a pigeon, this sign represented both a syllable and a house. I had the delicious sensation of entering a secret world. How powerful I should be once I had learned the names, even the dragoman did not know that a chicken was not carved into the rock for fun but because it was a letter and part of the alphabet. I was gloriously proud when the archaeologist (whose own name I never knew) told my father that if I stayed for the winter I should be able to read the easier texts. I pored for hours over the notes in Baedeker afterwards! I was lucky to have met this Austrian first. Some English archaeologists to whom I spoke upon a subsequent visit elbowed all laymen out of their way and sneered at me for asking whether they had found any scraps of poetry on their ostraca.

Sometimes the smell of bats drove us out of subterranean chambers where the ground was littered with chips of alabaster. Whatever we saw represented in the temples was duplicated in the life around us, the men stooped over their crops in the same way or, with the stiff, slow movements of a frieze, drove their donkeys to water. Once an Egyptian came nervously up to us with two evil-looking dragons, they were scorpions, fighting on a pottery sherd. I was lifted up to see a polished basin into which they put the babies in the summer so that they did not crawl on the ground among the vipers. There were many deaths from snakebite, much malaria and plenty of smallpox; these things were kept hidden from that gold mine, the tourists, but we heard about them from Dr. Boyce. (For some reason, they did not seem to alarm my family as much as measles.) Ali gave me a piece of freshly cut sugar cane to eat; to my disappointment because I felt disloyal to the Swiss Robinsons, it had a sickly, unpleasant taste. Neither did I care for fresh dates.

We rode home slowly in the evenings past the Colossi of Memnon while I wished that they could find an inscription that would set the stones singing again. The Romans had heard them, then the sounds had suddenly ceased. How exciting it would be to know the real pronunciation of Egyptian words! My head was full of such thoughts as we trotted across the plain that stretched about us like a fisherman's shallow hamper, sand, grass and stalk overlapping each other in a pattern of ochre and green with an occasional kingfisher rising above the rushes.

The day came when we took a Cook's steamer from Luxor to

Assuan. We stopped at Esna to see the temple and the small boys ran up to us with tall black and white baskets or faked scarabs just as they had pestered Roman legionaries on their way to the Cataract or Arab travelers in the Middle Ages. The next place, Edfu, was a hawk. It was the temple of my hero, Horus. His bird faced us, black, polished and still on guard after two thousand years in front of columns whose shadows were the color of water. I scrambled up to the tower and down to the colonnade. I was angry when some of the tourists laughed. It was as holy to me as it had been to the Egyptians.

Most of all, however, I liked standing beside the rail of the steamer while we moved gently along the Nile. A drove of asses repeated the familiar oval of an Egyptian text. A pole creaked, men stopped, the buckets of precious water for the maize and onions passed to and fro. Tiny camels followed their heavily laden mothers and where the villages ended, black and white hoopoes with amazing crests waited as if in audience upon narrow, gritty sandbanks.

I read of course but was mainly dependent upon Tauchnitz. I had translations of novels about ancient Egypt by Ebers, *Uarda, The Sisters* and *An Egyptian Princess*. There was our invaluable guidebook, *A Thousand Miles Up the Nile* by Amelia B. Edwards. It had been published in the early seventies but the scenes that she described had scarcely changed during the intervening thirty years. "This experience will give her more than two years at school," an American lady said to my mother. Two years! What an understatement! The background was there for life.

Kom Ombo was a frontier post where the river civilization and the sand met in uneasy alliance. It had a temple dedicated to two gods, Darkness and Light, the crocodile and the falcon-headed, a wonderful frieze of ducks rising out of a clump of rushes into the sky and a pool where they had once kept live crocodiles.

I did not like these creatures. To me, as to the ancient world, they were a symbol of some dark force able to alter destiny in a few seconds. The bravest hunter was powerless against them if his boat upset and although I knew that now they were never found so far north, I glanced prudently up and down the Nile as I came on deck.

It was early morning, there was nobody by the gangway. I ran ashore alone and started to explore the country, being careful, however, to keep our steamer in sight. This was the frontier of "Bow Land," the ancient name for Nubia and a camp for the caravans traveling to and from the Red Sea.

Three small children came towards me, glistening with castor oil. The boy's head was a mass of fuzzy hair, the tiny plaits, that were as many as the leather strings of the aprons that were their only dresses, dangled to and fro whenever the little girls laughed. They pointed at me. I smiled back and asked politely in my most carefully phrased Arabic if I might play with them? They howled and ran away.

How strange I must have looked! I was still dressed in woolen combinations, a bodice, knickers, and white petticoat, a blue dress with white braid, coat, black ribbed stockings and high boots. As a special concession to the African climate I had been permitted to leave off my flannel petticoat and had escaped that morning without gloves. I may even have had a Baedeker in my hand. My Arabic was unintelligible because they would certainly have spoken a dialect but I knew at once that it was my color that had driven them away. To them, black and almost naked, rubbed gloriously with oil like the Greeks at the funeral games, my white face under an overlarge, green-lined sun helmet can only have seemed a mask created by some medicine man to ward off the plague.

Color prejudice is inconceivable to me. (I doubt if my conviction springs from this incident because I am sure that I should never have had it.) Has either a black or a white face the monopoly of eternal values? Supposing that a creature arrived from another planet with a green hide and pink spots, are we to refuse his offer of friendship because his appearance differs from our own?

Naturally I did not think of such problems at that time. I was merely disappointed that they would not play with me and that I could not smear my head with castor oil.

"What do you expect me to do for you?" my analyst asked, almost angrily, many years later. "As a child you have been in Paradise!"

This was true. We rode every day across a desert that was not the flat plain that Westerners, accustomed to a beach, associate with sand but lightly smoothed ridges rising into hills. At noon these were gray but they turned into a fawn at sunset that darkened into glowing red. All an Arab's feeling for the "black tents" was flowing through my

73

blood. How could it be otherwise? I had loved adventure from my cradle and the realm before me was the kingdom of the tribes. I led, always. This was understood for the peace of the caravan. It was less the hunger to be first, I knew little then about competition, than a headlong urge to throw myself immediately into everything unknown.

Ali came abreast of me one morning as we trotted past the half-buried column in the alabaster quarries. I was wishing that I knew how to carve one of the many scattered chips into a foal or perhaps a bird when he stooped in his saddle to inspect my donkey's straps. The animal bore the unfortunate name of Ginger Brandy but it had a beautiful necklace of blue beads strung round its white neck to keep off the evil eye. "We are going a long way," he said, "but you will enjoy yourself. We are following the caravan track as far as the first halt."

It was particularly clear. The sand beneath my donkey's hooves was a fine, transparent apricot. Further away, in a hollow of the valley it reminded me of the topazes that a Cairo merchant had shaken into his palm from a black and white box. I was scolded suddenly for not answering and losing myself in a daydream but who, on such a morning, wanted to talk? Oh, if we had only got tents with us so that we need not go back to the hotel but could ride on week after week until we came to my other love, the sea. A donkey boy shouted, we stopped. Ali stood up in his stirrups, exactly like a trader from the friezes in his billowing robes. "Look!" he pointed and there, motionless and taut, I saw a long, tawny-haired dog. "Jackal!" There were whispers in Arabic and English. "What is it doing? They seldom come out except at night." Had it smelt us trotting too near it in that lonely valley or had some beast disturbed it in its lair? We watched, it turned its head swiftly towards me, then with a bound it disappeared among the cliffs.

The jackal was an omen of an adventurous day. More than an hour later we reached a pile of what seemed to be sticks, glistening on the sand. "Insh'allah," Ali muttered, "so near their destination." I saw now that the heap was the ribs and skull of a camel, polished by the sand to an extraordinary whiteness. Ali shrugged his shoulders and I knew, of course, that he was thinking about "Mektoob," or fate. Presently one of the donkey boys came up with a stalk of camel plant, full of thorns but with rubberlike leaves. The animals were fond of it and nibbled it when turned loose. Otherwise there was nothing but grit and dust, our own shadows and the burning sky, though we passed another bush that a boy slashed with his knife until an evil-looking sap oozed from its stem. I must notice it, Ali said, as if he were Pastor Robinson, it was poisonous and must never be touched because its juice could blind a man and it was the sign of a traveler that he could distinguish the difference between good and bad plants.

We had never been so far into the wilderness and it was past midday before we dismounted at the entrance to a deep valley to rest in the shade of an overhanging cliff. Why was there always too much food at the hotel and never enough on picnics? Ali told me stories about the Fayum while the boys unpacked the basket, he pulled an uncut turquoise from his pocket that he had picked up in Sinai, he mentioned an oasis of which I had never heard. He was still a Khalif's messenger with a hundred tracks in his head. He might have been twice from Cairo to Alexandria by train but he had never entered a car.

The shadows lengthened, the boys collected the donkeys, I buried my eggshells carefully in the sand. A cloud of dust came towards us from the gorge. Ali gave a sharp command, we remounted, the boys yelled. The whirlwind swept towards us, it turned into a group of shrieking Bedouin, they flourished matchlocks, some had swords. It was ridiculously familiar, like one of those pictures labeled *African Fantasia* that hung in the Paris shop windows but this time it was real and directed against ourselves.

We formed ourselves into a compact group. I was not frightened, I was very, very happy. I snatched a stick, I kicked my donkey's sides. I was ready and willing to meet the charge. My donkey boy pulled me back, swearing at me in Arabic. "They are going to murder us," my mother gasped, couching her sun umbrella like a lance. It seemed probable because they were pointing their guns at our heads. "Keep quiet," my father commanded, producing a revolver to our intense surprise, "and remember, whatever happens, the British army will avenge us."

This statement did not seem to cheer my mother up at all. I was still struggling to fight but the donkey boy held my arms. The dust was suffocating as they charged to within a foot of us before they reined their beasts back. Ali, he had a dagger in his hand, pointed to our lack of baggage, protested tactfully that we had no alms to give them and suggested meeting them that night in the Assuan bazaar. Their white clothes were travel-stained, their camels thin. For a few moments, to quote the popular press, our fate hung in the balance, then Ali must have convinced them with his quiet explanations that we were not worth looting. The leader looked us over, gave a sharp command and they thundered away. One man, I noticed, had a shield.

Were we in danger? Yes, up to a point. We were further away than tourists were in the habit of riding and without the armed guards that accompanied a proper expedition. I do not think that they would have killed us but they might have held us to ransom, in which case we should have spent several uncomfortable days hidden in a cave, certainly with lice and fleas and possibly with scorpions and vipers for companions. We sent them something that evening, not much, because appeasement might have endangered the lives of other travelers, but enough, I expect, to have given them a meal.

We did not resume our homeward journey until they were out of sight. The hills turned from a glowing apricot to a brick and powdery red. There was no sound except for the scratch of hooves against a pebble or the jingling of a rein. Many things may befall me but until the gods take memory away I have had a day in Heaven, as much beyond imagination as Paradise is beyond life. Some, though not all, of us are born to the wilderness. The world may break us but we are seldom to be tamed because it is an inheritance that does not depend upon reason. What is a wild gallop through an unearthly land but the physical symbol of the spirit of man?

There was plenty to learn about the present as well as the past. Every evening while my parents were at dinner, the chambermaid came in to see that I had not disobeyed orders and turned on the light in order to read. She was Swiss, we chattered together in French and I learned a lot about her own surprising sphere.

It had taken her nine years to get to Egypt. Every new hotel was a steppingstone because the "higher" it was in the season, the more she earned. Assuan was good, yes, but it was below Cairo, Monte Carlo or Saint-Moritz. No, they paid her her fare but hardly any wages, she depended on tips. Could I believe it! That miserable Frenchwoman down the corridor, the one who had taken the morning train, had I noticed perhaps that she already dyed her hair, well, she had rung her bell four and five times in an evening and what had she finally left? Five piasters and a bundle of worn-out stockings to be immediately thrown away. Five piasters! And the woman had been in the hotel three weeks. She knew merely by looking at us that our treatment of her would be correct. I must not think her avaricious, all she asked for was her due. Did I know that she and the floor waiter played a game of glancing at the new visitors and estimating what each would give or that they marked the trunks downstairs when the tips were poor? I should remember these things, someday I might marry and have to arrange the *pourboire* myself. Ah, but that was a long way off, she wished she had a baby of her own as active and as plump. I writhed with indignation over the word "baby" but curiosity kept me silent.

The stumbling block was the *Direction*. One had to accommodate one's self to the chef, the concierge, even the undermanager and thus, gradually, one arrived at Saint-Moritz. No, she had never been out to the temples. If she did have a few hours to herself she wrote to her mother or sewed, I must tell my mother that she was always happy to oblige a client. The young couple next door would give her a good present, I could make no idea to myself of how considerate they were. Finally we would hear my mother's footsteps, hurrying up from dinner (my parents annoyingly assumed that I would get up to mischief if I could), the covers were pulled up to my ears, the maid disappeared and by the time that the family peeped round the door I was seemingly fast asleep.

A few quiet breaths, the imitation of a dormouse and then, as soon as the danger of parental interference was over, I crept to the window. It was too dark to see the Nile but I could listen to the wild songs of the Nubian rowers as they brought the last visitors home.

French, Arabic, English, I moved so easily between the worlds. My donkey boy was perhaps eighteen, I, at ten, was roughly at the same level of development. The *corvée* had ended, he twitched Ginger's rein and we turned down another alley, but his brother would be called up for military service in a year and how was the family to be fed? There were many children, some younger than myself. The visitors were generous with bakshish, yes, but a boy had to give so much to the sheikh and so much to the dragoman; otherwise a strap would be slit secretly, the saddle would slip, he would be disgraced and sent about with the second-class tourists. The donkeys had to be fed in summer when there were never any travelers and people were mistrustful if a bridle had been mended. They wanted everything to be new. Wouldn't I ask my father to buy me Ginger Brandy? He gave me every gift I desired (sadly I wished that this were true), and I should never regret having a donkey of my own. Were we not always the first away, when had Ginger ever stumbled? His family would sell the animal to me for a good price, they would make a feast, oh, just a little one and he would chew sugar cane, he promised me, in my honor. Then on a fortunate day they would find a cheap donkey to train up for the following season.

We understood each other, though neither accepted at full value the other's protestations. I never made the suggestion about Ginger because I knew that the animal could stand neither a long voyage nor the English climate. Besides, I preferred a pony. I was cautious about bakshish, fearing the wrath of the dragoman, but I used my wits in the traditional Eastern manner and when the boy saw us off at the station, he was not, I think, displeased. It was part again of the common background of children brought up in the Orient; every word had its double meaning and we moved powerfully but also with discretion between the palaces and the souk.

It was not all sunlight. We were strolling along the river late one afternoon when the sky turned to fire. The news of an explosion at the hotel reached us by mouth-to-mouth radio, a mile in a minute. People began to run, we followed, a fiery wind like one of the Bible plagues beating against our faces. We actually saw a pillar of flame. A boiler had exploded in the laundry, two men had been killed, they were fighting desperately to save the hotel. A regiment of Egyptian soldiers had been called out to prevent looting, men were carrying invalids out on stretchers whose very existence had been unsuspected, and hauling up improvised beds. Some of the staff were holding down the brother of one of the victims; he was screaming horribly and had tried to throw himself into the blazing ruins. Darkness came, the electric plant was flaring in front of us, the hotel would have followed if it had not been for the skill of a visitor, an American engineer. He sent hundreds of men into the desert to collect buckets of sand and these eventually extinguished the flames. I went to bed that night by the light of a small candle, I could see the ring of soldiers round the trampled courtyard, I felt death was near. It was the dark side of the mirror, it threatened my ordinary world of riding, sailing or chatter and as I looked at the wreckage I decided solemnly that I understood now all that Ali meant when he spoke to me about Fate.

This sense of circumstance beyond human control was intensified when we visited Philae. The temple was about to be submerged through the barrage that we crossed on a little trolley and that was the symbol of a new, nationalistic Egypt whose birth we unknowingly watched. It is strange to think that a few engineers were able to change a land completely that neither the Emperors, the Khalifs nor Napoleon had altered. The Egyptians spoke uneasily of desecration as we wandered for the last time between the graceful columns of the little temple. I was torn, as usual, between the past and the future; I loved everything connected with ancient Egypt but the dam had its own excitements when we rode along it. A row of pelicans watched us from their safe and distant ledges to the roar and buzz of vociferous machines. Perhaps it was the fire or knowing that I was looking for the last time at a colonnade soon to become part of the river but a little of my child's sense of invulnerability cracked, I began to be conscious that I was as subject to destiny as Ali, although I was ten and he seemed, in his fawn- and water-colored robes, older than my parents.

The Luxor hotel was full so on our way back to Cairo we stayed at a bungalow in the grounds. It stood in a garden of palms, roses and bougainvillaea which was, my mother said, swarming with snakes. We teased her for being afraid but it turned out that she was right. It was the custom at that time for tourists to meet and stroll beside the Nile punctually every evening at six. English traditions were relaxed but we spoke, I believe, only to fellow guests. Occasionally a dahabiyah arrived, then a discreet whisper passed along the road, "Do you know who's on board?" It was already considered an ostentatious way of traveling and our humbler multitude delighted in exaggerating its difficulties. "I should be afraid, dear," the lady was in billows of white muslin, "think of sleeping so near a native crew without a policeman on board." Her companion would lift her parasol an inch higher to stare at the intruders before murmuring, "And they say that they were caught in a sandstorm, *miles from a hotel.*"

One after the other, small black boys ran up to us with their hollow, pink palms full of imitation scarabs. Would we like ostrich feathers, a colored reed basket, this beautiful prayer rug (it had obviously come from Birmingham), a string of blue beads? We met friends, discussed the badness of the food, took our films to be developed and agreed that Egypt was wonderful.

I was to take no ordinary farewell of the Nile. One afternoon I heard my parents whispering together and with the special sense children develop under such circumstances, I knew that they were discussing a problem connected with myself. "Shall we tell her?" I heard. Tell me what? I pretended to be absorbed in my book and waited.

The sheikh of the donkey boys had brought me a scarab in token of recognition. I was one of them, he said, I belonged to the East. Of course my family had some tiresome explanations although they added generously, "He really wants to give you a present," but I was glad that they were unaware of my hold over the villagers. It was so useful being able to chatter in a language that they could not understand. Naturally these were my people, I looked at the boy holding Ginger Brandy in front of the bungalow and smiled. Why did they call me conceited? It was a fact. They could not change me any more than they could change that alabaster chip. It would remain a stone, it would never be a growing leaf and so it was with me while I went my adventurous way, seeking for some absolute although I was only ten, there would always be something Eastern in my heart. I strolled onto the terrace and thanked the sheikh royally though not in pride, we understood each other and I was grateful. What were the winds of England to me and its cold narrow streets?

There were times, however, when I blotted my copybook badly. I was more tiresome than usual one afternoon and was sent to bed early without a book. It was asking for trouble. I looked round for something to do and found that the sheet was loose. I draped it about myself and turned off the light.

Presently there was a knock at the door. The Egyptian boy who came round every evening to pull the mosquito nets and empty the washbasins because there was naturally no running water, hearing no reply, entered the room. He did not turn on the electric switch, probably he was afraid of it, and enough moonlight came through the slats of the blind for him to grope his way to the cords. I crawled slowly upwards, uttering little whistling grunts. The man turned, saw me, dropped his pail. A yell, rather than a cry, startled the guests in the distant dining room. He trembled, staring at me, too frightened to move.

I heard (triumphantly) my mother scream, "The child's been murdered!" My father dashed in only to find that he had to rescue the Egyptian and not his daughter. He went out saying disgustedly, "She has turned a black man white."

Next morning there was a solemn conference that I was forbidden to attend. No native servant would approach the bungalow. I had bewitched it and might bewitch them. My victim had wailed all night, he was very ill. It was known now that I was a small but powerful evil spirit. Would my family remove me immediately? The manager had to consider the rest of the hotel. Ali offered a loan of a well-seasoned hippopotamus-hide whip, excellent, he insisted, for the bringing up of girls. I remember that he scolded my mother for her mistaken kindness when she refused it. I flicked my leg with it experimentally. It hurt.

According to Greek tradition, Fate itself took my punishment in hand. The net had not been drawn and I had deemed it prudent to go immediately to sleep. The next day my eyes were closed up with mosquito bites and my arms were so badly stung that I had to have them bandaged for several days.

It was fortunate for me that we had already intended to leave for Cairo that evening.

Egypt was an ideal beginning. A child thinks in nouns and sees in pictures. I had the excitement of learning to read a second time with fingers as well as eyes as I moved along the sunlit temple walls. Here, and I tapped it, was a jackal but it was also the sign for knowledge, as well as being a bird the flamingo was the color red, and because of the dual meanings I began to understand abstractions. I followed the recovery of the ancient Egyptian language with the breathless attention that I might otherwise have given to a penny dreadful, there must be other secrets in the world and perhaps I could discover them, I would be an explorer of more even than seas.

How much I owe to my parents' courage. Imagine the fuss today! "Take your child to the East! Think of the games and companionship the poor little thing will miss, besides, how can she make her lessons up in time to sit for the eleven plus with the rest of her class?"

It was a question of love rather than of wealth. Not all of us can cross the seas but a simple day's holiday at the beach can be as rich as an Oriental palace if the parents explain its wonders vividly and with affection to the child. I knew that my family wanted me to be with them. Society did its best by constant stories of danger and supposed lack of educational opportunity to persuade them to leave me behind. I might have caught typhoid or malaria, we were nearly kidnaped, there was always some peril from snakes. My mother was warned to keep me away from the Assuan bazaars where a number of Egyptians were dying from smallpox behind the open booths.

Yet think of what I gained! I was reading history from books written not for children but for scholars by the time that I was ten, I could chatter in Arabic, I knew some hieroglyphics. More important perhaps than knowledge I had been near to poverty, fire and death; I may not have understood them but I had heard the Sufis speak. What school, what routine, could have given me so much?

I cannot remember Arabic now; it is the common experience of children once they have left a foreign country. To retain a tongue it is essential to be able to read in it and there is a gulf between "donkey-boy Arabic" and the beautiful language with its usually unpointed texts; nor did I study hieroglyphics after I was twenty. Yet a carpet of sounds, colors and smells is at the back of my mind ready to recur as sharply as ever once certain impulses touch my brain.

We sailed for Naples and England. My next visit to Egypt was in 1923 and by that time the world had changed. It was not disappointing, it was like an album of old photographs, familiar yes, but with no emotional content. I had squeezed the Orient dry in childhoood, there was nothing to add and I have no desire now ever to return. The background will always be a part of me but we alter as we develop and as I grew up I was drawn towards the West. Yet emotion is stronger than reason as I knew when I heard the voice of the muezzin, fifty years later, at Lahore. We need mercy in this ever revolving world and though the woolen thread of the dervish is now lost to me, I still remember the color of its compassion. How can we obliterate what has once been home?

 *Four*

The winter of 1905-6 was a disaster. Perhaps it was inevitable after the exultation of Egypt. We set off in early December, this time with a governess, an English girl of about twenty who subsequently became a great friend both of my mother and myself, to travel through Spain to North Africa.

I had prepared for the trip by reading Prescott's *History of Ferdinand and Isabella* and Washington Irving's *The Alhambra*. (I wonder if people appreciate now how widely some American books circulated among the English at that time.) There was also a Henty about the Carlist wars but it is perhaps significant that it is almost the only story of his that I cannot remember. We had looked forward to the journey but we were unhappy in Spain. It was partly the poverty, people shivered in their grimy clothes and were too numb and unhappy even to beg. Yet there was something more; we felt a hostility that was hard to define and for the first time I was miserable and bored.

Madrid was piercingly cold and we caught influenza. We swallowed huge doses of ammoniated quinine, the favorite remedy of the period, and after the fever subsided spent our mornings at the Prado. I tried to copy the horses of Velásquez and I liked Goya who had drawn the crowds that we still saw in the streets but my impressions were external. I missed the depth of Egypt, the liveliness of Naples. The solitary moment that filled me with awe was when I saw the sword of Cortes in some armory. We went to a game of pelota but it only made me homesick for a windy English field and the footballers racing by us and the ball in our team's control.

The Escorial was terrifying and I was not even scolded for wanting to run outside into the sun. I remember only the synagogue in Toledo, perhaps because it was the first that I had ever entered. We all have one place that is nearer to our hearts than any other and it is natural that the reverse is true as well. I had just the same sensations when circumstances compelled me to cross Spain in middle age. It was as if I had to suppress all emotion on both occasions until I had left the country.

Once Christmas was over we went south. I remember being shaken awake in the middle of the night because the trains always seemed to leave at four in the morning and crouching over a brazier filled with lumps of charcoal at a hotel at Cordova trying to get warm. Of course I liked the Arab arches in the mosque there that had been converted into a cathedral and the tangerines, glistening as if beneath crystal, under a slowly falling rain. Seville, however, was a nightmare. The Spanish-American War had not been over long, the English usually left their daughters in the nursery so that I was taken for an American child and people leaned over the balconies and spat at me. After I had received a full blow in the face, twice in one afternoon, I howled.

I know that it will horrify all lovers of the Mediterranean but I could have knelt in Gibraltar and kissed the clean streets. I was so glad that I was English because of the warm and reassuring kindness of the faces about me and I was in my element when we drove out to watch the apes. It was not insularity, I had felt perfectly at home in Italy, France and Egypt. No, it was some underlying cruelty of which I was conscious in Spain and that was all the more sinister because I could not explain it, even to myself. I only knew that I was unhappy there and that it was, in all the meanings of the word, an alien place.

We arrived in Algiers early in January. It was snowing. This would have been endurable in England, "What else can one expect of the British climate?" but we should have had the comfort there of thick carpets and a blazing fire. The hotel was almost without heating, the wind blew under windows warped by the summer sun and we shivered. In addition, the city seemed entirely French with only an occasional fez to remind us that we were in Africa. We were not allowed to visit the mosques and after the richness of Egypt the tidy streets and dark clothes were a disappointment to us all.

My father talked easily to Frenchmen. They reminded him, I suppose, of his boyhood. He had spent it at Caen. I listened, as a result, to dozens of discussions as to whether the French or English method of government were better in the East. The English remained aloof and encouraged the inhabitants to retain their native cultures whereas the French mixed with them more freely but distrusted the Orient, they wanted their Arabs to become as *Parisien* as possible. "We assimilate," a bearded, sunburnt engineer proudly declared one day after lunch, "you are a nation of sanitary inspectors and police. One day," he shrugged his shoulders expressively, "you will go. We shall stay." Now, fifty years afterwards, the French system seems to have lasted a fraction longer in time.

There was no donkey boy to tell me about his village nor any archaeologist to show me some painted hieroglyphics. "We might as well be in Paris," I grumbled as I walked up and down the avenues in my best coat and hat looking at shop windows. "Wait till you get to Biskra," they consoled me at the hotel, "that is the gateway to the desert." Full of anticipation mixed with some misgivings, we set off hopefully one morning and ran at once into an unexpected adventure.

Algeria is swept every winter by tremendous storms. The visitors are always told that these are exceptional and floods are never mentioned. One moment we were looking out of the window at a drab and stony valley, the next instant the train shook as if an avalanche had hit it and a swirling river of shrubs and pebbles sucked at the rails. People rushed into the corridor, were we still moving? Had we stopped?

"*C'est dangereux.*" The conductor, a portly Frenchman with an immense black beard, stuck his head into our compartment, looked reproachfully at my mother and groaned.

"Does he expect me to scream?" my mother asked icily, continuing to embroider a rose upon a piece of cream-colored silk. I thought that I saw a dead camel but it was only an uprooted bush. My governess got out another rug, it had turned very cold. "*Dangereux, dangereux,*" we could hear our friend moving up the coach. Yes, it was dangerous, a French engineer agreed, he had left his seat and was talking to my father, the floods naturally might undermine the track. All the same, he leaned out of the window to stare at the turbulence below us, he thought that the rails would hold. There was no need to alarm ourselves. We should reach our destination in due course but evidently, a thorny mass of branches hurtled past us as he spoke, yes, evidently, we should be late.

The Biskra that I remember must have greatly changed since 1893 and André Gide's famous visit. It was more like a small provincial French town than a gateway to the East. The hotel was low and square with a row of palms standing outside the terrace. There had been no train to Algiers that morning on account of the storm so the rooms that had been intended for us were still occupied. The proprietor rushed us into a bedroom that was full of plaster. *"Le vent!"* He waved his arms expressively, somebody had opened a door, the draft had blown in a window and had brought down part of the wall. After that, as he expected, we accepted our cramped and improvised quarters without grumbling too much. The provisions failed. We lived principally upon dried dates, a picturesque but monotonous diet. We sat in coats and even gloves trying to keep warm while everything that we touched was covered with half an inch of dust. I had read my books twenty times and my father's cheerful explanation, "If we had not come here we should not have known what it was like," irritated us beyond measure. He could amuse himself by talking to another group of engineers marooned, like ourselves, by the weather. We were disillusioned and angry.

The wind dropped eventually as suddenly as it had begun. A guide in a new, scarlet fez, baggy fawn trousers and a light coat that was almost French in cut, so different from Ali's soft robes, proposed a visit to Sidi Okba, a neighboring oasis. We longed to go anywhere outside the too familiar hall of the hotel and set out the next morning in a carriage drawn by two horses. We had first to splash our way across a shallow ford outside the town and then to drive for some hours across the dunes.

Sidi Okba was famous for the tomb of a marabout and for its dates. "Oh, she will be crushed!" my governess screamed, it was her first experience of the Orient, as a heavily veiled woman stepped into the middle of a group of donkeys. Each of the animals was trying to rub its triangular pack of fodder off against a wall. I sat with the aloof expression of the experienced traveler to whom such scenes were an everyday occurrence as a haughty figure on a big, white pony trotted past with his burnous drawn, hoodwise, almost across his face. A child, a slice of the flat, native bread in his hand, looked up from a game and laughed. The irrigation ditches had overflowed and the carriage wheels jolted from one pocket of mud to the next while the smell of stagnant water and rotting palm fronds tempted us in some places to follow the native example and breathe through handkerchiefs.

While we were looking at the outside of the tomb that we were not allowed to approach, the guide drew my father aside. Some village elders had warned him that another storm was about to burst and it would be safer for us to remain in Sidi Okba for the night. We could rent an empty native house. We looked at the mud floors and my father decided that it might not be the question of one night but several and we turned at once to hurry back to Biskra.

We drove about halfway and the weather seemed unchanged so we paused in the shelter of a sandy ridge to eat a hurried meal under the pale sunlight of what could have been an English winter day. There was not a soul in sight when we continued our journey. We rumbled on with much jingling of reins and I was thinking regretfully of my rides across the "real" desert during the previous year when the carriage halted abruptly. "Stop him!" my mother cried as the coachman leaned forward and began to lash the horses unmercifully. There was a strange sucking noise and we began to sink. I still do not know exactly what had really happened. Two hours before, the track had been rough but sandy; now the entire plain was a treacherous swamp. A thin glutinous mud, the color of lava, coiled ominously forward. Deep runnels of water were beginning to appear around us while the carriage wheels were locked and the frightened horses could not extricate their legs. I was lifted out and stood on a hummock a few feet away. The others jumped. I felt a slight but disturbing pull on the soles of my boots and, for once, even my father seemed uncertain what to do.

We stood in the cold wind while the carriage sank further and further into the mud. Fortunately for us, a French officer appeared on horseback, leading a troop of mounted soldiers and two mules, each of which had a strange stiff bundle strapped to its saddle. It was not precisely cheerful to be told that these were the bodies of two French priests who had been swept away by a flood and drowned, some days previously. The officer rode over to us to ask what had happened but as soon as his men halted, their chargers began to sink. He gave a sharp order and they all moved off again while he shouted to us that he would send us help.

We waited on our hummocks, dragging first one foot clear and then the other. The horses were quiet, their haunches were held as if in a vise. The guide's fawn trousers were a mass of slimy patches although he had rolled them above his thin knees. It cannot have been more than half an hour (although it seemed much longer) till men and ropes arrived from a neighboring village. They heaved, they hauled, up to their waists themselves in mud, the traces broke, they mended them and pulled again until the horses struggled out at last onto firmer ground and a dirty, dripping object like a trampled mud pie emerged slowly from the bog. It was our once-polished carriage. Our guide produced a dagger from under his coat, we did not know whether this was a symbol of his authority or a sign that he expected trouble. We jumped into our seats while they were reharnessing the animals, paid our rescuers and drove off as fast as we could, while they quarreled violently about each man's share of the francs, a few feet from the quagmire.

Our own troubles had not ended. We still had to cross the ford. The four inches of water from the morning had deepened into a yellow torrent. Yet what were we to do? The bog lay between us and the oasis and we could not camp out in the desert for the night on account of both bandits and the cold.

The driver yelled. We plunged forward. The force of the river flung us sideways, we put our feet up on the seats because water was swirling over the floor. I almost disgraced myself by squealing as we seemed to topple; I thought the landau was going to turn upside down with us inside it, unable to get out. "You shouldn't have brought the child into this," my mother protested and for once I almost agreed with her but my Henty training reasserted itself as the carriage staggered forward and we reached the shallows.

Our fellow guests were lined up in the lounge, discussing our probable disappearance by the time that we reached the hotel. Who but the mad English would go out in such weather? There was even an enterprising journalist waiting with his notebook on the steps. I never shared the Victorian horror of reporters and would have liked to talk to him myself but was whisked upstairs immediately lest I chatter. I thoroughly enjoyed reading about our adventures in the local paper the next day and only resented the fellow's too fertile imagination. Of course we had never screamed "from the bottom of our stomachs," it had merely been a painful surprise to be almost drowned in a desert.

The line to the coast was still cut in several places on account of the storm, there were no newspapers, a hardship in those pre-radio days and worse still, from my father's point of view because he was primarily in Algeria for business reasons, there were no letters. We went to Constantine directly the railway opened only to find that we were trapped again. The wind blew round and up the famous cliffs, dark Jewish faces watched us suspiciously from doorways and we caught glimpses of plump women with bare arms, covered with silver bangles, in spite of the cold. By this time my father had either reverted to his Caen boyhood or succumbed to an Oriental fatalism, we were not sure which, but my mother had reached the limit of her endurance. She dressed us both in our best clothes and went to call in person on the stationmaster. He was very kind, he had a fire lit immediately in his office and discussed our predicament with sympathy and understanding. Constantine was one of the coldest places in Algeria, there was naturally nothing for Madame to do but he had had a wire to say that a train could get through to Bône on the following morning and he advised us to return to the coast. It would be warmer and there would be more shops. We returned in triumph to my father and packed.

Bône was a pleasant town of small white villas, each built inside a garden, facing the sea. It was completely French in atmosphere, the hotel was full of people whom I was to recognize in novels when I was a little older, men with newspapers propped up against wine bottles at lunch or women staring for hours into half-empty coffee cups. Conversation centered on the weather or crops. At least we could brush the sand out of our hair and refuse, with ostentation, to eat dates. We had only a very old guidebook and it was not my favorite Baedeker but it mentioned a forest just outside the town that had been full of lions. We drove there one day but it was as quiet and peaceful as any country park. I forgot Bône completely until 1923 when Norman Douglas gave me a memoir of Isabelle Eberhardt to read. She had spent her first months in Africa there with her mother and, as sometimes happens, the place flashed back into my mind with a more than pictorial intensity and I felt myself kneeling again on the shiny, black leather seat of the carriage, staring between the trunks of the trees, in the hope that one lion had survived.

"If we had not come here, we should not have known what it was like." As so often, my father was correct. It was natural for me, aged eleven, to miss the desert rides and all that Egypt had given me but the time was not wasted in spite of my grumbles. I knew the danger of floods, Isabelle Eberhardt was drowned in one, and the somehow thinner atmosphere of the Algerian dunes, when I read Gide and other books about the country in the nineteen twenties. "Never mind, Miggy," my father said at the end of a particularly dull afternoon, "we are going to Tunis tomorrow and then you will get back to the bazaars."

I did not think of Tunis, I thought of Carthage and of Henty's Malchus hiding in the reservoirs. Alas, it was another disappointment. It was partly because we all had influenza again, I seemed to have my nose permanently inside a handkerchief, but it was also because I felt myself "outside." Nobody talked to me, the Arabic was harsher and I could not understand it; besides I knew immediately that I was just an unwelcome stranger. We walked up and down the street of the scent merchants where they weighed essence of jasmine in tiny amber phials against one or more gold coins. It was interesting to watch once but there were no saddles, the houses, robes and turbans were white, there were none of the delicate colors that had made such lovely patterns along the Cairo streets, the atmosphere was not Oriental, it was French. I heartily agreed with my family when they said that the Midi would have been warmer and the journey less exhausting. I was seasick all the way to Marseilles and thoroughly happy to return to England.

Our disastrous winter had not ended. A few days after our arrival I caught German measles from a maid. It was worse in actuality than it had been in imagination because, apart from a third cold, I did not feel ill and yet I was shut up miserably in my bedroom for several days without the garden, my dog or my books.

 *Five*

Now what of summer? We went to the Alps, to Zermatt or Pontresina, long before these places were fashionable and explored them on our own legs. We got up at dawn, started up the hills with rucksacks on our shoulders and nails in our boots (it was before the days of Vibram soles) and came back at milking time with the goats. The Switzerland of my childhood has disappeared. This is a pity, it was such a gay world for a child. There are not many walkers today. It is a cheap way of seeing a country and tourist agencies discourage it, the young go to ski resorts with their lifts while motorcars have made roads too dangerous for us to use. We ought to have organized a group throughout Europe to protect our interests and to see that there were paths as well as *autostrade*. The essence of rambling is its freedom: to take a train to a national park and regain a station at some fixed hour makes it unnatural at once. Yet the real way to know a landscape is to cross it on foot; how is this possible when cars dash madly along even byroads and the air is full of petrol fumes and dust?

It is no wonder that I am adventurous. What a life my father had had! After his father's death when he was seven, my grandmother had taken him with his two sisters to Caen in Normandy. There he had made friends with two French boys rather older than himself who took him out hunting and fishing. He acquired not only the language but a Continental view of life. He looked perhaps more European than English with eyes that I saw as the green of a wave but that others said were blue and the short, pointed beard that was usual at the period. He was a fencer, swimmer and climber and as a boy had gone in for other sports. It was his dream, oh, how often he talked to me about it, eventually to retire from business and live in France. It was fitting that he died there. He was English in all his principles but French in his love.

Some years later the family returned to Birmingham where he entered King Edward's school. "If I had gone to a public school," he used to say when I was older, "I should never have got so far in business," adding sometimes, "The younger one starts the better." He left home at fourteen after a slight disagreement with my grandmother over smoking in the drawing room. (He smoked one cigar after lunch and one after dinner, never more nor less, just as he drank one glass of wine at midday and two in the evenings. Apart from the traditional bottle of brandy for medicinal purposes that was almost never opened, we seldom had spirits in the house and then only for guests.) Characteristically he had stayed at school until he had passed his examinations and then articled himself to a chartered accountant. This man, William Smedley, was a Victorian eccentric in his own right. He was convinced that Bacon had written Shakespeare's plays and showed me the first Elizabethan book that I ever handled, a Latin grammar whose owner had scrawled pictures of his schoolboy comrades in puffed sleeves and ruffs over the pages.

At least the Victorians were free from the modern fallacy that childhood must be artificially prolonged. When a relative died and left my father a small sum of money (I suppose that he was about sixteen) he was able to dispose of it as he pleased. Mr. Smedley happened to want some funds to finance a new project at the time so my father offered to lend him the necessary sum on condition that he could come to the office an hour later in the mornings (in those days they often opened at seven thirty) and have four months of holiday a year. The bargain was faithfully kept.

So my father went to Switzerland and climbed. He is said to have made a first ascent on the Italian side of Monte Rosa, he was carried away by an avalanche, he outwalked a well-known guide for a bet. These activities did not prevent him from passing his final examinations with the highest possible marks. As a reward, he went to India to try some peak in the Everest region. (I suspect that he hoped to to get to Everest itself.) It must have been about 1882. The party was trapped on a ledge near the Tibetan border and his toes were frost-bitten. He did not lose them but it stopped further high-altitude climbs. He walked several miles a day to the end of his life and, apart from France, was at his happiest in the Alps.

I never climbed with him, I was too young but although my short legs could not match his long, trained strides and I must have held him back continually, he usually took me with him up the hills. To me he was Pastor Robinson, full of the facts that I loved and a guide to high valleys and easy peaks. How much more I learned from him than if I had been at school. Did I notice how small the fields were? That was because instead of the eldest son inheriting the farm as he would have done in England, it was divided equally among the children abroad. There were the laws of the mountains, "Be careful, Miggy, never kick a pebble off the path, you might kill some goat," and tests of endurance, "I've told you not to chatter going uphill, no, we can't rest until we have done two zigzags more." Once I blacked out from sheer exhaustion but I soon recovered and it was an invaluable train-ing for later life. Besides, it was fun, I slung a green canister over my shoulder that contained my lunch and could also be used for flowers, occasionally I let my hat slip on its elastic to the back of my neck. Yet it is the scents that I remember most, the wooden smell of the Alpine rhododendrons, the extreme freshness of the highest grass. And the water! The moraine beside it was not as gray or clear; it turned sud-denly to silver in the hollow tree trunks that led it from a hillside to the fountain near some barn.

Sometimes my mother claimed me and, while my father climbed to a hut that was just a dot below a glacier, we looked for gentians and picked bilberries. If I could manage to keep still long enough, we might see a marmot, perched, a perfect sentinel, in front of a rock. One perfect afternoon, a little goatherd led us up to a cliff of edelweiss. It looked so different growing in a cushion over the steep lip of a gorge from the solitary, stunted specimens that walkers find today. It was a world where all was color. The yellow globeflowers in the Zermatt meadows reached to my waist and I thought the bog cotton in the mountain pools was like some tiny shepherd's crook.

The Rhone valley seemed a golden place. It was always a hot summer afternoon when the train moved slowly through it on the way to Visp. The shutters on the chalets were painted in wavy bands of red and black, there were baskets of apricots in the orchards, avenues of poplars and, first to one side and then the other, the turbulent river rushing towards the lake. It was a scene that became a foundation stone of childhood because it was there, the July that I was eight years and ten months old, that I first read *Beric the Briton*.

I owed more to Henty when I was young than to anyone except my father and mother. He taught me history. I can still place dates and epochs by remembering the titles of his books. Yet he was not precisely a simple writer; looking over his books today, I am surprised to find so much powder and so very little jam. He knew, of course, what we wanted. Solid fare and plenty of facts. He was just to the other side and how far afield we ranged with him. To Carthage and Venice as well as to Mexico and Rhodes. He was also far from taking the conventional view of his fellow Victorians. He introduced me to Peterborough and to "Cochrane the Dauntless," a seaman I knew that I would rather have followed than either Nelson or Drake. People complain that his characters are alike but surely they have to be? We cannot expect a man to be a Kafka or Proust if he is writing for boys.

I read books by other writers, Ainsworth, Ballantyne and Kingston, Gordon Stables and Manville Fenn. I enjoyed them all, particularly Fenn's *Dick O' the Fens* and Ballantyne's *The Young Fur Traders* (I did not like his *Coral Island*), but I was never absorbed by them as I was by Henty. I have since tried to analyze what made his work so alive to me. I think that it was because he wrote from a background of personal experience, he had been in the Crimean War and as war correspondent on various campaigns, and that he was *entirely on our side*. I think children seek violence today because their legitimate literature usually preaches to them against their normal instinct for adventure. His views were strict, his heroes had to undergo a period of preparation, they had to learn foreign languages (most valuable advice) and harden themselves physically but afterwards they had their opportunities and rewards. People may laugh but much of whatever I may have accomplished during my life has come from never sitting still and expecting a sugarplum to fall into my lap without my having worked for it.

94

Of course these things were not clear to me that summer afternoon. I felt myself running near Beric in the wood because, curiously enough, I never felt inside his heroes but always beside them. I sorrowed over the burning of the rolls when the Roman villa was sacked and when I got to the great scene in the arena it was as if destiny had had me in mind when the book was written. Had I not scrawled *Rufus Was a Gladiator* on the strength of half a page of Baedeker the previous winter? It is sad that such unself-conscious absorption in stories is usually lost by the time that we are twelve.

The Rhone valley was one of the most beautiful places in Europe. Now the poplar avenues have been cut down to widen the roads and the apricot orchards have disappeared to make way for filling stations and factories. The population of Switzerland has increased by almost a million in the last twenty-five years and I have never been one to deny the necessity of industrialization. The people in the towns have to develop along modern lines but there could have been a pooling of interests; Nature has its rights as well as Man. It needed only a little, possibly national, care and one edge of the valley could have been left unspoiled.

Oh Helvetia, Helvetia, what have you done with your inheritance?

I must be one of the last people to have driven in a diligence or "post" carriage. We crossed from Thusis in the Engadine to Visp and the journey took about three days. I loved the horn that rang out as we clattered up to each stopping place and I was once allowed to sit on the coachman's high box seat and watch the straw hats bobbing up and down that the horses wore to keep away the flies. The balconies on the chalets recalled my long-discarded Noah's Ark and I wished that I could run up the outside steps to my bedroom instead of using the prim staircase inside a hotel. The children wore the dresses of their cantons as a matter of course; the striped skirts were faded and the bodices rumpled because they were their everyday clothes. They went barefoot in the meadows, otherwise they wore (as I did) heavy, nailed boots. Women waved to us, their rakes over their shoulders, peasants pulled their mules to the side of the road, the high pack saddles piled with bags. I can still feel the quality of that early morning air or taste the small, sweet greengages that were then at their prime but alas, so many other details are lost. Yet what could anyone ask more than to drive on and on in the sunshine and never sleep more than two nights running in any particular place?

Whatever we may think, the influences of childhood are the strongest elements in our lives. We may rebel against them; even so, they are the forces that have created our revolt. I wrote my own myth unconsciously in those hot, peaceful days among the petal-shaped lakes that became so much more familiar to me than an English meadow. The Greeks knew a lot about the spirit and it was not by chance that Artemis had a band of nine-year-old girls among her followers. Some of us belong to the soil and should remain where we are rooted but others are born wanderers and would rather ramble roundabout to heaven than be carried there easily in a chariot. Up in the high valleys, among the dark red mountain pinks, I was wild and free. Not lightly, but with a not to be restrained and unchildlike passion, I had to give myself, the heart to Artemis, the body to exploration.

Six

Fate was kind. I did few formal lessons in my childhood with the result that my mind developed freely and was ravenous for knowledge. There was always a governess but after my first Fräulein most of them were English, we liked each other and I have remained in contact with several till this day.

We are only discovering now the profound influence that England had on Europe during the nineteenth century and much of this was due to her export of governesses and nannies. They controlled children at the most susceptible period of their lives and I suspect that many of the revolutionary movements of that time can be traced originally to the ideals of justice that these strict Englishwomen implanted in their charges. A governess was also an integral part of middle-class life when I was a child and I feel that we have lost a great deal from a psychological point of view from her disappearance. The older child belongs to the classroom but the younger ones may find such a teacher less anxious about them than their parents and a convenient bridge between the lost nursery and the often baffling outside world. I valued my governess for the selfish reason that she talked to my mother and thus left me free for my own important affairs: a run with the terrier in the part of the garden where nobody could see us or a snatched forbidden moment with a book. I am afraid that my pranks as well sometimes reduced her to tears. I learned a certain amount of French and German grammar but arithmetic remained a blank. I had only to see a number on a page to forget what I was supposed to do with it. My mother insisted that I have piano lessons. I had no ear, I loathed these hours with an extreme violence and I was infinitely grateful when I was allowed to give them up, being at the same point as where I had started, five years previously. I discovered subsequently that I was a "color hearer"; that is, I saw and heard words as colors. It is common, although with most people it is confined to a few words such as the months or days of the week. It was general with me and has been recorded of many writers and painters but seldom of musicians. The modern explanation is that it is due to a slight confusion of the nerves of hearing and sight. I have always been extremely sensitive to words. I "hear" them in several layers as, I suppose, other people hear music and I can feel the discord if there is one syllable too many in a sentence.

We are not always born to our own land and I have known much about exile in my life. My father bought a small house at Eastbourne in 1903, it was almost on the Downs, and we lived there in the intervals of our frequent journeys abroad. I hated the town at sight. It was not built up then as it is today but it had all the disadvantages of a city without any of its rewards. I had to wear a hat and gloves if I went to the pillar box, the frequent east winds blowing the length of the front made me seasick and after the plain, bright colors of the South, I disliked the chalk that turned everything into pastel shades.

There were some compensations. My family believed in exercise and like a little Tudor page I rode, fenced and walked for miles every day. There were lessons every morning but more often than not either my father or mother came in after an hour or two and ordered me to "get out into the air." It was a reaction against Victorian stuffiness and the beginning of a new health-conscious age. It was natural that I wanted to fence, my father had been a swordsman since his boyhood but I was so small when I first insisted upon lessons that my mask and jacket had to be specially made for me. My master was an ex-army instructor who had no patience with protective measures. A mask, yes, but "you are given a sword to protect yourself" and if I made a wrong movement he flicked a bit of skin from my bare knuckles. It hurt and I seldom repeated the fault. He had no use for style so that when I moved eventually to a *salle d'armes* in London my teacher exclaimed after a first bout, *"Mais ça, c'est de la boxe."* I found the French fleuret too formal and switched to the dueling sword, the épée, dreaming of challenges. Fencing gave me both a feeling of confidence and the knowledge, when I studied Elizabethan afterwards, of what it felt like to have a weapon at one's side. A smith is said to have made William Morris a suit of armor when he was seven and whether people like his poetry or not, he knew how men wearing armor moved. Imagination may have wings but it also needs experience as a teacher.

Alas, what we lose through ignorance when we are young! I must have been one of the last people ever to watch a demonstration of old English quarterstaff. My first instructor used to practice it occasionally with one of his pupils. I do not know where he had learned it. Perhaps in his village? It was noisy, it was exciting, the sticks whirled and were parried in a light crackle of wood and there I stood, deserted of Clio for the moment, enjoying what I saw without a thought of the morrow, when for the asking he would have shown me the moves and the holds. It was a last not faint but thundering echo of feudal England like the maypole that I had passed that year on a village green and I had no more sense at the time than to thank him and run thoughtlessly home.

Up to about 1910 the ability to handle a horse was as much a part of education as learning to read and write. It was purely a practical matter with no suggestion of aristocracy about it. How was a tradesman to reach his customers, for instance, if they were beyond walking distance unless he drove or rode? I was put on a pony as a matter of course when I was eight. My first steed was gray, it had just come out of a circus and danced if it heard music. It was also so small that we once enticed it into the house after a lump of sugar.

I liked galloping across the Downs, especially in summer when they were covered with wide, almost flat wild roses and the gold pea-shaped gorse. The flowers of southern England rolled across the mind like the transparencies on sale at the village shop; a hollow full of viper's bugloss that looked as if a giant blue shovel had been at work on the hill, straggling clumps of mignonette that marked the track where we could not gallop, clumps of columbines where I learned to jump. I never had a pony of my own. My father said that I should gain more experience at a riding school but I knew that this was an excuse. A car, it was always breaking down, stood in what should have been our stables. Generally I was allowed to have Primrose, she was a race horse who had broken down in training and cantered, I thought, like the wind.

I lived through the switch from hooves to engines during these years yet, oddly enough, I do not remember resenting it. Change was in the air. I never rode after I was fifteen. I had not the slightest wish to drive a car and although I once took a few lessons to please my father, I was immediately turned out of the class as potentially dangerous and it took a lot of self-control not to say to him triumphantly, "I told you so." I love footpaths and detest roads. But flying! I took my first lessons at a small airfield near Lausanne in August, 1939. They were among the happiest hours of my life. "Flying is like riding," my instructor said as we rose into the sky, "the hands must be light." I felt the plane, I landed her myself, it was a *cheval de bois,* a switchback, yes, but I got her safely down and they said that I might make a good pilot in spite of being forty-five; then war broke out and took my happiness away. The bureaucrats of 1946 denied me a second chance on the grounds of age. Perhaps it was as well. I sometimes get the feeling in the air that divers are supposed to feel at certain depths. It is a quite irrational exultation and I might have gone up and up, only aware of the sky, until there was no more petrol left in the tanks.

There were compensations in England. I liked the food so much better than what I called "foreign messes" and after the too familiar "No, darling, that is too heavy to pack" I had my library jealously arranged in a special order in my own bookcase. Reading was limited to twenty minutes after lunch and the same amount before bedtime. I had to be in the open air. This rule taught me concentration because the time was so precious to me that a dozen people could have banged drums above my head and I should never have heard them. To this day, I avoid a quiet place in which to work. I also learned pages by heart to repeat to myself during walks. It was a form of oral transmission ideally suited to the training of a writer but at that time I dreamed only of going to sea. I had discovered Dana's *Two Years Before the Mast* and used to get out of bed at night and sleep rolled up in a blanket on the floor to prepare myself for a voyage round the Horn. It proved an excellent training for the wars to come and a couple of Arctic voyages.

It was not the custom then to give children the presents that they get today. I had a shilling a week pocket money but it never stretched far enough to buy the things that I wanted: books, plants for my garden, presents for my family and extra biscuits for my dog. I rolled the lawn, picked peas and ran messages to add to my supply. My mother was partially deaf from an attack of scarlet fever and the maid was frightened of the telephone so I took over that instrument. Probably any business instinct that I possess comes from a saturation in messages from or to my father. I did not always understand them but I knew that I had to be accurate or lose the post of which I was so proud.

It annoys me when people boast that they know nothing about money as if it were a virtue instead of a symptom of bad citizenship. Mankind has used some form of barter since prehistoric times and I feel most strongly that economics should form a basic part of elementary education, to be learned with reading and counting. Wealth may consist of technical skills or gold but the essential test is the use that we make of our gifts. It is the evasion of responsibility that is evil.

I was always more interested in money, I think, than my father. He was a mathematician and his interests were in abstractions. I have seldom known anyone more remote from the things of this world. The success or failure of an equation meant a great deal to him, its rewards to himself very little. He possessed the detachment that lifts finance into an art, creates "risk capital" and is one of the nation's most valuable assets. In antiquity, I suppose that he would have been an austere Pythagorean.

I never remotely belonged to such a sphere. Words had wings for me but never numbers. All the same, I wanted to go into business but my father forbade it because I was a girl. "Women will never be accepted at conferences," he said. I wriggled my way in to some extent after his death but, as psychoanalysts will understand, never in England nor in any industries with which he had been connected. I learned what little I know about finance largely alone and, oddly enough, I found my study of history of great practical value. It helped me to assess the future and to be aware of change. My destiny was to write books rather than run a factory but I have always been passionately interested in economics.

The chief interest of this time of my life, however, was fossil hunting. I was dinosaur-mad from the age of eleven. "But what happened *before* the ancient Britons?" I asked continually until I found the answer in an article about the earth in some children's magazine and chanted "Triassic, Jurassic, Cretaceous," whenever we went for a walk. My mother gave me Hutchinson's *Extinct Monsters* and I copied the illustrations endlessly with sticks of charcoal on red flower pots, in imitation of the vases that I had seen in Italian museums.

Did people know that Triceratops had overspecialized himself? He had developed three horns and these had made his head too heavy to lift so he had become extinct. (I often think of him if I meet some arrogant specialist today.) A Brontosaurus was so big that it needed a swamp to support the weight of its tail. Could I go and dig in the Pevensey marshes? I might find a bone. Those little dinosaurs were very dangerous although they looked like kangaroos, they often ate beasts bigger than themselves.

I found an ammonite under a clump of blue borage at the bottom of a landslide. I added Hutchinson's *Prehistoric Man and Beast* to my library and stormed the British Museum with an arrowhead that turned out, alas, to be an ordinary flint. I made my peace with fairy tales; mermaids were Eskimos in kayaks that a gale had swept to Scotland. Cuvier and Buckland became familiar names. The stories were so exciting; I could understand Hugh Miller's struggles to get an education because I was eager for explanations that I could not always find and who could be more adventurous than Marsh, digging up a skeleton from the Arizona sand while his men kept the mounted Indians from charging him? What I could not comprehend was why people had laughed at them and sometimes at me. There were many who *preferred* to believe in dragons rather than know that there had been life on the earth millions of years before man. How could they say that it was an attack on the Bible when fossils were just as much a part of creation as myself?

It is sad that paleontology is often neglected in schools, because it is the proper bridge between science and art. A complex discipline is needed to reconstruct a monster from two bones. A pterodactyl can fly to the utmost heights of some philosophical speculation. How secure the Cretaceous age must have seemed to its inhabitants. Then either slowly, or was it overnight, a change in temperature rubbed out a landscape or a sea, leaving a few footprints or a shell as the epitaph of a continent. It is good for our pride to realize what newcomers we are, how fresh to this ancient earth.

I was sent occasionally to stay with my uncle and aunt at Edgbaston near Birmingham. It was the Victorian world with a vengeance, far stricter than home.

My Aunt Ida was the elder of my father's two sisters. She was born on July 28, 1856, and died on February 3, 1959, aged a hundred and two years. At the time of my first visit she was a slight but imposing figure dressed in the fashion of an earlier day with skirts that trailed over the ground and what I called "a coachman's tippet." Unlike my parents, she did not believe in either exercise or fresh air. I know that she wanted to win my affection but she frightened children, perhaps because she thought of us as naturally wicked beings who had to be scolded in order to be "saved." She had a fund of stories, each more gruesome than the last, about the fruits of disobedience. Most of the boys and girls whom she had known seemed to have fallen out of carriages into rivers where inevitably they had been drowned. She did not approve of the way in which I was brought up and considered my navy blue clothes too gay. One alarming afternoon she walked me round and round the big lawn questioning me about my knowledge of the Bible to make certain, as she said, that I really understood the meaning of an oath. Fortunately my Victorian books had prepared me for such an occasion and I was wary, I would not give my word in advance. She wanted me to promise her solemnly that even if my father offered me an oyster, I would never eat it. If I did, she warned me, I should inevitably die from typhoid. I must also never touch salad. (I think that this must have been a memory of her own childhood when cholera was still rampant throughout England.) If I were her daughter, she would never allow me to go abroad (I heard this in horror), I ought to have been sent to school but now it was too late (I was ten), she was so sorry for me, how I should regret my ignorance when I grew up. I listened patiently and with reasonable politeness in the hope of hearing something about my father's boyhood. Alas, all that she ever told me was that he had been very fond of a monkey, the pet of a friend.

Southern England might have abandoned itself to the Edwardian age but Birmingham remained a fortress of the manners and customs of the eighteen seventies. The day began at eight with family prayers. I had been up since six and was ready for the huge meal that followed, bacon, eggs, sausages on Sunday as a special treat, bread, butter and marmalade, all of a quality that I have not tasted since 1914. Breakfast has always been for me, unlike most people, the most important meal of the day. I walked with my uncle afterwards to the neighboring station and waved to him as he went off to his office, he was a solicitor, on the puffing, local train, then I played in the garden or read in the library while my aunt was busy with her household duties. We never went outside the gate without a definite errand. The more respectable a family was the more afraid they seemed not of gossip, that was unthinkable, but that somebody's cook might remark casually that she had seen us going up the road. In such a case, there had to be a precise reason for our expedition, there was no idle walking except in the countryside. We did visit friends, "my brother's child" had to be inspected to see if it had grown but oh, what trouble I got into for confessing that I had never even *heard* of the ritual of calling and leaving cards. Twice a week the maids came into the dining room to be taught scripture and needlework and once a group of my aunt's friends met to read a severely censored copy of a play by Shakespeare. On that occasion I was sent happily upstairs with a plate of cakes. There was no set lunch for the grownups although I was always given something to eat at noon but directly my uncle returned from Birmingham a four-course dinner was served at about five thirty when the news of the day was discussed; I was allowed to ask questions but never to interrupt, "A child should be seen and not heard," and at seven thirty I was sent to bed. My elders had "tea" at nine and the cold meat and tarts that I saw arranged on the dining-room table always looked nicer than the meal that I had just eaten. It was a familiar atmosphere from one of Mrs. Molesworth's stories but very different from either Henty or home.

The house was a dark, rambling place with engravings from Landseer hanging on the walls. It was a time when animals meant more to me than people and I admired them very much. The garden was larger than ours and full of tiny, gold raspberries. I have never tasted so sweet a berry since. There were beds of old-fashioned mimulus as spotted as its name and a greenhouse where I crouched under big maidenhair ferns because their hot, green scent suggested a jungle. The cocker spaniel, Roy, had a trick of standing on his hind legs to nibble the choice bits out of pears. It is rare for a full-grown dog to eat fruit and I was afraid that I might be blamed but my uncle knew the spaniel's habits.

Every visit Aunt Ida took me over a factory with the double purpose of demonstrating *The Child's Guide to Knowledge* and convincing me that I must never value material possessions. I saw pencils being made and spoons being plated. The workshops were exciting; question after question came to my lips but I was too shy to ask them in front of my aunt and to crown my misdeeds forgot to say "thank you" properly after one of these tours. I think a lot of bad manners in children is due to shyness. I remember lingering beside a little girl who was fitting pencil leads into cedarwood cases. I thought that she looked happy but as soon as we left the building, my aunt explained that it was my duty as soon as I grew up to see that such children went to school and not to work. I wondered whether adding sums up on slates was not much worse than sitting on a factory bench but was prudent enough to keep such thoughts to myself. The nineteenth century did more than we do, I think, to keep children in touch with manufacturing processes, we were nearer to the times when most articles had been made at home or in the villages, but actually to be told that a pious heart was better than a golden sovereign made me sigh regretfully that I had so few opportunities to earn more funds.

Fate seemed bent, however, in 1905 on making an Arab out of me. My uncle was wonderfully kind. He loosed me in a library full of Oriental books, smelling of leather and dust. His father had been a scholar who had spoken sixteen languages. I could not find out much about him, they said that he had studied too hard and died from brain fever while still quite young. I plowed through the romance of Antar in a Victorian translation, it was very heavy going, tales from *The Thousand Nights and a Night,* not in a child's version, and pages from the Koran. It seems odd that this vast mince pie was not considered somewhat advanced reading for a ten-year-old but in my aunt's eyes I was retarded and babyish. "Your grandmother was head of a household when she was little older than you are" was a favorite reproach.

They wanted to be kind. They took some Hentys out of the library to which they belonged although one was a three-volume novel that I found strangely disappointing. Gorged with books and feeling slightly guilty because I had disobeyed my mother's instructions "to play in the open air as much as possible" I was glad when the time came to return home although I knew that trouble was inevitable after my aunt's invariably adverse report upon my manners. Nobody stopped to think that the standards in the two households were not the same. Life was one long scolding for the Victorian child; it toughened us, I suppose, but it had its dangers. We were often genuinely bewildered and the seemingly irrational prohibitions led only too often to neurosis in later life.

 *Seven*

We arrived at Palermo in December, 1906. It rained for seventeen days on end and there was no heating. One evening we managed to get a stove installed in the sitting room. My mother discovered that there was no chimney and I shall never forget her saying to me, "Don't tell your father, darling, it is New Year's Eve and I long just once to get really warm." I was in my outdoor coat and my dressing gown at the time. We both thawed out peacefully until my father returned from one of his "brisk walks." (I realize now that one reason for the clarity of his mind was that he lived like an athlete in training until 1914.) He sniffed the smoke, examined the heater and extinguished it immediately. That night, in spite of the occasion, we were all in bed by nine o'clock.

Palermo at that time was a mixture of races and cultures. I am not in love with unity when it comes to experience and the different patterns in countries such as Switzerland and the United States have always attracted me. It is the early instilling of a tradition into a child that is important, not the geographical site. I feel the essence of England the more deeply because I have lived most of my life in Europe, apart from two wars. Understanding depends upon a measure of detachment; emotion, and we need both, upon unreason.

I had read Freeman's *History of Sicily* and watched the crowds eagerly as a result for a Carthaginian face. The idea of the lingua franca also gripped me. How wonderful it would be to travel from one end of the Mediterranean to the other, speaking a mixture of Arabic, Punic and French! Palermo was terribly noisy, coachmen cracked their whips, peddlers yelled their wares, but it was also a realm of donkeys. A red-robed king, a Moor whirling a scimitar through the air, all the folklore of the Sicilian past appeared on the panels of their tiny carts that were full of oranges or artichokes or threatened to tip up under the weight of an entire Sicilian family. The people were poor but gay, there was less of the desolate misery that had so oppressed us in Spain. My nurse had once brought me back a bottle of colored sands on her return from her annual holiday when I had been about three and I often thought of it as we shoved our way along some alley; the boy in front of us had a Greek head and a straw-covered amphora of wine under his arm but the three women at the corner with black shawls over their heads might have been watching there since the eighteenth century for a pigtailed English sailor.

The drawback of that winter was the weather. If it did not rain, there were blistering winds. A small tornado actually lifted me off my feet one day and into the air. My father caught me but we had to cling to some railings till the tempest dropped. The Mediterranean must have been a hazardous place for the ancient ships and it is not surprising that so many epitaphs in the Greek Anthology are addressed to sailors.

We explored the countryside bravely, in spite of the rain. A few orange flowers were in bud among the damp leaves. We got out of the carriage once to walk across a sandy bar to look at some view and I picked up a piece of coral. It was faintly splashed with rose but I doubt if I should have recognized the corrugated lump in my hand if I had not read that the place was a "coral beach" in Baedeker. For some reason, I suddenly linked my experience of the English shore to this southern strand, they fitted together like the two halves of a shell. I have often wondered why I remember this incident so clearly when so many days full of sunshine and maturity have vanished without a trace? It is, I believe, because such an impression in childhood is really new. Repetition may not blunt pleasure but the moments flow into each other without any sharpness of impact. A never-previously-experienced sensation can be just as vivid in old age as in youth.

One late afternoon as it was dusk, we were taken into the catacombs. Nobody had prepared us for the sight that met our eyes. The walls were surrounded by skeletons that, in the half light, appeared to move or even to beckon to us. A shipload of earth had once been brought to the churchyard from the Holy Land and in order that as many people as possible could share its virtues, the corpses were disinterred after so many years and the bones set up in the vault. It was really not a spectacle to commend to the nervous but it was all part of the lingering medieval tradition and we took it philosophically if without enthusiasm.

I developed what my mother called, in tones of resignation, "a new craze." I tried to teach myself bookkeeping. I imagine that I was too proud to ask for explanations but double entry was baffling; my exercises never seemed to come out as they should. Still, as my mother said, they kept me quiet. I had decided that my best chance of getting to sea was to become a merchant. If I could sail round the Mediterranean selling oranges and fish at every port, I could combine being a mariner and historian. Henty and my father had both contributed, however, to a conviction that I had to prepare for the day when my wishes might be granted. I knew that a trader had to keep accounts and so I sacrificed some of my few free hours struggling with the arithmetic that I hated.

It grew a little warmer and we went to Girgenti where I wandered among the temples with Freeman's *History* under my arm and the memory of Africa in my head. Otherwise we were still in the eighteenth century. There were armed guards on the train when we crossed the island by way of the sulphur mines to Catania and people discussed bandits, flowing lava and the orange harvest with equal indifference in front of us. All of these were everyday facts. Once we had octopus for dinner, my mother refused it but I was always experimental and decided that it was like a rather tough chicken.

It is a great advantage to have been an Iberian slinger in one's pinafore and I came to my own at Syracuse. We stayed at a hotel above the quarries where the Athenians had been confined and nothing could keep me away from the spot. I stood there for hours, looking down at a tangle of grass and half-wild geraniums, wondering if it were true that some prisoners had been saved because they could repeat the words of a new play and if they had ever got home? At such moments I felt that I had only to make some sign or turn my head a certain way, to enter the actual past. Curiously enough, I do not think I wanted to become a Sicilian, what I passionately desired, as in my Swiss Robinson days, was to share in the adventure *as myself,* or else to stand detached from it to observe what had actually happened. It was certainly a wild and melancholy place. The sixteen-year-old son of an English doctor and his wife, fellow guests at the hotel, used to go out with a penknife and return with a handful of human bones.

It was near Euryelus and the ancient walls that I knew Clio for my life's mistress and that ecstasy, in the Greek and terrifying sense of that word, seized me by the throat. I saw a vision and could hardly breathe. History from Tyre and Carthage to the Pillars of Hercules spun in front of me, waiting for an interpreter, not in separate, narrow lengths but in a single, flowing-together wave. To translate the old into the new, I had to feel as a rower had felt bending over his oar, the heat at the point of a sculptor's tool, the range of a ruler's mind and the helplessness of the slave. To write of things was to become part of them. It was to see *before* the beginning and *after* the end. I almost screamed against the pain of the moment that from its very intensity could not last.

It was youthful, yes, but in that hour I ceased to be a child. Perhaps, like the South, I flowered early but I have never felt so utter a dedication to wisdom again and I still believe that on that day my mind reached the height of its powers. Freedom, especially of thought, is always disliked and the conventions of the time retarded my development for another twelve years. Destiny may have played some part in the matter, it is true; in my efforts to liberate myself I turned to psychology that is also the study of the living past, instead of drifting into purely historical research. All the same, I can forgive the world for many of its blows but not for its attempt to keep me back from my rightful maturity.

Eight

The next two years are blank. Even a dedicated scholar needs a fraction of encouragement but people laughed at me as a rule or accused me of "showing off" (sometimes I did) and I had no idea where I could find the books that I needed. Libraries were forbidden, "You are not to go into those dusty places, full of germs." It was not entirely a wasted period, however, the motoring age had begun and we traveled a lot in France.

We still never expected to complete a journey without breaking down at least once. Our first car was a Panhard, almost as high as a dog cart; our second, I think, was a Daimler. Horses reared, boys threw stones at us, policemen stopped us continually and the veils and goggles that we wore were really necessary on account of the dust. Some people considered us heroic, others immoral. "The body cannot stand a speed of thirty miles an hour," my aunt warned me solemnly, "beg your father to leave you behind or your heart will give out and you will spend your life on a sofa." Such warnings did not discourage me in the least. More and more people joined us on the roads and at last the reign of Queen Victoria was truly over.

I had no French friends as yet but the sounds, sights and smells as we drove across the countryside rapidly became as familiar as the

Sussex villages. Every town had its story, they were like a row of gaily jacketed books. Children in sabots and black aprons chased hens out of the way and once on a clear stretch of road, to our awe and amazement, the speedometer touched forty miles an hour.

I began to think in French but found little to read until I was given *L'Histoire d'un paysan* by Erckmann-Chatrian. This was a book about the French Revolution from the French point of view. It was full of facts about smallpox, famine, the first planting of potatoes and the effects of the blockade upon poor craftsmen. The young respond to the primitive meaning of words. All my life I have been interested in Robespierre because his nickname of the "Incorruptible" so impressed me in childhood.

We did not go to Switzerland either of those summers but we drove once as far as Cornwall. I felt my spirits lift as soon as we crossed the Devon border; the raspberries and cream may have had something to do with it but the West seemed to welcome me and I longed to live in one of its sheltered lanes. Perhaps unconsciously I recognized that its sea was a Mediterranean blue. Otherwise those years were a time of hibernation while I rode, fenced and grew into a tough and cheeky boy, clamoring to enter the apprenticeship of life.

How did I discover poetry? I don't know, it came. At the beginning I supposed that it rhymed. I also decided that it had to have the same numbers of letters in each line but this, as sound, limped unpleasantly. I found the clue (somehow I would!) at the back of my French grammar. There was a chapter on various meters. "How do I know what a great poem is?" I inquired, thinking of some carefully hidden sheets of foolscap.

"Poems? You give them away with a packet of tea," was the amused Edwardian reply. Again how thankful I am that nobody encouraged me. I should have been insufferable.

Except for Shakespeare or an anthology or two, little poetry came my way until I was fifteen. I was growing out of Henty, however, and one day, after many entreaties, my father gave me Freeman's five-volume history of the Norman Conquest. I flung myself into it as only the young can read with an intensity that was near to the battle rage of the warriors. Freeman, we know, was wrong about the palisades and a few other details but none of the soberer authorities that I studied later in life had his sweep and fire nor much that was new to say about the conflict. I knew the countryside well because we often drove over to Battle for tea. I suppose that it was imagination but I was always uneasy on the legendary site, it was usually damp and I felt sorrow rising into the air with the mist although I never spoke of this, fearing that people would laugh at me.

The only part that I liked was the road that led down to the Pevensey marshes. That landscape has always remained vividly in my mind, the yellow flags, the grass that oozed water if we trod on it, and even the disagreeable old woman who, in sheer fright, pulled her perfectly calm pony and trap into a ditch as our motorcar advanced (we might have been going fifteen miles an hour) and then cursed us as we dragged her out of it.

I often wondered since if we ever passed a walker in her tweed together with "the coat and mushroom straw" on the Hurstmonceux side of the lanes? The Quaker farm that was the setting of Dorothy Richardson's *Dimple Hill* was in that neighborhood, she was there at about the same date and we often speculated afterwards what would have happened had we met at the time instead of in 1923.

It was in 1909 when the shadow of my century first fell across my own horizon. We were out one Sunday morning looking for mushrooms in a field below the Downs. "I don't like the news," my father said uneasily, "I'm afraid there may be a war." I listened, of course, but it seemed as vague as any national disaster, the earthquake at Messina for example or a fire that nobody knew anything about until after it had happened. We had passed through Messina before it had been destroyed and it was equally hard to think of its solid buildings in ruins as to imagine "the Continent" that we had visited so frequently being the scene of battles.

It was a particularly cold winter that year. We went to Folkestone for a couple of months and I sometimes wondered if I should ever feel warm again. One day my father came into the schoolroom with a newspaper in his hand. "Read this article, Miggy; Blatchford is a socialist but he has grasped the situation. You must try to understand, it is very serious."

Stamford Bridge, the Saxons and the Normans were easy but even the Boer War had been a continent away and although I understood the surface of the warning its meaning did not really penetrate my consciousness. How could I have imagined the young men whom I saw hurrying to work with black umbrellas and what seemed to me a total lack of any adventurous spirit, taking to uniforms and rifles? I listened to my father but then, with the thoughtlessness that was, after all, natural to my age, I forgot his anxiety. Besides I soon had enough to do without bothering my head about a possible conflict between the Great Powers.

Most of us have only one April, mine came early. Fifteen can be a turning point in youth and several factors combined to make 1909 a different year from any that preceded it. My father and mother were married in that year although I did not know this until I was twenty-four. They were hardly separated for a day during the nearly fifty years that they were together. They were always passionately in love and it was a truer marriage from the first than most of those that I have seen, before or since. I prefer to state the facts rather than to have an aura of mystery. Long afterwards, I was offered the chance to ask for my birth to be regarded as legitimate. I refused with indignation, preferring the affection and the glory.

My brother was born after the marriage in December, 1909. My mother was ill for a considerable time afterwards, we did not go abroad that winter but my father bought a house in London. I was told that I had been allowed to run wild too long; it was time that I conformed to contemporary customs. The shift from the formerly freer French atmosphere at home to a rigidly conventional English one was revolutionary and startling. I was scolded incessantly for unreasonable or trivial reasons. Life changed in fact and not in imagination.

I can see now that I presented a problem. I was not so much an ugly duckling as a voracious cuckoo with an open beak, clamoring for lessons in Arabic and drawing. Since I had said good-by to Sylvia, aged six, I had scarcely spoken to a child of my own age. My mother would have liked me to be interested in clothes, I hated what I called "dressing up." I had always had the energy and the frankness of a boy and the high-necked Edwardian blouses and my now longer navy blue skirts made me look ridiculous although they were the uniform of the period. I tried to be unobtrusive, it saved many scoldings, but I had only to enter a room to upset my mother's visitors. "She knows what I think," one of them complained bitterly afterwards, "she stares right through me." It was perfectly true. I had felt her deciding that I was an awkward, clumsy girl who needed to be sent to school and beaten into shape. My relatives blamed me for my lack of education while at the same time every sign of intelligence was immediately repressed. Apart from my parents and my governess, I cannot remember a kind or an encouraging word. It was harsh treatment because I was still very young but it forged my spirit; I shall be a rebel, I think, until the end of my days. The sands were running out but one last moment was granted to me. I think that it determined my life.

I saw a sign, THE SCHOOL OF ANIMAL PAINTING, written up above a studio in Baker Street. I persuaded my governess to let me make inquiries and my father, with more difficulty, to let me enter one of the classes. Six weeks of pure happiness followed. You cannot talk to me about heaven, I have been there, but just as in the myths so profound an experience has to be paid for with sorrow.

Most of my fellow students were elderly gentlemen except for a rosy-cheeked country girl a little older than myself. According to the custom of the time, we did not speak to one another. We had not been introduced. There was a muttered "thank you" if somebody picked up a pencil or an "excuse me" if an easel were bumped in passing, otherwise we worked in silence or spoke to the dog, a beautiful basset hound who slept on the model's stand during the whole morning except when he rose from time to time, stretched himself and had to be enticed to lie down again by an attendant with biscuits.

I was quite the worst student in the class because I had never learned the rudiments of drawing. I had merely scribbled incessantly and looked at pictures. Now they give colored chalks to children as soon as they can crawl but I belonged to the sterner age when we only had slates. Paints were "messy" and it was "less selfish" to go for a walk on the Downs than to pore over a sheet of paper. These lessons were the first time that I had been allowed to draw for two hours together without reproof.

Mr. Cameron, our teacher, used to walk up Baker Street with a cloak flying from his shoulders. I was accustomed to seeing men wear capes in Italy but it shocked my governess when she came to fetch me. She reported him as dangerously eccentric. I liked him because he would tolerate no covering up of mistakes. Everything had to be stripped down to essentials. The rest of the class found him arid. He taught, in fact, anatomy rather than art. He looked in horror at my board when my turn came, demonstrated faults with a flick of his pencil and tore the paper in two. I was enchanted. This was learning as I had imagined it to be and I wanted to cut my teeth on the hardest criticism possible. I understood the rules but my hands were clumsy and my lines appalling. "All she does is to draw little black lumps," Mr. Cameron complained to my governess, "and yet somehow she has the root of the matter in her."

I sometimes wonder what would have happened to me if I had been allowed to continue drawing. I should have become quite a different person from myself as writer. The written word is colored by the conscious mind, by reason and by all that we learn through observation and experience. In painting with me, the unconscious would have been dominant. I know who my master would have been, Toulouse-Lautrec. Say what you will, no woman yet has had the same opportunities as a man to use her mind. I have always been handicapped in writing because, although due to some psychological training I know what a lumberman thinks, it is impossible for me to stay beside him while he works or drinks and listen to his conversation. It is not important to reproduce his swear words, these are monotonous and stupid, but I must be able to hear the rhythm of his speech if I am to reproduce it afterwards. Social taboos have cut me off from much of the material that I should have liked to use. They are also the reason for the greater concentration of women writers upon landscape and mood. Drawing is different, it is a silent art. If I permit myself to scribble on Sundays I am indifferent to beauty, it is the greed beneath some placid face that holds me, the envy under a smile. I long to catch the "is" and not the "should be" and I suspect that I should have gone deeper and deeper into the underworld to record such impressions. It is possible that I should have been a much greater painter than I can hope to be a writer but how would it have ended? How much would it have mattered?

In 1910 I knew *how* I wanted to see—in an instantaneous flash of lines in the Japanese manner—and that I needed for this long years of hard, technical training. This was not the whim of a child, it was mature and in spite of my awkwardness every hour of work was pure happiness. Changes in development have always happened to me with the speed of lightning although the approach to them may have been slow and unperceived. Now to my intense surprise, I grew up in a day.

The beginning of life is brief. It is only the moment when the spirit is neither male nor female but a unity and my April lasted barely its thirty days. I think my mind might subsequently have died had not destiny sent me scuffling along the shelves of my father's library towards an old, leather-bound book. It was Hazlitt's *Dramatic Literature of the Reign of Queen Elizabeth* and in it, waiting for me, was Bellario.

The mature reader of Elizabethan drama comes back to Shakespeare with an added appreciation of his power but that does not mean that at a certain phase of our existence, other writers of that time may not have a closer message for us. I was drawn to Bellario as I never was to Viola or Rosalind because from my point of view she had all the virtues, she was loyal, she was not afraid of a sword and she had some of the loveliest lines to speak in all English poetry. Philaster was tiresome but youth can alter material as it pleases; I transformed love into fidelity to the muses. It is strange that in the darkness that followed, it was a figure from a now almost forgotten play who kept me anchored to the world of reality. It must be remembered, however, that both people and circumstances during the next nine years tried to force me to conform to a conventional pattern whereas I, almost with ferocity, felt myself to be dedicated to art and freedom.

I inhaled the studio turpentine as if it were Arabian jasmine while I tried to strip everything that I saw or read to its skeleton, to the reflection behind the bone that Egypt had taught me to call the Ka. Alas, I became so absorbed by this process that I forgot to say "yes" and "no" at the right moment so that people complained to my parents that I was not "quite normal." Send her to school, they advised, it will knock the edges off her.

Mr. Cameron's classes closed for Easter and I wondered how I should exist until the summer term began. I had been promised that I might go back to his lessons. On Friday we returned to Eastbourne, on Saturday they told me that my drawing days were over, Saturday and Sunday I prayed that I might die . . .,

> " 'tis not a life,
> 'Tis but a piece of childhood thrown away."

On Tuesday I went to Queenwood.

Nine

The bomb crashed. We were lying on the floor. The walls of the room seemed to rush towards us. Small objects fell from the tops of the cupboards. "If this is the end, it is not as bad as school," flashed through my mind. Unexpectedly the walls stopped moving. The foundations rocked slowly backwards and forwards till they settled. We got up, choking with dust, but alive.

The house had held although there was a large crater underneath the windows but I knew now what my last thoughts would have been. I had neither seen my life flash past in a second nor recollected friends nor happiness. What I had remembered was Queenwood.

School for me was a violation of the spirit.

The scarlet geraniums on that May morning shone in the sun. I knew as I passed them that a part of myself would be dead before evening and there is something even in the most adventurous among us that shrinks from so final a change. Time seemed to move and at the same instant to stand still. I was never to be the same person again and I was looking back at what had been an intense spiritual experience through an ever less transparent veil. I walked through the school gates as into an enemy town. Nothing remained to me but courage.

I had hardly entered Queenwood before I was hustled out once more to march two by two in my first "crocodile" as far as the Town Hall. It was May 6, 1910, the date of the proclamation of George the Fifth as King, another landmark if I had had the wits that morning to think of my mistress, Clio. The vacant space in front of the building was entirely filled with children, standing by schools in separate groups. I could hear only a confused murmur of words, I remember nothing of the pageantry and this is what happens, I suspect, to most of us on such occasions. The end of an age may be a clear-cut symbol to the scholar but the people themselves are absorbed by their own affairs: they may notice a face but it is rationing, the call up or higher taxes that teach them history, not their having been part of a crowd at a given moment in a certain place.

It is hard to make people understand what I felt like during the next weeks because mine must have been a somewhat isolated experience. I had lived most of my life outside England and I had never had friends of my own age. Now I was flung into a crowded boarding school to sink or swim alone. I kicked and spluttered in an agony of bewilderment and very nearly sank. Nobody gave me any explanations; it was a perfect preparation for Freud. The experience could have driven me to insanity or suicide and it was as crippling for a time as a paralytic stroke. I did not recover from it until after a long psychoanalysis and I survived only because I was tough. I am a poet, even a visionary, but I am not an intellectual type. Had I been some sensitive misfit, I should have gone crazy during the first month. The more I learn about the mind, the more surprised I am that, hardy as I was, I survived the first shock.

I made no secret of my determination to become an artist. It was as natural as breathing and it never occurred to me to conceal it. Mistresses and pupils alike roared with laughter. I am thankful now for their mockery, it drove me to learn my craft the hard but sound way, alone. The world said I was too young to study art. Too young! It was the whole of my desire. I knew that my powers of reasoning were mature, something flamed in me that was perhaps the spirit and because of this I understood that years of technical training were necessary before I could draw. Yet I was too much of an Elizabethan to wait. They might take my pencils away but they could not stop me thinking. Perhaps if I wrote a book I should be free.

There were eighty boarders and a few day girls at Queenwood and we ranged in age from nine to seventeen. We were too few in number to be considered a public school in the English sense of that term but we conformed to the system, with the disadvantage that as we were all in one house, we were under strict and continuous supervision.

The training was harsh but it had two advantages, in view of our unsuspected future of wars and financial disaster. We were hardened physically and they stressed the fact that we were all equal links in the unit, Queenwood, and that the aim of life was service.

The hardening process was simple and efficient. Windows were kept open throughout the damp, English winters, there were abundant drafts, we were not allowed a fire in the classrooms unless the temperature fell below sixty Fahrenheit and then the ones in front roasted while the back row shivered. I do not think we had even heard of central heating. A favorite trick was to fill small medicine bottles with hot water and keep them in our pockets to warm numb fingers. The rain might fall in torrents, there might be a raging gale but we were either sent to the playing fields or for a walk across the bleak, exposed Downs. "I cannot think why we did not all die of pneumonia," a mistress said to me long afterwards but somehow we survived although we often had colds. Thoughtful mothers stitched strips of flannel inside our uniforms and we wore thick underwear and black woolen stockings. It was particularly hard on the girls who had been born in India. If we went to the drawing room on some special occasion we collected the cushions to pile outside in the hall because we were not allowed to sit upon anything soft.

Of course we hated the discomfort but afterwards, when the wars came and we had to wait in queues for our rations, it was almost a familiar experience. One day, holidays—or peace—would come again, and in the meantime we stuffed our shoes with newspaper and if we got wet through shrugged our shoulders and did not expect to die of pleurisy. It had happened so often before chasing a ball on the hockey field or trying to stand upright against a nor'easter on the cliffs.

It is true that we came roughly from the same social group but while some parents were wealthy, others were officials whose meager salaries were barely sufficient to pay the year's fees. It did not matter. We all wore uniforms, so that there could be no competition as to clothes and, to within a few pence, we had the same pocket money. I have never lived in so classless a society before or since.

A bell woke us in the mornings, a second one sent us to our knees where we stayed until released by a third bell, five minutes afterwards. We had breakfast, made our beds and were drilled; no time was allotted to the needs of nature; it was a standing joke that Authority supposed us to be without digestions. Classes started at nine and continued till one, with a short break at eleven. After lunch there was hockey in the winter, cricket and tennis in the summer or a walk. The team took precedence; Authority considered that it was healthier and morally superior to be better at games than lessons. (I think now that this was right within reasonable limits. What is the use of erudition without health?) Little attempt was made, however, to teach us to play correctly; we were shoved onto a field and ordered to run. I used to wonder if sport were so sacred an institution that instruction in it was irreverent. Tea was at four, there was preparation till supper, then the younger girls went to bed. The over-fourteens had various duties, there were missionary lectures or, bribed with cakes, we met to speak French or German. The bell sounded at nine to summon us to our dormitories. There was no leisure for outside interests or hobbies, I was lucky if I got a quarter of an hour once in a while to read a book. This routine continued throughout the year for three terms, each lasting about thirteen weeks.

The weekdays were dull but they were joyful compared with Sundays. We were allowed to get up half an hour later and after breakfast and one of Miss Chudleigh's famous talks about our sins during the week, there was compulsory letter writing home until it was time to go to church. Lunch followed our return. Afterwards there was an hour's silent reading of a good book, a Bible class, tea, and compulsory hymn singing until we went to evening church. We had supper as soon as we got back but were then sent immediately to bed. What all this had to do with religion in any real sense it is hard to imagine.

Queenwood could boast one virtue rare among English schools. The food was simple but while we were pupils the quality was good and it was well cooked. I heard afterwards that the standards deteriorated during the first war and that the meals became as tasteless as in other institutions. This was not the case when I was there.

My verdict upon the intellectual standards at Queenwood used to be pitiless but now I am less sure. The very few who went on to a university had to spend an additional year elsewhere preparing for the entrance examinations but it was the usual custom at that time. We forget that in 1910 the battle for the equal education of men and women was far from being won. Many parents objected to intensive training of the mind and if we spoke wistfully about jobs we were sharply reproved and told that we must not take the bread out of a poor girl's mouth. Yet one of the babies of the school, Martita Hunt, became famous as an actress on both sides of the Atlantic, the writers included Sylva Norman and Nellie Kirkham, there was Doris Banfield who created a number of new daffodils, Dorothy Pilley whose name is well known in mountaineering circles for her climbing books and her ascents in the Far East and the Alps, and Dorothy Townshend who was a pioneer in the psychological treatment of children and the author of an excellent study on the education of girls in France. After we had left some of the subsequent pupils wrote best sellers. With such a record, can our education have been as bad as I then thought? I simply do not know.

It would be unfair to judge the school by my own particular case. I arrived there completely lopsided. My brain was mature as far as literature and history were concerned but I had the emotional development of a boy of nine. My two years at Queenwood were an intellectual disaster but it would have been the same anywhere else. I was not a model pupil, far from it, my marks were seldom above average for my age group. First of all, I had never been taught to prepare neat answers, then my mind raced along much faster than my hands so that although I knew the details perfectly well I often forgot to write them down and I was apt to plunge into the intricacies of chain mail when all that was required was the simple date of Hastings. Still, I could read French as easily as English, I knew a fair amount of German and I am afraid that thanks to Henty and the wide reading to which he had led me, I knew more about history than my teachers. I was a day girl in the Fourth Form my first term. In September I became a boarder and moved up to the Fifth; the following year I was in the Sixth. It was lucky for me that I did not belong to the next generation. I should then have ended in some class for the maladjusted because I was totally unable to add up figures and might have hated learning for the rest of my life.

It was a simple place. Nobody expected us to be trained for either marriage or a career. What we were grounded in was virtue and though we may not have been glamorous, we were tough, and came through "the revolution of the forties" with honor.

My first exploit was to present our Headmistress, Miss Chudleigh, in perfect good faith a plan for the reorganization of the dining room. At breakfast and supper two girls were sent in turn from each of the tables to fetch the food from a hatch. They crowded haphazardly together so that there were long waits and the meals got cold. I worked out a scheme whereby we could have been served in rotation in about a minute.

Miss Chudleigh received my piece of foolscap in amazement. She read it and remarked with reasonable gentleness that service was more important than organization. Oh no, I replied, I could not agree, I had no objection to taking my turn with the others but what I wanted was efficiency. If she would try my suggestions, she would find that they would help us all.

I was genuinely surprised when she sent me back to my school-mates.

There were many other difficulties. First of all, there was the strange language. I had never heard slang before and, as I had seldom read a school story, I had never even seen the terms "funny old fish" or "bags I this seat" in a book. Often I literally did not know what they meant. It helped me to understand the feeling of those savages who were trapped and dragged aboard a pinnace by Elizabethan sailors but this was not very useful in ordinary life. There was also the question as to what I was called. I had grown up under a variety of nicknames to which I still answered when at home. I thought that my real name was Winifred but I was not sure, and it seemed silly to ask.

Compulsory games were dull after fencing or riding across deserts. Still, although bewildered, I was not unresourceful. How could the Games Mistress watch everywhere at once?

Queenwood was built in a saucer of land below the Downs. The hockey fields were outside the walls but this was summer and the tennis courts were beneath the school in what would otherwise have been a lawn. They ended on one side in a tangle of bushes and long grass. A ball flew into this shrubbery and I scrambled after it, another new girl as unhappy as myself followed on all fours. We crept most carefully into a place where the Games Mistress could not see us and moaned in unison, "School is horrible." My companion was perhaps the youngest child there and I was among the oldest but already, as the Elizabethans would have said, she was "all fire." Was she as beautiful then as she is now? I think it came later, created by her own inner gifts. All that I remember is hair tied back tightly into our regulation black ribbon knot, the white flannel shirt with our red and black school tie and a quivering, indignant face. "What are you going to do when you grow up?" she asked me passionately as I ducked to avoid my head showing over a bush. "I want to go to sea," I think I answered, it was a moment when I saw no future but only a daily battle with both school and home. "I am going to be a great actress," she declared and looking at her, I never for a moment doubted it although I wondered what obstacles her family would put in her path. Fate was kind and ultimately she had her wish. It was Martita Hunt.

Does some natural instinct lie behind the separation of age groups? I arrived at Queenwood free from prejudice but a taboo that I never questioned was the one that divided the Upper from the Lower School. This division swept Martita and myself apart and we seldom had an opportunity of talking together afterwards. I know now that I ought to have sought her out, she found the environment even more cramping than I did, but though it was my first encounter with genius, I was too immersed in my own misery to profit from it.

I remember very little of those first three months. The major incidents of childhood have never faded from my mind but at Queenwood I dropped into a trance in which I felt nothing, realized nothing, cared for nothing, a form of Lethe in reverse. "Everybody is unhappy the first term," people said. It did not help that this was often true. It is easier now to understand from a distance of years that it was not calculated cruelty but the custom of the age that the objective of the school was to break a pupil's spirit. I had never heard of the unconscious mind and I had to work every step of my rebellion out for myself. It was part of the Game if you wish. I had asked to be tough since babyhood and I was getting my desire. Only two things sustained me and they were neither love nor fear. I remembered the Athenians in the quarry at Syracuse and Sir Richard Burton's expeditions to the "black tents."

Halfway through the term an incident occurred that increased my bewilderment still further. My mother was anxious about germs, having lost her hearing through a second attack of scarlet fever. For years I had been forbidden many trifling pleasures because "you might catch something, darling," and I had the grimmest memories of my week with German measles. I had treated plague and smallpox with indifference, rats, scorpions or thunderstorms had no terrors for me, but when I heard during our morning break that there was a girl in the sickroom with a rash, I slipped away from the others and ran home, it was only ten minutes away. I burst into the hall, screaming "measles, measles" and I honestly expected to be praised for my prompt action. My mother looked up in surprise, remarked, "I have made you too nervous" and marched me back to school without a word of explanation. It was as if I had landed on the unseen side of the moon.

Destiny, however, had not quite forgotten me. Being a day girl that first summer, I stayed at home on Sundays and we sometimes drove across my favorite marshes. It was the moment when the yellow flags rose out of the ditches in full flower and whenever we passed through this landscape, with the sunlight catching the points of the reeds, I used to hear a word, "Ru-an, Ru-an," echoing in my ears. I did not know consciously for another twenty years that it was a Cornish word meaning running water. It was simply a sound ringing like a bell with its promise of shelter to a fogbound traveler.

I had been flung into the whirlwind to be made "like other girls." I had guts enough to resent so forcible a transformation of my character and decided to confine my conversation to such brief answers as were required to reply politely to questions. The system worked perfectly for some weeks until we were sent to church unexpectedly one morning instead of into our classrooms.

It was a rule that we could choose our companions for our afternoon walks but we sat at meals or went to church according to our age. My father had inadvertently entered me in the register as being a year younger than I actually was but although he immediately rectified the mistake, like all red tape matters, this took time. I only had lunch at Queenwood so I had been passed from table to table wherever there had happened to be a vacancy but I was paired that day with the girl whose birthday was nearest to my own. We started in silence but we were hardly outside the gates before my companion said cheerfully, "You live here, don't you? I come from Penzance."

It had never occurred to me that I should meet a Cornish girl. All that I knew was that I regarded the West Country with awe. It had everything that I desired, color, the sun, sheltered valleys and little, wandering paths; above all, it seemed closer to the sea. Besides, even Miss Chudleigh was not able to resist my companion's dark, merry eyes or her enchanting smile. Her name, she said, was Doris Banfield, this was her first term as well as my own but she had an older sister, Ethel, who had already been at Queenwood for two years. Did I like dogs? She had a fox terrier called Sampie with a black spot above his tail and she thought that he must miss her very much.

Yes, Fate must have been behind my father's mistake. Even a year's difference in age can be a barrier at school so if it had not been for that first walk, I might never have gone to Scilly. Think what I should have lost if Doris had not taken me all over the islands or if we had not groaned in seasick sympathy on the rolling deck of the *Lyonnesse*. We were inseparable by the time that the transfer to my correct age group had been completed but Miss Chudleigh gave us permission to continue to sit together at my family's request although she sometimes complained that we encouraged each other in irresponsible pranks. We have only grown nearer to each other throughout the intervening years.

So the days followed each other, each a long training in rebellion until the term ended in July and the holidays began.

I spent August sulking with Shakespeare. Caliban attracted me because there seemed some resemblance between his state and my own and I knew that I could never return to my island innocence, no matter what future enchantments might be in store for me. It was no wonder that I felt confused. The long painful obediences of childhood had been wiped away at a stroke. It was useless to explain my feelings, nobody believed me. "She is spoilt and resents discipline," people said smugly yet oddly enough, in some ways, life at school was less strict than at home. "It will be the making of her," they added and this was true, though not with the meaning that they intended because I rejected their standards for ever. My parents kept saying that they wanted me to be happy. "Then let me go back to my drawing classes," I begged but they shook their heads. I was not to hear the name of Freud for another ten years but Queenwood was the perfect preparation for me to become his adherent as I fought to find out how the unbearable frustrations could be eased.

I think now that it was society itself and not my family that was to blame. It endeavored to enforce conformity through pressure at an individual's most sensitive point, his children. It needs great courage to disregard the opinions of the day and yet, as I have seen so often, the virtues of one epoch become the crimes of the next generation. I was also mature in a number of ways but, like most of my generation, ignorant of what were called "the facts of life." I suspect that my parents were afraid that I might make "undesirable friends" at any school of art. I learned subsequently that I was not more stupid than my fellows. After all, as I said afterwards, the Victorians outwardly gave up sex and received an empire in exchange.

Of course I was difficult and my parents began to wonder whether Queenwood were a good idea or not (it was, if one could survive it), so in order to sweeten the final summer days my father took me to Cornwall. I began to breathe as soon as I reached the West. We went to Tintagel, I remember, and as we stood on the top of the cliffs I knew that there was no adventure that I would not dare and no opinion that I would not question. I looked up at the gulls in a state of exultation but then, the next minute, the approach of a new term flooded me with terror. I should have run away there and then, only, having a practical nature, I knew that I should not get very far on the ten shillings in my pocket.

Our journey ended at Penzance. It had never occurred to me to question Doris about her family but I did have her address. "Oh, you mean Mr. Banfield the shipowner," the hall porter said when we inquired the way to the house. My father was delighted, in the whole school I had picked out the one pupil whose father was a colleague and likely to have interests identical with his own. Nobody was at home when we called but Mr. Banfield came to see us that evening. His wife, Doris and her sister were over at St. Mary's but it was arranged that Doris would come to us for part of the Christmas holidays and that I should accompany them to Scilly the following summer.

The second term at Queenwood passed more easily than the first. I learned to lie, easily and efficiently, it was a valuable accomplishment. I also became a boarder, strangely enough, I felt freer and it lessened the tension. A day girl has to cope with three dimensions at once, all pulling in different directions: her own development, the wishes of her parents and the laws of the school. The moment that I was inside Queenwood, I became one with my companions; we were usually in a state of dissembled revolt but the struggle was shared, I was not fighting alone. It deepened our friendships and I have noticed since that whereas those who have been educated at day schools often lose contact with their classmates, I have only to cross a room to greet someone I have not seen for thirty years and, because of our shared experience, it is as if we had parted yesterday. There is everything in favor of the properly run boarding school from the child's point of view, exceptional cases apart; they lessen considerably the strain of growing up. Contrary also to European opinion they strengthen rather than decrease the ties with home because both sides are more tolerant of each other when they are not permanently under the same roof. Doris and I remained inseparable but two others joined our group, Dorothy Pilley who first took me up a mountain and Dorothy Townshend who with her vivid imagination and intellectual interests was even more rebellious than I was at Queenwood. We were conventional as to names. There were eight Dorothys and six Marjories in the school but luckily for me only one other Winifred.

I rapidly evolved a technique of avoiding our dreary rambles over the Downs. My favorite device was to jerk off the bow at the bottom of my pigtail, then, with luck, by the time that I had been sent to replait my hair and find another ribbon, the walk would have started. The games were almost as dreary, apart from a few girls, we all played badly. I faced a hockey ball not with a stick but with my eyes towards the heavens, declaiming Beaumont and Fletcher.

> Hence, all you vain delights,
> As short as are the nights
>   Wherein you spend your folly:
> There's naught in this life sweet
> If man were wise to see't,
>   But only melancholy,
>   O sweetest melancholy!

It was intolerably smug but they merely yelled patiently, "Get on with the game," and there was an occasion when my meditation was rudely disturbed by a cricket ball falling into my pocket instead of my hands. On the whole, however, I adjusted in fits and starts and as I had to find something to occupy my mind (I had been suspended from the history class under the pretext that I had learned as much as was necessary!) I persuaded Miss Johns to teach me Sanskrit.

It was a pity that I did not learn Greek. I might have mastered the verbs at that age that are so intractable in later life but I had read some dreary translations of Greek plays and the East still dominated my imagination. I never considered Latin. The tongue of the hated Romans was a key fumbling at the wrong door but Arabic, the growling consonants that came straight from hippo-hide drums, or whatever was Oriental, helped me to escape from school through another language into my former life.

We had exercise books bound in different colors for different subjects. (Does one still use the term? It is years since I have heard it.) I drew out the mottled brown one reserved for Latin and wrote Sanskrit on it in enormous letters. After all, pride in adolescence is a stimulus to learning. Unfortunately I found the language extremely difficult, I had not heard messengers and water carriers shouting the words at each other and though I was able to cope with vowel points, the Sanskrit habit of running the words of a sentence into a single line of letters proved too much for me. I struggled through a third of our "Elementary Reader" to end triumphantly, but I imagine for ever, at "The two elephants smell the perfume." It was an illustration of the dual.

I grew devoted to Miss Johns though I was her solitary adherent. She had taken two degrees, at the time this was most unusual for a woman, and specialized in philology. She was plump, good-natured and Miss Chudleigh's shadow although often scolded by her because of an incapacity to control anyone, pupil, parent or dog. I found out after I had left that she was of Welsh descent. Eventually she was relegated to the domestic side of Queenwood in spite of her learning. Is it imagination or did I really see her bustling about in a white apron with a bunch of keys at her waist? I think of her in retrospect as the housewife who would have busied herself sorting apples when some survivor brought the news of the Norman victory at Hastings but who would have understood the consequences of the battle better than her master the thane.

Miss Johns was a scholar and remarked shrewdly enough that I should never take kindly to academic tuition because my mind shot off in too many directions at once; I was considering reincarnation while she was explaining the locative or dreaming about Egypt instead of learning my declensions, but I owe to her, rather than to Mademoiselle, a further advance in my apprenticeship. We had to read a good book for an hour on Sunday afternoons but I got permission to read French. I suppose the basic idea was that we must not enjoy what we were doing. One hot summer day just before the bell rang for reading to begin, I was summoned to the dining room and handed a copy of Flaubert's *Salammbô*. I am sure that it must have been Miss Johns because I doubt if Mademoiselle would have dared to give it to me, even though it were a classic.

I sat on a hard chair in a crowded form room smelling of varnish and ink. It was not the words, it was what they caused to happen to me. All young artists have such moments of awakening and mine were intensified because of my extreme isolation. On that Sunday I entered into the creative dream, into the veritable handing down of the secrets of art from one generation to another, partly because it gave form to ideas that because of my inexperience were naturally nebulous and also because of its reassurance. I almost yelled a battle cry in triumph. I was right, Queenwood was wrong, I was not a solitary rebel.

I have read since that Colette preferred *Salammbô* to Flaubert's other novels and I think that I understand the reason. Bourgeois life had changed because all Europe has been affected by two wars and their migrations. Flaubert helped to prepare the ground for modern psychology, he was not a doctor's son for nothing, and it is a measure of his greatness that we respond to different books of his at different times. It was another fifteen years before I understood *Madame Bovary*. Perhaps his study of Carthage and the mercenaries (how one can smell the lions!) is nearer to us now with our memories of blitzes and invasions than his greater but narrower studies of French provincial life.

I am profoundly grateful to Miss Johns. She knew and gave me what I needed although I was still too undeveloped to realize that we both belonged to the same band of scholars or to show her the slightest return for her kindness. She did all that she could to make my lot easier and I wish that she had lived to read *Roman Wall;* she would have criticized it furiously but what a talk we would have had about the Roman Empire afterwards!

I was not the only child to beat against the intellectual starvation of an Edwardian education that was sometimes worse than physical hunger. There were a dozen girls there with better brains than mine though none had, I think, my impudence. I ought to have known

Nellie Kirkham but she remains a fleeting impression of a lovely, fair-haired creature whom I passed occasionally on the staircase. Some years after leaving Queenwood she wrote a novel, *Unrest of Our Time*, that was both modern in approach and an extraordinary study of Derbyshire lead miners in the Elizabethan period. Perhaps it appeared too early? It ought to have been a best seller but it seems to have been overlooked. She is now a recognized authority on lead mines and their history but where are her other novels?

I also like to think that Sylva Norman's witty and tolerant observation of human nature began in our drafty corridors, perhaps while we were waiting "to peck" Miss Chudleigh when we said good night or, if we had colds, shake her hand. I have always been envious of those wonderful first chapters in *Tongues of Angels*. Possibly only someone who has lived in Switzerland can appreciate how remarkably she has portrayed certain phases of Helvetian life. It is simply not true that books survive on their merit. Why has her *Nature Has No Tune* never been reprinted? It is an enchanting account of a pension in the Italian hills in the far-off days of the twenties.

Martita with her developing art and Dorothy Townshend with her clear Latin mind both suffered more than I did from our diet of crumbs. It would have been the same at the time in any school either in Europe or England, we were girls and so sacrificed to the prevalent spirit of the age; knowledge might make us discontented. To use the current phrase, it was "dinned" into us that it was selfish and disloyal to the community to take a job. Woe to the conformers! Thirty years later that same community punished the obedient who had listened to them. Fortunately for ourselves, most of us were rebels.

Yet Queenwood was a modern school for its time. Greatly daring, Miss Chudleigh took us to a reading by Ellen Terry for the benefit of the suffragettes. I remember only a little old lady and a voice, nothing was said about votes but we listened to Portia's speech and the proceeds from the tickets went to the cause. It was enough to have made many parents remove their daughters immediately. At the time, I did not worry about political rights. I had to be self-centered to survive and there was nothing in any manifesto about votes giving me the chance to be a sailor.

Queenwood, however, had its lighter moments. "Girls!" Miss Chudleigh came forward to the edge of the school platform. "Girls!"

Our lines tautened because it was better to give the effect of listening even if our thoughts were far away. "Mr. Smith has consented to give a lecture with lantern slides for the benefit of missionaries in Somaliland this evening. It will be a silver collection. Preparation will begin in consequence at half past four instead of a quarter to five." There was an almost audible attempt on our part not to groan. Miss Chudleigh removed her glasses, wiped them, and took a step nearer the edge. (We always hoped that she might fall off but she never did.) "And girls," the voice sank to its famous, whispering tone, "I had presumed that coming from homes of every possible refinement, it would be unnecessary to teach you the elements of social courtesy. I was surprised yesterday . . . and sadly shocked . . . to hear a titter, a perceptible titter, when the page boy had the misfortune to drop a leg of mutton on the floor. Surely you know that *no lady* ever laughs at an accident?" Slowly, majestically, Miss Chudleigh descended the steps, no Queen ever left an Assembly with more dignity.

A pause, a sign, the youngest child led out first, two thin plaits jerking behind her ears. At the far end of the hall, the head girl of seventeen and a half with precisely the same expression, the same black bow on her hair and the high-collared blouse that was the symbol of the constriction of our days, waited her turn to leave. It was army life but it had its compensations.

Only three men ever entered Queenwood, the doctor, the clergyman and a teacher of music. Parents were confined to the drawing room and the garden. Apart from brothers or an occasional cousin, few of us ever mentioned a boy. If even our mothers had used make-up, they would have been requested to remove their daughters from the school. On that particular day a rumor passed round the corridor that the music master had somehow missed his train and would have to stay to lunch.

"Chud's put on her striped linen." There was nothing that we did not observe.

"No talking in the passage," the mistress on duty snapped, "ten lines for anyone who speaks again."

We sat down. The girls began to pass the plates of soup. The striped linen shone among us with its newness. Miss Chudleigh and the master discussed music in strained, polite tones. Chatter subsided or broke out in painful gasps. The ladies of the staff seemed more uneasy than their pupils. We finished the first course, the page boy gathered the plates, the top one half full, into his clumsy arms. It was a pity that the pyramid overbalanced precisely as he passed Miss Chudleigh's chair. The room froze into silence. Nobody moved. The page boy stood staring at the damage. Drenched with soup Miss Chudleigh was pinned between the table and the plates, until, after what seemed minutes, hands began to snatch the pile away. "Coming from homes of every possible refinement, no lady ever laughs at an accident," we muttered over and over to ourselves for fear of possible reprisals if we smiled. The music teacher glanced covertly under the table for possible damage to his trousers, Miss Chudleigh rose, apologized to her guest and left the room. "I think we are going to have rain," Miss Hulbert remarked loudly with immense presence of mind. The tables burst into hysterical giggling as if it were Saturday and not the middle of the week with nothing to look forward to but a damp walk on the Downs and a missionary lecture in the evening. Did I hear the babies in the Third Form humming "When the cat's away, the mice will play"? A week later, the page boy left.

White walls, the misty Downs and the wet asphalt or else moss roses climbing through the windows of the School Hall on a summer day, these are my exterior impressions and I see them more vividly in memory than the lines of my companions in white blouses and blue skirts. I felt aloof to my last day there and what my comrades thought about my attitude was completely indifferent to me. My elders argued that it was selfish not to try to fit into the group. I shrugged my shoulders (a foreign gesture that they disliked) and remembered the conscripts in the Paris streets. There was a continuous sense of being in the wrong place with no appeal possible to justice, mercy or even to common sense. One of the fundamental differences between school and myself was that I accepted all races and religions, had I not mixed with Moslem, Christian and Copt in the Cairo streets, and although so deeply English that I often aligned myself with the lost, unpopular cause, my concern was with freedom. Queenwood preached acceptance of the customs of the age.

Languages saved me. The upper forms were given Racine to read when their vocabulary was perhaps two hundred words. Our accents were ruined for ever through an idiotic rule that we must talk French during certain periods of the day. There was no phonetic training and most girls simply tacked French endings onto English phrases. Everybody hated the lessons and so if I wanted to escape some *corvée*, I found substitutes in plenty if I roughed out their translations for them. Europe rescued me from many difficulties and I was very grateful for her assistance.

I had read enough history to know that it was wise to get as close to the throne as possible. Freeman's *Sicily* had explained the position. Our Headmistress was a Tyrant and the staff her bodyguard. I left the beings alone whom I had innocently called governesses on arrival but, after a sharp reproof, "the ladies of the staff," and whenever I wanted anything, knocked at the library door. Dear Miss Chudleigh, I discovered afterwards that she also came from Cornwall, we were adversaries but we respected one another and miraculously she let me argue with her almost daily. Most of her pupils trembled in her presence, it never occurred to me that we were other than equals. There was one difference; temporarily she had power over us but she, in turn, was dominated by our parents. Had I known it, her life was a novel made to my hand because she had fought her way up from a remote Cornish day school to being part owner of one of the best private schools of that day's England. I did not grasp it at the time but sometimes when people grumble now about the madness of the world, I remember her stern features. *We have made progress.* In 1910 we were on the threshold of a new era in education and if a particular pattern of Puritan zealousness had not been stamped across "Chud's" soul, she could have been one of its leaders. She had a grasp of organization, she tried out new teaching methods (not always popular with us), and unless a matter touched her religious convictions she was just. It was the discipline of her youth, she must have been born about the middle of the eighteen seventies, that had hooded her intellect and warped her views. Her Sunday talks were famous and twice a term she lectured us about "unhealthy friendships." None of us had the faintest idea of what she meant.

Miss Chudleigh took us for literature class, twice a week; in one we read a Shakespeare play, in the other Tennyson's *Idylls of the King.* I do not know if it was due to my pugnacious instincts or to my study of Saxon weapons but I distrusted the ability of Tennyson's knights to stand in the "shield wall." I asked Miss Chudleigh where he had found the stories and she suggested Malory. I was still not satisfied and, was it destiny again, I found *The Legend of Sir Gawain* by Jessie L. Weston on a back shelf in a bookshop. It cost four shillings and made an enormous hole in my pocket money. How can I make people understand what gates it opened to me? It seems a simple enough book today, it was published in 1897, but it led me straight to modern science. I discovered that a story accumulated new details whenever it was retold but by patient sifting (how wonderful this was to a would-be historian) it was sometimes possible to trace the outline of some ancient event. Once I had grasped this fact, it was easy to understand the idea of the unconscious mind, a few years afterwards. It was also a summons. The victors of Hastings were trying to claim the Arthurian stories for their own. They had defamed the character and stolen away the exploits of the real English hero, Gawain. There were pages on sun worship and the islands of the dead and I was at the age when one is interested in the soul. Somehow I got her *Sir Percival* and flung myself into it with almost as much enthusiasm. What were the *Enfances* but a picture of my own childhood? I, too, had grown up in solitude and had had to learn the usages of not a court but a school, under the mocking eyes of half a hundred Sir Kays.

Years later, when I read Mr. Eliot's *The Waste Land,* I smelt ink, furniture polish and disinfectant soap again as I sat in the School Hall at preparation with my comrades around me, all dreaming of half term and the numerous trifles that make up a schoolgirl's life while I was proudly turning names over in my head, Ferdinand Lot, Bédier and Gaston Paris. I must confess that though I could crawl through some of the less difficult parts of Chrétien de Troyes, I found them boring. It was Miss Weston's historical ideas, her linking of Gawain with the remote past of Britain and her refusal to accept knights as missionaries that gripped my mind. She became the shining flag of all my rebellions. Besides, she was a woman and where she had gone I could follow. All that I knew about her was the word "Bournemouth" that appeared underneath the introductions to her books and as I knew little about scholars, I pictured her as a retired governess living in that watering place. It never occurred to me, it would have occurred to no Victorian girl, to write her a letter.

I dragged *Diu Krone,* an obscure poem in which Sir Gawain achieved the Grail, whether it was appropriate or not, into every class. I was eloquent about Tennyson's misuse of his sources. Miss Chudleigh gave me the lowest marks possible and trapped me over the meaning of an obscure Elizabethan word. Then she made up by calling me into the library and letting me read Miss Weston's newest article in some learned publication. Of course I was a nuisance, of course I deserved a smacking, but all these encounters sharpened my wits. If I had been left free and encouraged to sit in a library, I should probably have played truant and never opened a reference book in my life.

England has forgotten, after two wars, the terrifying power of the Victorian church. The school's attitude to religion shocked my Eastern soul. It was the solitary emotional outlet permitted to the girls and it turned into a whirlpool of fear and sentimentality. God cared only for those who obeyed Authority and went to church on Sundays. People mouthed supplications as if they were turning a prayer wheel but without a Tibetan's faith. The mind was always to be discouraged from inquiry, the mysteries were unimportant.

This creed was not quaint. It was a deadly reality. It could effect both marriages and the getting of work. We were allowed to take one book back to school with us and I chose my favorite *Extinct Monsters*. I was hardly surprised when Miss Chudleigh confiscated the volume, everything that we liked, however harmless, was taken away at once. I was astonished, however, when she called me into the library and explained that although it was proper for me to read at home whatever my family allowed, she could not allow it to circulate freely at Queenwood because there was a reference to Darwin in a footnote. She would give it back to me when we went home for the holidays.

I simply did not know what she meant and I believe I only fully understood her action when I read about the Piltdown forgery in 1953. I am convinced that this was due to frustration. The antiquity of man had been accepted by most learned societies in 1912 but there was still much opposition in England where it was considered anti-Biblical. I suspect that Dawson was so irritated by the views around him that he wanted some tremendous proof to convince the people at large. It may be that his action was a help to his fellow scientists at the time. It is so easy to forget in a freer age that our forefathers had to work secretly and often in isolation if ever their researches appeared to challenge contemporary theology. Even today I meet people who regard prehistory as a dubious myth and we have the conflict raging, although in a stifled and less violent form, over the Dead Sea scrolls.

Miss Weston herself is out of fashion at present for an almost similar reason. She felt that there were traces of Eastern and probably Indian influence in the very early Arthurian material. Some of her details may be wrong, she was writing over forty years ago, but the original "Matter of Britain" goes back to our remote past when traces of religions brought in by foreign traders under the Romans still existed in isolated Welsh and Cornish valleys. Most scholars now work on the later versions that arose after the Norman Conquest and that were deeply affected by the Christianity of that time. To like and study one or the other is a matter of individual preference but it is unscientific to ignore the fact that the first tales belong to an age when Norman Christianity was unknown in Britain and to blame Miss Weston for being more interested in the beginning than the end.

There was one thing to be said in favor of the Victorians. They believed in their causes. In those days, you were either "for" Tennyson or Browning and no literary group that I subsequently joined ever discussed the merits of two rival poets so vehemently. Browning was said to be obscure; this aroused rage as some people felt that they might be tricked thus into reading heretical views. Let us give Miss Chudleigh her due. We studied Tennyson because he was "set" for examinations but she also took us to outside lectures on *The Ring and the Book*. I loved Browning, to me he was crystal-clear and, reading him, I was nearer again to Italy, the Italy of my childhood. I think now that he was a forerunner of the documentary film, he photographed what he saw and the problems had an unexpected twist to them for that age. Suppose he believed in happiness, I had need of such a faith at Queenwood. I did not know what was going to happen to me, except for a little reading (yes, this was much), Authority planned almost every minute of my day and the world around me revolved according to incomprehensible laws.

> " 'Tis only the coat of a page to borrow,
> "And tie my hair in a horse-boy's trim,
> "And I save my soul—but not to-morrow—"

Leave to the sixteen-year-old a flash of color, and to the would-be escaper (without the price of a railway ticket) the feeling that he, or she, is not the only runaway alive.

Yes, Browning was a great comfort when one was young. Waring reminded me of Burton. He was real, unlike the maidens with their tapestries, and how often, after I had been told for the hundredth time, "Showing off, Winifred, is not ladylike," I had first answered cheerfully that the last thing on earth that I wanted to be was a lady and had then retired, muttering to myself,

> "True, but there were sundry jottings,
> "Stray-leaves, fragments, blurrs and blottings,
> "Certain first steps were achieved. . . ."

because I too had a beginning in a notebook. As soon as I had time, neither at home nor school, alas, was I allowed any leisure, I was going to write a book about "the ladies of the staff." I felt profoundly sorry for them. One day the door would open and we would bang out of Queenwood but what had they to look forward to but an eternity of terms? I had even heard one of the senior mistresses humbly ask permission to go to supper with some guild at the vicarage and every contact with their pupils outside lessons was sternly controlled. I knew the basic rule in art was to write only of what the author had experienced. I had never, alas, led a charge of Hannibal's elephants but now by fits and starts I was beginning to learn my trade.

I attempted to slide back and forth within the school, using its code as coloration as I had shifted in Egypt between the East and the West. It did not work. I had grown too analytical and the circumstances were more complex. Still I tried to get behind the teacher's skin and to imagine her sensations. What did she think about when she saw our row of faces? Did she ever dream, perhaps in the train that took us towards our holidays, of some eventual freedom? Oh, if I could get her down on paper (I still regret that book) I could reform the world. I did not yet possess a typewriter, my observations, my heroine and myself got into such a sorry tangle that I could not straighten them out but it is not the flat-topped cap that makes the apprentice but grimy hours of false beginnings and unproductive work.

After all, it was the start that mattered. I was tired of reading first chapters and about how others had begun their adventures: Marco Polo, for example, who had just walked off and followed a caravan with nobody yelling "come back" at him. I was old, old, by Elizabethan standards and the future seemed a blank wall. Yet if discovery was nowhere else, it was in the wind. It smashed across the trees at night, swept along the grasses, covered the Downs beyond us with leaves. I could hear it whispering, "Do you know where Tierra del Fuego is, have you been round the Horn?" Time was rushing on, time was being spent and what had I to show for it? Only frustration as the bell woke us all from dreams and "Get up, girls, get up," echoed along the corridor.

There has to be a responsive frame of mind or historical events pass unnoticed. We saw the Coronation procession in July, 1911, but I was in conflict with my surroundings and the details are imprecise. Instead of emperors and kings, I remember rather with malicious clarity that Miss Chudleigh, who had been invited to go with us, swallowed a fish bone at supper and had to be rushed to the nearest first-aid post by my mother. I was thus eyewitness of the fall of great-ness and smarting, together with my schoolmates, from reproofs— "Winifred, where is your hair ribbon? Dorothy, have you a button missing from your sleeve?"—we exulted together, as soon as we were alone, that the rulers, as well as the lowly, were subject to the world's ills.

We went on to watch the Naval Review from the deck of a steamer. One of the Queenwood mistresses who accompanied us still speaks of my family's kindness and of the occasion being one of the happiest days of her life. My only clear memory is of going aboard an American battleship. I had heard so many stories about the States from my father that I was delighted to be technically upon "American soil." We were asked afterwards to a party on board but my mother felt that it would be improper to take my schoolfellows without the consent of their parents to a "grown-up" function. I was not quite sure what a party was but felt that it was no place for a cabin boy and intended to wriggle out of it, but my companions were bitterly disappointed. We were allowed to watch the illuminations, however, until quite late at night.

It was during these same summer holidays that we went for a short cruise to Norway. I liked seeing a new country but what was more important than the waterfalls and the harebells growing out of some barn roof was that, in looking for translations of the sagas, I discov-ered William Morris. He taught me first, I think, to listen to the pattern of words. I could not get the sound of his early poems out of my head. I think that it is his fondness for a few archaic terms such as "sithence" that disturbs the modern reader although most of us have a favorite word that we use too often. At sixteen who notices such things? I read for the pictures, the two children shouting to each other across the "sundering flood," the riders in the woods, a ship in a gray harbor. One thing I knew from my fencing, Morris understood weapons. I did not like his renderings of Arthurian romance but comforted myself with the thought that he had lived before Miss Weston had made her researches. His damsels could be ignored, they were merely a blazon, a device, or occasionally useful for a rhyme. What I felt and liked in his poetry was his courage.

It takes a Shakespeare to write for the seven ages of man. Morris is youth, speaking to it or to old age, to that moment when, as they tell us, Queen Elizabeth could not listen to State Papers any longer but only to folk stories and ballads. It is not a question of arrested childhood. He expresses unconsciously but fully the first phase of maturity. People say that he wasted his gifts upon too many things but what else do any of us do, if we have guts, when we are twenty? He never attained again the greatness of *The Hollow Land* that I read then as an adventure story and now as a myth of the pilgrimage of the soul but he chose to fight in many different ways and made it easier for the twentieth-century artist to break through to a greater freedom.

And thus I came from Morris and the sagas, late that summer, for the first time to Scilly.

My first voyage to the islands was an initiation rite. I sat watching the granite cliffs towards the Land's End from the deck of the *Lyonnesse* in happy anticipation of the marvels that Doris had promised me. Suddenly the increasing motion blotted everything out except a determination not to be seasick if I could possibly help it. I was quite a normal child. I could have borne the captain or Mr. Banfield watching me hang over the rail but if this should happen, my Queenwood companions would tease me gleefully for days. I need not have been ashamed; men had been known to sail the oceans of the world and then succumb to the choppy crosscurrents off the Wolf but I pretended at first that I was all right, then I repeated lines of poetry in a wild attempt to keep my mind off the roll, then I closed my eyes and gripped my chair until finally a voice said cheerfully, "You'll feel better in a minute, we are entering the Sound."

Scilly is a continent in miniature. The islands formed a single land mass, ages ago, and due to the influence of the Gulf Stream, except to westward, the gardens are full of palms and tropical plants. I have never felt a similar atmosphere anywhere else, it is drenched with age, yet of the moment young. On that day, however, I did not notice the white crescent of Samson nor the clear, emerald patches on the eastern side of the channel. I was just able to wave halfheartedly to Doris and Ethel on the quay and to struggle ashore, absolutely green but technically undisgraced.

It was the first time that I had come within a cabin boy's view of the sea and I was out of my mind with joy. There was not a single feeling of disappointment, it was everything that I had wanted and more. The Sound had the color of a gull's wing and something of its movement, the edges of the waves were like the shells. Sometimes we steamed out in a small launch to fish beyond Annet and then we were tied with life lines to the rails, in case we got seasick and fell overboard. If like a plant we can draw life from a particular soil, I have drawn mine from the islands. There were no tourists in 1911 and no cars. We drove across to Pellistry beside hedges full of a lemon-scented honeysuckle and carried our parcels in a donkey cart or we rowed about in our own punt. Many of the inhabitants had not only never visited the mainland but had never left their own islet. We would not look back when the time came to leave but promised ourselves that when we were "grown-up" we would never leave Scilly but live there till we died.

The years passed. Naturally the higher I went up in the school the easier life became for me but at seventeen we thirst to remake the world and I had that illusion badly. I was all zeal. If my companions did not like history it was because their imaginations had never been awakened. (In a sense I was right.) Let us develop our intelligence, find out what had never been discovered before and if I had to cuff a few heads in the process it did not disturb me in the very least. I resented the waste of time and the vast amount of preventable unhappiness. A touch here, an alteration there, and the organization would have revolved so much more smoothly. As for the curriculum, I should have scrapped it at once. Hours were spent upon useless snippets, one girl through a transfer from another school spent three years on the Wars of the Roses and many of my companions left unable to look up a train in a timetable and without knowing how to order a book from a shop. I wanted to introduce business correspondence and have them study the world instead of merely England. I also tried to organize a strike against the carrying of umbrellas. We were used to rain and what were they, I argued, other than an emblem of respectability and, therefore, to be deplored?

"What is your aim at Queenwood?" I asked Miss Chudleigh audaciously as we were plodding across the Downs on the walk that she took alone with every girl from the top form who was about to leave.

"To turn out the greatest number of girls conforming to an average pattern," my Headmistress replied as precisely as if she were annihilating some troublesome fly.

"But then you will lose the few above and the much greater number below," I protested but Miss Chudleigh shook her head.

"The individual is less important than the group."

Her arguments left me cold. Every person alive had the right to personal development and besides, was standardization, to use the classic English expression, "fair"? Authority just twisted facts to suit its own ends. Tradition, I proclaimed, was just another word for laziness. We ought to examine every action, I thought, instead of looking at the ball that I was supposed to hit (was I not the young scholar literally sacrificed to the Games?) and discard what was merely a convention. Give me a class to teach and I would show "them" results. Meantime let us forget that awkward incident of zero at arithmetic. I had no trouble in remembering the dates of historical events.

What happened to us all? There were about eighty pupils at Queenwood during the two years that I was there. As I have written earlier, Martita became an actress, half a dozen of us wrote books, Dorothy Pilley climbed in the Alps and in the East, Doris created new daffodils. Some ran schools, others worked both with radio and films, they farmed, they nursed, they settled all over the Dominions. The moment that a new type of work opened for women, one of us was usually there. Nearly all my companions married and had families. Miss Chudleigh and Miss Johns both died during the thirties and I never saw them again after 1918 but I am still in touch with several of "the ladies of the staff." In general, they also married or went on to other schools and escaped the "eternity of terms" that I had projected for them in my novel. The school itself ceased to exist but there is still an active Old Girls' association that meets twice a year.

There are certain psychological factors that make a type of life less bearable for some than others. Fortunately I arrived at Queenwood with my character already formed and by some miracle much of it survived. Yet the children who came when they were nine and left when they were seventeen, how could they keep even hope? I used to blame Miss Chudleigh for her mistakes. Now that I am the historian that nobody wanted me to be, I understand that it was the age and not my poor headmistress who was at fault.

Perhaps each epoch has a particular mold that all its citizens must share. What was school but a foretaste of those army camps where millions in subsequent years faced their training also in circumstances where justice and mercy were largely unknown? One thing was spared me. What my comrades thought about my attitude was entirely indifferent to me. I demanded judgment from my peers. I could see no escape except through knowledge but I felt instinctively that this had to come through life and not from books. I intended to question the validity of every thought, to fight for my freedom and, if I could not get it, die.

There had to be a bridge between the isolation of my childhood and the everyday world. The friendships that I made at school have lasted all my life. I can concede at present that the gain was greater than the loss. Yet there was less than a knife's edge between psychological disaster and survival, my story might easily have had another ending and though as age has chilled the emotions I can accept Queenwood as a necessary part of my experience, the impact was a shattering one and it was hell while it lasted.

Ten

To leave Queenwood was not to regain Paradise. I had supposed that I had only to leave school to be happy again but I sweated out the next seven years in complete frustration. They were the first endurance test of *The Book of the Dead*. How could I have known then that though experiences sometimes repeat themselves, it is always with a difference and never in their bright, primal colors? The war was responsible in part; until it ended the pressure to conform increased but there was also a change in myself. I cannot remember ever having felt lonely in childhood or even knowing what the word meant. Now I wanted passionately to be able to talk to my own generation.

The modern world does not understand how narrow existence was for the Edwardian woman. It was not a question of class, or even money, this should be emphasized, but of public opinion. From slum to palace almost everything outside the home was forbidden ground. It was only after analysis, many years later, that I realized how much of this was due to sexual taboos that were all the harsher for never being explained or mentioned in conversation. I was not allowed to go to public lectures or to accept invitations to lunch in restaurants. (This taboo did not apply in France.) I was reproved, aged twenty, for writing a business letter to a publisher to inquire about the fate of a manuscript. "What do they expect us to do?" I used to ask Dorothy Pilley, the freest among us, when yet another harmless pleasure was put out of bounds. Her only answer was to shrug her shoulders. If my Queenwood friends came to see me, we sat sedately on chairs hoping that our almost-floor-length dresses were not getting crumpled, this meant a scolding, "Can't you girls ever learn to sit still," and that the hairpins holding up our heavy plaits were conformably in place. Our generation, as always, was supposed to be unbelievably wicked. My mother's friends alluded to scandals in oblique terms after glancing in our direction. They could have discussed them in the plainest words, we should not have understood them. We were much too frightened of our parents to worry in the modern fashion about how they might behave. Our rebellions took place in our thoughts, it was only after 1920 that they passed into deeds. I was a dutiful daughter (strange though this may seem) and renounced almost to the memory all that made life endurable only to hear after every fresh submission, "Why can't you be more like other girls?" These wanted less than I did, they were not vowed to Artemis; besides how was it possible to change a cheerful and obstinate hippopotamus (my totem animal) into a graceful Edwardian miss?

In one respect I was fortunate. Nobody had less sense of caste than my family. My mother was, as my father often ruefully remarked, "an anarchist at heart." He was blamed for promoting the office boy who had shown initiative instead of the gentleman's son who was a university graduate. I often heard him say that if he had been to a public school he would not have been flexible enough to create his business. I should have been smacked, whatever my age, if I had dared to suggest that I was any better than my neighbors. We came from the stolid, Protestant middle class and we stuck to its training. Some of the rules I understood and still accept; if I happened by chance to have more funds or intelligence than the people around me it was so that I might help them. I must never "show off." (I wonder if a little "showing off" is not good for the extreme young?) The conventions that I fought were either conformity of dress (I was supposed to put on a hat and gloves if I went in the country to the post box at the corner) or all that kept me from adventure or that interfered with the freedom of the mind. Mercifully, within rigorous bounds and hours, I was allowed to go out alone although this was considered shocking by many of my mother's friends. Sometimes when she sent me to a neighbor with a message, I had the humiliation of waiting while they telephoned to inquire if it were really true that I was permitted to take walks unescorted.

Pioneers are usually Puritans, they have to be, but neither common sense nor the exemplary lives most women led helped them in the least. We were literally freed by the war. So many families then lost all that they had, so many daughters were forced to go to work through sheer economic necessity that some though not all of the restrictions collapsed. Alas, in an age of prosperity, they recur.

The logical action if I could not advance was to retreat. Consciously I wanted to grow up but unconsciously I was drawn back to an earlier happiness and suggested to my family that if we ever went East again I could be valuable as their interpreter. They showed little enthusiasm but I had discovered that there were Arabic classes at London University (it must have been through Miss Johns) and they consented reluctantly to my attending a course. The group was so small that the professor preferred to take it at his own house and I suspect that this was the deciding factor; it meant that there was no chance of my mingling with other students and "getting ideas."

Professor Arnold fulfilled the popular conception of a scholar. He was dignified, incredibly erudite, absent-minded and even shyer than myself. He faced his three pupils helplessly in his library; I seem to remember this as a sunken room somewhere near the Natural History Museum. It was hung with dark but glowing carpets and packed with books from floor to ceiling.

We were all three there for practical reasons. There was, first of all, a nervous youth whose name I never knew who had been ordered to take an examination in Arabic before his leave expired. He had been working at a consulate somewhere in Africa and already spoke Swahili. His interest was law. I remembered perhaps a hundred words and had never learned my letters properly but I wanted to read the battle poems, the *Seven Odes,* in the original. I imagined myself quoting them from the top of a racing camel somewhere in the desert. Our leader was the Egyptologist, Margaret Murray. She spent the winters excavating beside the Nile; in those days we were too polite to speak of going on "a dig." She herself was like some hieroglyphic bird as she turned her head restlessly from one side to the other, missing

146

nothing, always wary and full of common sense. "I can't talk donkey boy Arabic to the sheikhs," she explained and added when I said wistfully that I wished that I could join her, "Wear a scrap of veil or even a bit of mosquito netting the next time that you are in Egypt. It can be as transparent as you like but the Arabs will talk to you more freely once they see that you respect their customs." How many political difficulties might have been avoided if Western officials had taken her advice?

The University syllabus had prescribed a course in classical Arabic founded upon the Koran. It was the equivalent of giving an Elizabethan Bible in the spelling of that age to some cheerful French family visiting England for the first time and confirmed my opinion that universities were stupid places where people went on being children for the rest of their lives. We sat with our books in front of us and understood perhaps one word in ten; the "set book" was the Islamic version of Joseph and his brethren. Professor Arnold seemingly spoke every language of the Near East and to help us Miss Murray gaily persuaded him to tell us stories. Grammar was his love; from the root of an Arabic word he swooped off to Sanskrit or hovered longingly above Persian. The character of a race, he explained, was visible in its language, the soft Syrian vowels became a grunt of consonants in the harsh Moroccan sands. He could be kept discoursing on a single verb all the morning or, if luck were with us, turn into a storyteller straight out of the bazaars.

Sometimes he would remember that we were, after all, his pupils. "Try to say gh-rr-r," he encouraged us, "begin in the throat and throw the sound to the back of the nose." We hesitated, it is extremely difficult for three people to gh-rr-r in unison, then we ghrowled. "Oh, no," I can still see Professor Arnold shaking his scholar's head, "perhaps if you went to the Zoo it would be helpful. It is really a camel sound."

The youth scribbled something in his notebook. Was he writing down "Practice five minutes daily at the dromedary enclosure," I wondered, with "*mouth open*" underlined?

"How do you get the camels to cough?" Miss Murray was always practical.

"I leave the details of their studies entirely to my students." The professor permitted himself the suggestion of a smile.

We never managed to gh-rr-r very well but we covered pages with exercises. It was old-fashioned and comfortable, there was none of the modern drilling in a few basic sentences, we were supposed to run, driven by our enthusiasm, long before we could crawl. I enjoyed myself but the shock of Queenwood was exacting its toll. I had lost my habitual concentration and had never learned so badly nor dreamed so much. I copied signs and thought of saddle straps as I drew the curves but my mind was not awake, I was stiff and frightened and the others thought me stupid and bored. Even my enthusiasm began to slip away when my confusion increased in spite of all my hard work.

Occasionally there were other complications.

"She lifted the pomegranate," I was very glad that I had actually seen the fruit, the consul-to-be noted its equivalent in Swahili, the professor bent over his Koran. "Beholding Joseph's beauty, the knife slipped . . ." he looked up in agitation, "Miss Murray, Miss Murray, this is very different from the Jewish version, do you think we ought to omit the next six lines?"

Miss Murray caught my eye and grinned. Joseph, although he ultimately resisted temptation, gave a precise description of his physical reaction to love that was highly distressing to British reserve. We started again, Miss Murray began to laugh, we leapt a whole page and eventually reached harbor in some pious sentences about the wisdom of virtue. The difficulty was that words such as "zealous" and "abnegation" were hardly the terms that a traveler needed to order a glass of tea or find his way out of a *souk*.

After a second such experience the professor shut his book gratefully and turned to his colleague, "I suppose you have heard about our new Persian course?"

"I have seen the prospectus, yes, but I have three classes of my own . . ." Miss Murray looked up with the defensive air that I saw then for the first time when lecturers suspect that they may be asked to take extra work.

"The authorities decided, I think unwisely, upon a formal inauguration. There was first the benefactor who had provided some funds on account of his interest in Omar Khayyam, then the Persian Ambassador decided to come with several gentlemen from the Foreign Office to support him and there was an unusual number of our colleagues. They all arrived at the classroom punctually at three."

"In top hats?" Miss Murray was irrepressible.

"I presume they came in appropriate dress. It seems that there was a single student. A lad going out to an oil company, I believe, near Tabriz. The Ambassador addressed him from the platform upon the beauties of Persian poetry and a diplomat spoke most feelingly afterwards about the influence of Eastern philosophical thought upon Western belief. Unfortunately we had a letter from the young man this morning, saying that he proposes to continue his studies elsewhere. It was his first lesson and I am afraid that he was rather shy."

My next adventure was *Sakuntala*. An Indian student rang our doorbell one evening and, to my mother's amazement, asked for me. Where had I met him, she inquired? Nowhere, I protested, she had seen my fellow pupils when she had taken me to the first class and she had known my exact whereabouts during every moment of the last month. No, I did not think that it was the brother of the Indian girls at Queenwood. They had been younger, in the Lower School, and I had seldom had an opportunity of speaking to them. I had never been asked where I lived but if the man were a foreigner and in distress, according to the Bedouin traditions of hospitality we ought to see him and offer him help.

My family seemed doubtful that this was the correct procedure. Duly chaperoned however by my mother and a friend who happened to be staying with her, we entered the library where he had been asked to wait.

It was "much ado about nothing." A terrified Hindu student with a letter from the University in his hand had called to ask if I would take tickets for a private performance of *Sakuntala* in an English translation arranged by some dramatic society. He had got my name from a list of those taking Oriental languages. It was a Sanskrit classic and had little to do with Arabic but perhaps, he ventured, I might be interested.

I had never been to India and its literature seemed remote to me but I took two tickets, I think that they were four and sixpence each, he bowed and left. The meeting had lasted precisely three minutes. Then the storm broke. Girls never went to amateur performances given by students. I should understand when I was older. (I was then nineteen!) Besides, who knew what was in the play?

"It is a religious drama," I remarked icily because I knew that this was a matter of principle and that it was essential for me to insist upon my right to see it. Why must I be forbidden every activity that took place outside the home? Eventually we reached the usual British compromise. I might see the play provided that I could persuade Miss Johns to come up from Queenwood, it was during the holidays, and accompany me to the theater.

The performance was a hilarious occasion. *Sakuntala* had been translated about 1860 by an English gentleman with a fondness for the word "sublime." The scenery had been borrowed and was not remotely like a jungle while most of the cast was English with an obvious terror of declaiming poetry out loud. The play also went on for five hours. I tried to be worthy of the occasion until the Queen flung herself onto the stage in all the glory of a dozen shimmering veils and a pair of sturdy, black walking shoes as she was being abandoned to the sublime ferocity of the more than sublime tigers. I reverted to childhood and howled. "Try to control yourself, Winifred," Miss Johns whispered, tears pouring down her own cheeks. The newspapers described it the next day as a very moving performance.

"Ah, what I expected," Professor Arnold remarked soberly when I answered his polite inquiry at our next lesson. "I think perhaps I was wise to immerse myself in my work."

One victory led to another. After such an innocuous experiment I was able to persuade my parents to let me join Miss Murray's own class in elementary hieroglyphics. It was actually given inside one of the University buildings and I had to endure a number of family lectures upon not allowing myself to be "influenced by people." None of my twenty fellow students ever spoke to me nor I to them. I do not think they talked among themselves. It seems crazy today but it was part of the fabric of that so-called "golden age"!

I did not find the hieroglyphics as difficult as Arabic. I remembered the pictures at once. It was easier being taught than learning them alone because I could ask questions if I did not understand them. I did not realize it at the time but drawing the signs probably allowed some of the feeling for art that I had so sternly repressed to emerge into consciousness. Sometimes a new symbol could illuminate a day.

At the end of the first term I was offered what might have been a chance of escape. We had been sent to a strange classroom and Miss Murray herself had offered to show me the way back to the entrance.

"Why not ask your parents to let you come all day and train properly as an archaeologist?" she suggested, "We need assistants badly and you would like the work." It was the last time for six whole years that any adult offered me help.

My family said no. I was too young. I must certainly stop at home if classes put such foolish ideas into my head. I might get stranded in some unheard-of place, lose my ticket, have things happen to me that they could not possibly explain. I fought back. I should be old enough because the training took three years, there would be a group of us in Egypt (I thought it wiser not to mention that we should probably sleep in tents), why was it right to be with all those girls in Queenwood and wrong to be with students interested in what I liked? They said no again but not quite so emphatically and I think I might have persuaded them at least to let me begin if an English family that my father knew had not invited me to spend the next spring at their place in Lebanon and they even offered to lend me an Arab horse. My father this time gave his consent but war broke out before I could leave.

Perhaps I had a narrow escape. A little easing of the intolerably frustrated state in which I lived and I might have become the conventional scholar so absorbed by research that I should never have had the adventures for which I was born. I began gradually from this time to divest myself of the Arab world, it was a dream's misunderstanding, as I came to analyze its attitude towards women. Of course I thought of it occasionally but in general it was a scrap of papyrus from the past upon which no complete text was ever written. My true destiny was the West.

What a disappointment I was to my parents! All their friends had liked me as a child but here I was with the raw aggressiveness of a boy, clamoring to be loosed upon a world that had no use for me. My father might have coped with the situation if I had had a mathematical mind but what was he to do with a young savage who was only interested in tearing society apart to see how it worked? It must have been disconcerting when a guest, meaning to be kind, asked me what my hobbies were and got the answer, "I want to find out how people think." Once in an unguarded moment I said something about writing. There was a roar of laughter and a visitor answered, "Oh, no, Miss

Winifred, I'm afraid that is a little out of your range but I'm sure you'll run the garden splendidly in a year or two." Usually I was careful and silent. I prayed to be forty, knowing that as long as I was young nobody would listen to me. I seldom had more than half an hour a day to myself. It taught me concentration because such moments were so precious no noises could disturb them and I usually spent the time memorizing pages of poetry to repeat during our interminable walks. It was a training in the ancient oral tradition but also a dangerous practice because it absorbed the energy that should have gone into creative work. Yet what else could I have done? It was morbid to read so much, they said, and selfish to want to write.

I do not know how I should have lived if it had not been for one of those little magazines that, as Gertrude Stein was fond of quoting, "have died to make verse free." It was *Poetry and Drama,* edited by Harold Monro. The English contributions were too conventional to touch me but F. S. Flint had written articles on modern French poetry and I found in them for the first time the magic word "Mallarmé."

Mallarmé's ideas exploded in my head. We desire perfection when we are young, not knowing that inspiration is the skin boat of the seal woman, here momentarily, as suddenly vanished. I had been groping towards the idea of a *poésie pure* and I was willing to give up everything else to find it. I was utterly alone and for that reason, *le verbe,* as the French would say, had become of supreme importance. I thought of it as Pegasus and saw it as a way to freedom. In my innocence, I took the words literally and supposed that *l'azur* meant that Mallarmé had wanted to be a cabin boy and run away to sea. Unconsciously, I imagine, I caught some echo of his own unhappy schooldays although I knew nothing then about his life. Perhaps I was not so wrong after all, remember the famous *yole*? I had so great a thirst for life that when it came to me through certain of the lines, I could hardly bear to listen to them. There was a sense of infinite adventure in the words, what were they but a huge Atlantic roller, curling over and bursting into foam? It was as if a captain had suddenly come up to me and said, "So you want to go to sea? Very well, go forward, we'll have to try you out."

Purity of apprehension by no means implies an ability to handle form. About this time my father paid for some of my incredibly bad verses to be printed. In retrospect, I do not think that this practice is necessarily wrong, all apprentices have to learn their trade and we cannot expect to waste paper at a publisher's expense. It is also less vanity than a desire to be accepted as an aspirant by one's fellow writers. I had never spoken to an author, praise then would have seemed patronizing, rather like a Queenwood mistress deigning to approve an essay, but if I were to develop I had to leave home and success might soften parental opposition. I was nineteen, it was my first book and I had hazarded, if you will, all I knew upon a throw of the dice.

A few days before the verses were published I discovered Mallarmé. I knew then that everything that I had written, under conditions of the greatest difficulty, was meaningless and that it was doubtful that I could ever produce a sentence that I might have carried to the Rue de Rome. It was a profound shock because it literally destroyed all the hope that I had in life. I tore up my manuscripts and apart from an almost factual account of my schooldays, I wrote little more for twenty years (Mallarmé seems to have that effect upon people) yet during that time my principles of conduct were founded upon his ideas. He had felt intuitively some of the steps taken later by Freud to liberate the mind from purely conscious thought. It is a measure of his stature, not only as a poet but as a leader.

Young fibers are resilient. Prowling around a bookshop, I discovered a slim, green volume, *Des Imagistes,* and flung myself upon its contents with the lusty, roaring appetite of an Elizabethan boy. I was discontented with traditional forms but this was new, it said what I was unable to write for myself.

The horror that the Imagist manifesto produced had to be lived through to be believed. Poetry had reached an incredibly low level in 1913 although it was fashionable to quote it continually in conversation. Verse then was distinguished from prose because each line began with a capital letter and it rhymed. It was improper to mention the modern world except in terms of horror; the writer should be down on his knees in the clover (odorous was a better word than scented) waiting to be stung by a bee. It was also important to use poetic language, we "quothed" rather than spoke. Naturally "free verse" was confused with "free love" and not to rhyme was felt to be a form of cheating.

I think that the cause of such opposition came from first lessons fixing a definite pattern in a child's head. It is natural to begin with ballads and these are usually written in some easily remembered form but they are a beginning, not an end. Our opponents forgot that alliterative poetry was the basis of English literature and that the ability to hear and use the slight pause or silence between parts of a line or the portions of a sentence is one of the writer's important tasks. We do not need to match love with shove but to vary this break so that it is never monotonous but always perceptible to the trained ear.

I have full respect for the popular arts but the function of the artist is vision. He must be in advance of his time and as to know is to be outcast from the world, why should he expect recognition? Fame is merely the badge of long service. His duty is to his art and that implies detachment; he is the twin of the designer of supersonic aircraft, his ivory tower is his drawing board, it is not his function to produce the commercial air liner or the family car. I have a profound contempt for the writer who speaks of making his work intelligible to the masses, he is not serving them but betraying their trust. Our job is to feel the movement of time as its direction is about to change and there can be no reward but the vision itself. It is natural that we should be both disliked and ignored.

Our youth makes us whether we like it or not. The rest is simply sharpening and experience. I felt the approach of another age and the Imagist poetry made me drunk with joy. Some of the writers were American; they also wrote of the Mediterranean that had been a part of my childhood and they used new rhythms and exciting sounds. There was a feeling of revolt in the air, nobody had spoken to me about it and to this day I do not know precisely why I leapt into the twentieth century without a single, backward glance. Perhaps we cannot escape from our generation, no matter how much we may be isolated from it, it is a universal movement and we have to drift with it or perish.

I risk giving the impression that I was living in the bourgeois environment that Flaubert described so well. This was not the case. Our house was full of pictures. They were traditional and friends said indignantly that they would not enter a man's home if he hung futurist daubs on his walls but there were frequent visits to galleries and museums. I was able to listen at the highest level to discussions on law and the political trends of the time. The cause of the rift between myself and my surroundings was purely sociological. In 1913, women belonged in the home. My family were truly frightened of the free-thinking little monster that had emerged in their midst and naturally did their best to discourage my "morbid ideas." It would have been the same wherever I had been born, in a cottage or a mansion, in Kent or France. Slavery may be a gentle thing but the threat of the rod is always in the master's hand. It was not until the war gave women the possibility of economic freedom that circumstances changed. I could not possibly have understood this at the time. I wanted to sail around the Horn or, if this could not be managed, go as near it in adventure as possible and then write about my voyages in an entirely new form. Nothing else mattered to me. No wonder I scribbled in my notebook, "I waste in a raw world, dumb, unendurable and old."

Under such circumstances, the young usually fall in love. I followed the pattern but with a country, not a person. America was my first love affair and I have never gotten over it. My mistress perhaps, because we have both been perceptive and also inconstant. I am deeply and traditionally English by temperament but whatever recognition I eventually received came from the other side of the Atlantic. Sometimes I think that Fate allowed me to have my desert training as a child for a special purpose. It enabled me to see both sides of two powerful civilizations that might understand each other better if they did not speak the same language. We are nearer our Atlantic cousins than we shall ever be to Europe but words change profoundly in meaning when there is an ocean between them. "I want to go to America," I said, to everyone's astonishment because until then I had always talked about the East. "You'll soon get over that enthusiasm," they laughed but I shook my head. I knew better, miracles happened in America. *Girls had jobs.*

I have spent a lot of my life trying in small ways to bring Americans and English together. If anything that I have done has been worth while, it was due originally to an economic fact and to Imagist poetry. Perhaps, as in the Middle Ages, a proper secondary function for the poet is to be an ambassador. H. D. had written:

> Hermes, Hermes,
> the great sea foamed,
> gnashed its teeth about me;
> but you have waited,

> where sea-grass tangles with
> shore-grass.

I, too, waited for another five years.

I never asked to return to my drawing classes nor have I ever willingly had pictures in my room. I tried to detach myself from possessions, this was reasonably easy apart from books, and as whatever I
enjoyed was usually forbidden, I never showed more emotion than I
could help. I suspect, however, that my father had wanted to be a
painter when young. I still have some of his sketchbooks, they are
mostly full of Indian landscapes, and his greatest friend had been Val
Prinsep, one of the Pre-Raphaelite group. He would not collect old
masters, "Always buy a painting by a living man, Miggy, what use is
money to him when he is dead?" but his taste was naturally traditional,
he never made the leap to modern art. Prinsep had died when I was
ten and I had never met him but my father was the guardian of his
eldest son, Thoby, who often came to our house. Val Prinsep had
given my father one of his pictures. It dropped from the wall for no
apparent reason the night of my father's death.

It must have been through this early association that we knew Sir
Luke Fildes. We often used to have tea on the lawn of his house in
Melbury Road that was so quiet that we might have been in a country
village. For some reason or other, I had to sit to him for a portrait.
I resented this at first but Sir Luke's quiet kindness soon smoothed out
the prickles. He belonged to another age and though he lectured me
gently upon the need to give up everything for art, his own life seemed
as constricted as my own. The flatness and fidelity of nineteenth-century paintings embarrass our modern eyes. We should not impute a
lack of integrity to Victorian painters because we have learned to look
at light and color in another way. It is not enough to give a life's devotion to the Muses. They choose, they touch one person with a feather
and leave the rest and often, to our surprise, it is the one who seems to
deserve it least. Many factors besides vision and skill go to make a
masterpiece and perhaps the man who is a bridge between two generations has the best chance of survival. Sir Luke had fought a hard battle
to be allowed to paint at all in a period of ugliness and horror. I have
never met anyone who approached art with more humbleness.

"You keep as still as a model," he would sometimes say approvingly as he cleaned my portrait face with a sliced raw potato. The birds sang outside in the garden and although he was usually silent, he lifted the veil one day from a corner of the Victorian world that was so deeply cruel underneath its placid surface. "I knew a boy," he said, wiping his brush on a piece of rag, "he wanted to write instead of going into the family firm and made things worse by marrying a girl from a different group than his own." It sounded like the *Little Meg's Children* that I had read in the nursery but I listened. "His people used their influence to stop him from getting work and his wife and the baby died from what they called pneumonia but it was really starvation." I nodded, I had always suspected that there were more happy endings in books than in life. "They crushed him into submission," he began to paint again with slow, careful strokes, "help everyone you can but it isn't always possible." By pure chance I was able to check the story shortly afterwards and every word of it was true. It is foolish to imagine that there was more security then than there is today. Horace Gregory, who has so profound a knowledge of the Victorians, told me years afterwards that its underworld was perhaps the most vicious of any in English history.

Sir Luke seemed like a grandfather and I was a restless modern who welcomed the machine age that he found destructive. Yet he set me an example of patience and when I think of him now, standing beside his easel under the high windows, I am ashamed that I often responded so roughly to his advice.

At least I got plenty of exercise. I went out with my mother in the morning, with a French lady for conversation in the afternoon, I wish she had done more to correct my accent while we wandered up and down the Serpentine among the waddling, peppermint-colored ducks, and after my father got back from the office in the evening we went for a stroll before dinner. Godliness was certainly inherent in the miles that I covered during the day. I was used to being in the open air but I longed to have time for my own work and friends with whom I could talk, all night if need be, about voyages and books. I am most grateful to my father for one thing. My cousin Jack, who was about my age and stayed with us frequently, taught me to type and then my father gave me a machine. It became at once an extension of myself. (It is recorded of me that I once snatched it from the hands of a page boy at a hotel, saying, "You can't carry that, it's my soul.") I suppose it was because it gave me the illusion of print but I soon became incapable of writing anything by hand. Even now, if I have to take notes in a library, I usually trust to memory, I cannot read anything that I have scribbled.

I do not mind the changes in modern London so much as the different colors. Neon lighting has standardized the sky. It is the red of metals whether we are in Knightsbridge or Fifth Avenue. In 1913 the horizon was a deep blue and the sunset between the lamps at the end of a distant street had the effect of a country orchard. Even the solitary car moving slowly across a square was more like a phosphorescent fish in the dusk than a means of transportation. We thought that the city was terribly crowded, people asked each other how humanity could stand the pace, they still grumbled that taxis had replaced the hansom cabs while I wondered how I could endure the dragging days that, if I had been allowed, I could have filled with life.

I was always repeating poetry to myself during these walks and there are certain lines that, if I see them now, bring back those Edwardian days as if they were happening round me. Hodgson's "Bull" is one of them and three lines of Vildrac that I had found through Flint,

> Las! tu n'as qu'un livre,
> Tu n'as qu'une vie
> A vivre . . .

and of course my Elizabethans.

It was easy to talk about people wasting opportunities because they rushed about, as my aunt said, "like maniacs," but suppose you were never given an opportunity to waste? I was scolded again for being inattentive and sent off to dress for dinner, I really regretted the Queenwood uniform, "What a pity the dear child takes no interest in her clothes," feeling that another day had dropped completely out of life.

In April, 1913, we went back to the South. This time, on account of my brother, we joined a cruise to Italy and Greece. The places had not altered but I had changed. I recognized the scents and colors but I had lost the ability to become part of the landscape that I had had as a child. It was a curious and empty feeling. Besides, there was too much dressing up on the steamer, I missed Doris who could not come with us because she had been ill and I thought longingly of the Scillies. All the same there were some exciting moments.

We happened to arrive in Naples at the moment when they were about to launch a new Italian battleship. The steamers were in line across the bay so we took our places in one of the lifeboats for the occasion. It was impossible to see the water. The surface of the sea was crowded with Neapolitans. Sometimes there were twenty people aboard a craft meant for four, boys paddled about on improvised rafts, one passenger declared he could see somebody floating round in a converted tub. It was ten in the morning and the sun was already hot. The spectators sucked oranges, munched salami, drank wine, sang songs and flung their greasy paper against their neighbors' oars. "This is how they welcomed Nelson," one of our party remarked, "you would never see an English crowd enjoying themselves so much."

"It's the sun, remember our fogs!"

"They'll stand up when the guns go off, capsize and sink," our officer grunted, doing good work with a boat hook. We had dressed ship that morning quicker than any other vessel in sight.

"You don't know Italians. They're so buoyant, they'll float."

A destroyer dashed up and down, trying to keep the lines. The boatmen yelled, backed and as soon as the wash had subsided, swarmed forward again. It was obviously every man for himself. A particularly dirty bit of sausage wrapping drifted against the side and one of our sailors pushed it away with a grimace of disgust. I looked across at Vesuvius, it was peaceful and quiet. Capri lay behind us, the rest of the bay was full of every type of craft. "It will be midday before they start and we shall all get sunstroke," another of our passengers grumbled.

It happened when we least expected it. Guns boomed, flags waved, we could just see the battleship sliding into the water. The Neapolitans not only stood up, they jumped. They broke all the rules of being in a boat. Yet oddly enough nothing seemed to capsize around us although we all got splashed and a raft just missed our stern. Then everybody made for the shore at once. We were about to wait with true British calm for the rush to subside but we were caught up in the push. We wriggled our way with infinite skill until we reached the haven of the steamer.

It was in the early days of travel and as we had been promised a visit to Paestum, it had been arranged that some of the local fishermen should take us ashore from the ship in their boats. I doubt if any of us will forget the experience. We were rowed for half an hour across a deep blue sea that was very different from the choppy English Channel, the mountains behind the temples seemed almost transparent in the heat, everything was calm when suddenly, and without a word of warning, we appeared to turn sideways on top of a wall of surf. Men prayed, some stopped rowing, others yelled, we expected the craft to fall back on top of us but somehow we were flung forward and were lifted out onto a circle of damp shingle, half a mile from the ruins.

There were no paths. It was still a time when people walked and none of us minded a scramble but we soon found that the sand was full of small, angry vipers that looked so much like scraps of dried weed that we narrowly escaped stepping on them. In ancient times when there were few remedies, they must have caused many deaths. I cannot imagine anyone enjoying the walk, it was unpleasant struggling through warm, slithery sand with hisses coming from adjacent boulders and knowing that we had to return that same way to the shore but it was an authentic approach to the temples that was very different from the motor road of today.

The myths of childhood had faded and nothing had prepared me for the impact of Greece when we landed at Corfu. Strangely enough, I felt that the island was alive, antiquity was there and I was not looking at it through a veil because it was also intensely modern. We went to Delphi, Athens, Delos and Crete where I watched Sir Arthur Evans excavating but did not dare to speak to him but this early visit was simply a preparation and my real Greek experiences belong to a later section of this record. In 1913, once we had left Greece, all that I could think about was Scilly and I was happy to get away from the formal atmosphere of the cruise and back in July to the islands.

 *Eleven*

1914. Life swept on towards war.

Was it the golden summer that some say? It was hard to understand the people who spoke of it later as a time of unparalleled beauty because to me as to many other girls of my generation it was a moment like any other with no particular promise to single it out from the ever-narrowing world in which we lived. We helped our mothers in the morning, we went for walks in the afternoon; when possible, whatever wishes flowered in us they destroyed. It was the pattern that England expected of her daughters or even of her sons. We were thousands of mass-produced little Victorias and Alberts already sitting on our memorials, certain conventions common to every class in the land, that had replaced understanding and compassion. I have always felt that it was a lesser tragedy that thousands died in the trenches than that these youths had never had the chance of any human experience before they were killed. How far in fact was this repression of nature, not in Britain alone but all over Europe, the underlying reason of the war?

All July we waited. We moved as if paralyzed among our neighbors who were sure that everything would "blow over" and that it was all "hot air." Our friends teased my father when he refused to go abroad for our usual summer holiday but, as some repairs were needed to the Eastbourne house, we rented a place at Totland Bay for August. "I cannot understand why the Germans want to fight," my father said while we were watering the garden together, "they will have world trade securely in their hands in another few years without firing a shot."

I hated the Isle of Wight. It was as conventional as Sussex without the consolation of my cupboard full of books. The grass was pale as if there was never any sun and the water bitterly cold. We tried a canoe but there was a strong current flowing through the bay and we were almost swept out to sea. Sometimes there was artillery practice at night. Then the windows rattled and there were sinister flashes across a cloudy, threatening sky as we began our apprenticeship to the dominant mood of this century, waiting for a catastrophe that we imperfectly understood, to crush or spare us, apparently by chance.

An odd word, "neutrality," appeared in conversation, like a ball in a new game. I knew that the universe about me was slipping away but what could I, or even my father, do? Yesterday, how was it possible to remember yesterday when my own hope of freedom was ending with these last days of peace? "You must realize, Miggy," my father said as we went on tying up the tomato plants, "nothing will ever be the same." Oh, how much easier it was in 1939!

The news grew worse. People poured back to the ports or crossed the Channel by the next to the last boat. Dr. Boyce got home but had had to leave his luggage on the way. I discovered to my shame that though the round turrets had always been a familiar feature of the landscape, I did not know the origin of the Martello towers. After I had looked it up, I wondered if there had to be a great war every century and, if so, would the pattern ever change?

We were still firmly rooted in a former age. Nobody had a radio and if we wanted to go for a picnic we rented a pony trap and drove to a different beach. It was sinful to be late for meals, people still wondered if the water supply was safe. One afternoon we started out for a drive, the roads were empty, the hedges white with dust. A motorcycle roared past us suddenly and stopped at a cottage at the end of a lane. These machines were rare at that time and very, very noisy. The pony pricked up its ears and had to be soothed. The cyclist was holding out a paper to a woman when I looked up. She began to cry. "Oh," my brother's governess said, "they are calling up the Reserve." The flowers were half withered in the garden, the rider swung onto his cycle again and was off, the woman stood still in the doorway of the house. Somehow it is this scene that I always see in memory when I hear the word "Mons."

That night I joined my first queue. It formed outside the stationer's shop when the evening papers arrived.

The sky was red, the weather thundery, there was nothing to do but watch each minute crawl slowly after another on the clock. Still a further new word, the "ultimatum," spread softly among the groups waiting together in the dusk.

I stood for a while among the crowd on the evening of August 4th, feeling that as long as I did not see the words "War is declared" there was still a fragment of hope. There were no lights, the rumor spread that we should hear nothing before the morning and so we gradually dispersed. I was quite unable to imagine a modern battle in spite of my history; faced with catastrophe all any of us could do was to murmur, "But it isn't possible."

"It's war." Somebody rapped on the door early the next morning, "Get up, we're having breakfast at once." I had a momentary feeling of relief that the strain of waiting was over although I knew that at every instant something of the familiar world was shattering into dust. The front door knob was smeared with blood when I went downstairs. It was an appropriate symbol. The government had summoned my father to London and the telegraph boy had fallen off his bicycle in the darkness and cut his hand.

People on holiday with no urgent business were ordered to remain where they were and not to crowd the trains. I remember no cheering in the Isle of Wight, only many tears. The place was full of sailors who belonged to the Reserve. The first hours were so utterly strange that I think we all hoped that Time could swallow itself for once, obliterate a day and let us return to peace. It was only after the first cruiser was sunk in the North Sea that there was a general realization there could be no turning back. A handwritten notice about the loss was posted up among tins of biscuits and packets of tea in the little general shop. Then the mood changed instantaneously; rumors began to circulate, German spies had been landed in a cove, all civilians were to be evacuated, silver coinage disappeared. We began to struggle with the blackout. In an age that has seen the triumph of electricity, it is odd to realize that we have had to live in artificial darkness for eleven of the century's first fifty years.

An English cargo boat came peacefully up the narrow channel between the cliffs and the mainland. It had left port several weeks previously and carried no radio. Why should it stop because a shot was fired across its bow? It was just the navy playing about on maneuvers, the captain was saying, no doubt, but in more picturesque language, to the mate. We stood on the cliffs, knowing that the area was mined, while the firing continued. At last as the vessel hove to, we seemed to feel its surprise. It was a perfect symbol for the advancing month.

London was a city of the dead. The news got worse and my father was not confident of victory. He wanted to send us to America but we all refused indignantly to leave him. "This is the result of our education," I grumbled, "what is the use of knowing every skirmish in the War of the Roses by heart and nothing about what is happening in Europe?" I knew that I was caught in a trap (if only I had not seen it coming) and that I was only a cipher in what future historians would call the general population, sharing a chronicle instead of writing about it but without the solace of believing England to be invincible.

A wartime pattern of life began to evolve. The shops were empty, the parks were full of soldiers learning their drill. The air was suspended in excitement, in the vibrating stillness of after an explosion. Ugly rumors began to spread about faulty ammunition and waterlogged trenches. People still greeted each other with "It will all be over by Christmas" and when my father said no, it would last several years, they remembered his German grandfather and refused to speak to us. I comforted myself with Freeman's history of ancient Sicily. It was just as modern as the newspapers. Artillery or Iberian slingers, the effect was the same whether Paris or Syracuse were in danger. It became so saturated with the spirit of that unhappy, bewildering time that I was never able to read the book again.

Business as usual. No, my masters, how quickly we misread the language of the past. Those words did not have the sinister meaning that is now ascribed to them. It was not a summons to profiteer.

We were in the first major war since Waterloo and it was an order to us not to panic but to get on with our jobs. Let the present misunderstanding be a warning to historians how much the moral meaning of a phrase can be distorted in a generation. I believe that the English took the First World War far more deeply and seriously than they did the Second. They learned in sorrow, the casualty lists were nearly three times greater than they were in the nineteen forties, the beliefs for which they had sacrificed so much and that they had been taught would sustain them in adversity were shattered in a night. They were then blamed for having had faith in them. There was more fluidity in 1939. People knew what to expect and took it as a necessary evil, like going to school. The real British revolution took place on August 4, 1914, and none of the survivors have got over it.

The winter was grim and hard. It is never pleasant belonging to an unpopular minority and we were disliked the more heartily when Christmas passed and my father's prophecy that it would not be a short war proved correct. At Easter, 1915, I had a brief respite. I was allowed to go alone with Dorothy Pilley to a cottage belonging to one of her relatives at Beddgelert in North Wales.

These holidays were another proof of the inconsistency of the laws that bound our daily lives. We were not allowed to go to a tea-shop in London even as a group but Dorothy and I enjoyed two glorious weeks of complete freedom in the mountains simply because we had been sent there to walk. Both of us loved rambling and this was no hardship. I tramped a great deal when I was young, mostly with a heavy rucksack. I think my record was fifty miles in three days.

How little we know about our native land! To our surprise we found ourselves among foreigners. The children learnt English at school but their parents spoke Welsh and we had to learn a few words ourselves so as to ask the way should we get lost. The minister called on us the day after our arrival and told us that he would excuse us from attending the services as those were in Welsh but that we must pull down our blinds, read our Bibles and not go out until after four o'clock on Sundays. Yet in spite of much apparent godliness, many of the neighbors would not speak to one another and the village was seething with scandals and feuds.

We wandered about the hills from dawn to dusk. The land felt old, a mist rose sometimes without warning and we wondered if we should be able to find our way back to the valley. Other mornings the sunlight brought out the smell of grass, fresh and cool in the growing time of the year. A pale blue clump of harebells marked the way along a narrow river where the water tumbled over ancient, moss-covered stones. Every generation has a special symbol that it cherishes and ours was Nature; we did not have to be "seen and not heard" on those long tramps, we could talk to each other, we were free.

Dorothy wanted to climb as much as I wanted to write. I thought that mountaineering was reserved for the Alps because at that time only a few enthusiasts climbed in England and it was little discussed outside their own circle. We happened to walk fifteen miles across open country one day and met three men from the Beddgelert hotel over tea as we were waiting for the bus to take us back to the village. They invited us to try a mountain with them on the following morning.

So we climbed Tryfan, and incredible as this must sound today, we climbed it in skirts. It is true that they were short. One man unrolled the rope, the leader explained the belay and we were off, clinging to the rock face with fingers and toes. I am afraid that I was hauled on several occasions but Dorothy went up as if she had been used to precipices all her life.

I imagine that we climbed one of the easier ways. It was exciting to sit on the summit and look across at other peaks instead of up at them. The descent was worse, particularly one pitch where we had to swing out in space without being able to see the next foothold, but we got to the valley eventually and had a short rest. It was about four in the afternoon but our leader suggested that instead of taking the path to the valley we should go up and over a place called the Bristly Ridge and back that way to Beddgelert. The name was enough for me. One of the party was elderly and he and I went ignominiously down by the easy track while the others roped up and started again for the heights. They did not return until eleven o'clock that night. Dorothy had found her destiny and was in a state of ecstatic happiness. I was praying that our parents would not hear about our escapade.

It is said that the English are a nation of amateurs but to share in some sport or art, no matter in how humble a manner, makes life richer and keeps us young. It is only after we have tried to climb, ourselves, that we can really understand it. I have never been a mountaineer because I do not have the requisite balance or a head for heights but the gain from my few attempts has been pure gold. My shelves have always been full of climbing books, I have walked for days with a rucksack among the rough hill paths of the Alps and at least I know enough to appreciate the difference between rocks that crackle in the sun like a dragon's mouth and the cold crevices just empty of ice. I have seen saxifrage growing out of a rift that was a deeper, purer color than its cousin in the valley and have felt the contrast between the nearness of the prickly surface to which I was clinging and the wideness of the surrounding space. Dorothy Pilley (now Mrs. I. A. Richards) got the feeling best of a sudden unity with a far from inanimate earth in her book, *Climbing Days*. Her ascents in the Alps and the Far East are well known to her fellow mountaineers. I was there the day that it all began and have always been grateful; she widened my world.

All wartime blurs together in retrospect but I would far rather go through the second war again than the first. There was a gulf between soldiers and civilians in 1914; in the blitz we were as one. After the initial, shattering start (not at Dunkirk but at Mons) there were four years of shortages, food queues, alarms and appalling losses, while we waited in stunned silence, never knowing what to say or do. Petrol pumps were left running at the camps, men played football with joints of meat but we, as civilians, dared not criticize the waste. I lost all confidence in governments then and afterwards. Less bureaucracy and more common sense might have saved so many lives.

As far as I and the girls I knew were concerned our already stern discipline was immediately tightened. It was wrong to be happy in such times and whatever tiny rebellions broke out were crushed before they were born. No deliverance was possible as long as England was at war. Little attempt was made to recruit female labor until 1917 although it was fashionable to volunteer for nursing and maids went into factories instead of domestic service. I answered the telephone and did odd jobs, my chief task seemed to be carrying heavy baskets of potatoes up a rather steep hill. It seemed to me that I was neither dead nor alive but struggling like Atlas to hold up some grain of individual identity against a monstrous cloud. It was useless saying that I could not endure; in the classic phrase of the Second

World War, "What else was there to do?" If I could grow again, I scribbled in another notebook, if I could only grow. . . .

It was one of the few times in my life when my landscape shifted from the country to the town. The noise of the passing traffic made the streets seem less lonely than the silent fields. I could not resist the illusion that someday in London I might meet a fellow writer although no stranger crossed the threshold of our house. In 1916 I read a review of Dorothy Richardson's *Backwater*. It was said to be critical of education so I immediately bought a copy. I defied all rules and read on until I had finished it. For the first time as I said excitedly to my schoolfellows, "Somebody is writing about us."

I have always told my friends abroad that if they want to know what England was like between 1890 and 1914, they must read *Pilgrimage,* and Dorothy Richardson has often been more appreciated on the Continent than in her native land. People do not want to know what really happened in that epoch that they persist in calling "the golden years." Miriam's England was the England that I saw. I never identified myself with her because she was twenty years older than I was and I was full of the revolutionary spirit of my own generation. We had faced the same reproaches, however, and shared the same fury that social conventions were considered more important than intelligence. Perhaps great art is always the flower of some deeply felt rebellion. Then there was the excitement of her style, it was the first time that I realized that modern prose could be as exciting as poetry and as for continuous association, it was stereoscopic, a precursor of the cinema, moving from the window to a face, from a thought back to the room, all in one moment just as it happened in life. Dorothy Pilley was as enthusiastic as I was; we had our favorite scenes, mine was the discussion as to how far the school's reputation might have been harmed because a child had taken off her hat while she played and both of us knew the sudden exhilaration in spite of the pressure upon us, as we rode down a London street, like Miriam, on top of a bus. Most of all I felt that a weight had been lifted for a moment so that underneath the daily frustrations I could feel my roots prickle and know that they were still alive.

I did not meet Dorothy Richardson until 1923 but she was the Baedeker of all our early experiences and I have read and reread *Pilgrimage* throughout my life.

It is difficult to pick out dates in the conglomerate of years.

My school friends were scattered, Ethel was nursing in Salonika, Petrie was at Oxford, Dorothy at work and Doris was also helping her father in his office. She was allowed occasionally to come up from Penzance and stay with us. One evening after a particularly dreary day of small but necessary tasks, we were sitting after dinner beside the blue and silver curtains in the drawing room that, in their turn, concealed the blackout when the door opened slowly and the butler entered. He bowed and announced with an old-fashioned formality, "My lady, the Zeppelins."

My mother was on her feet in an instant, "Get your coats, girls, come at once."

"Is it wise to go out?" my father inquired, lowering the newspaper that he was reading.

We did not stop to reply, we ran. By the time that we got into the street dozens of people were staring at the sky as if they expected an eclipse. Officers on leave stood beside girls in evening dresses, a scullery maid with her hair already in curlers had tried to tuck these unsuccessfully beneath a faded, woolen cap, a cook had come from washing up with flecks of soap still on her arms and the nurse from next door ran out, buttoning up her coat. We had no idea whether we were being attacked by one Zeppelin or seven, it was our very first raid and we did not think about damage. As usual in a time of crisis class distinctions were forgotten, we gaped and chattered, thought we had seen "something," were answered with jokes. The only person unconcerned was the postman; we had an evening delivery right through the first war and he continued his round with perfect dignity as if he were in an empty road.

Doris and I slipped out the next day and took a bus to the City to look at our first bombed house. It may seem callous in the light of later experience but when masses of the population had not even seen an aeroplane and the wildest rumors were circulating, we felt that accurate information was important and it seemed the proper thing to do. We could not find the place at first but few people could resist Doris when she smiled at them and a friendly policeman directed us to the street with a "mind you stop when you get to the rope." The back of the house was untouched, the front was rubble, a familiar enough sight in the forties but then it seemed vast, unnatural and completely new. I could not relate it to anything that had ever happened and as we boarded an ancient bus to return home with our tale I said, "Remember, Doris, we are a footnote to history," in the most pompous voice.

It was only a beginning. The raids continued and we began to take them seriously. "I shall not live to see the country recover," my father said, "you may." The external rules held, we dressed for dinner but we had strips of flannel stitched inside our clothes. The only fire was in the dining room, there was no other heating and I was never warm in winter except in bed.

"Wake up!" A hand shook my blankets. "Wake up!"

I did not want to emerge into another monotonous day. I wanted to be conscious instead that I was warm and asleep.

"Hurry!" I heard a tremendous explosion but as I opened my unwilling eyes I realized that it was only a maroon. Our maid, Emma, was standing over me, a Bible under her arm and a dustpan in the guise of a steel helmet upon her head. My blankets had never felt so luxurious but somebody else would only come to fetch me if I lingered. My dressing gown and a coat, the usual routine, were spread over a chair.

I grabbed a book of American poetry, if I were going to be killed it should be while I was reading about the New World. "Hurry!" There were shouts from the staircase and we shuffled down to the dining room as we had been advised to shelter at the bottom of the house. How innocent we were! There was a glass chandelier in the middle of the room. I do not think we imagined what it would be like if the house were hit (it was in 1940, and partially destroyed but by then it was empty), we went downstairs purely to please the government, quiet in demeanor as per headline advice and, as I added, with yawns.

I went along the corridor to my father's office. The lights were out so I drew back the curtains and stared at the sky. It was as blue as a deep wave and the rooftops looked like towers. People were always blaming me for talking about the past but here we were in the middle of things and a bomb splinter could kill one in exactly the same way as an Agincourt arrow.

Something zigzagged across the window and I leapt backwards like a modern kangaroo. The park guns started, I felt the foundations of the house rock under me, I wondered if we should even hear a bomb in all the noise. It was a little lonely and I returned to the dining room to report.

"Have they hit anything?"

"If they have, we shall not hear for months!"

"We'll know. The rumors will be everywhere."

"It's a thunderstorm, darling," my mother said reassuringly to my brother who had been rolled up in a blanket, he was about seven, and put into the big armchair.

"It's not, it's a raid."

Ah, I thought, you cannot trick a child as I wrapped myself up in a rug. The noise moved away. The firing continued in the distance but there was a strange, unearthly silence along our street. "Go and tell Emma it is over," my mother suggested, "she always gets so frightened."

I crawled along to the kitchen in the dark as I was not sure if they had remembered to draw the blinds and found Emma, still in her dustpan helmet, moaning to herself. "It's all right, they've gone," I shouted but she did not hear me until I shook her by the shoulder and she lifted the pan an inch.

"Gone, miss, don't you know what they are going to do?"

"Come along," I knew if I gave her the slightest encouragement that we should never get back to bed.

"But, miss, you don't understand! My brother-in-law wrote us from France. The first lot come with bombs. The second are going to sprinkle a powder, or maybe it's a gas, over all of us. Whoever breathes a particle of it and you can't see it, mind you, or smell it, will die of diphtheria, after 'orrible sufferings." (Normally Emma was most precise in her speech but there were occasional lapses.) "I wished I had stayed in America when I went to see my brother there but I couldn't get a decent cup of tea."

"It's cold, come along, we may as well die in our beds," I suggested cheerfully.

"You go, miss," Emma tilted the pan back on her carefully rolled bun of hair and opened her Bible, "I couldn't sleep a wink if I did get upstairs but mind" (she was more authoritarian with me than my mother) "don't you go turning on your light till you're sure the curtains are drawn."

"All clear!" The boy scouts were riding round on their cycles. "All

171

clear!" A dog barked, it sounded so old-fashioned after the guns. I peeped round a blind on my way upstairs to see the gray of a civilian dawn breaking over the houses. Somewhere people were digging through wreckage and marking the places where bombs had fallen on a map. How stupid it was! We were not in the Dark Ages, this was the twentieth century. I gripped the banisters but even the hardness of the wood did not convince me of reality or that I was actually myself. I had forgotten my doubts by the next morning only to have them return as if a switch had been reconnected as I stood under the same conditions on a similar staircase on my first experience in 1940 of the blitz.

Twelve

I knew the Scillies in war as well as peace. Fishing was forbidden, notices were posted up advising us to take shelter in suitable caves in case of an invasion (how we longed for the alarm to go off) and the commander of a German submarine was said to have told some torpedoed sailors that he had been round and under the little *Lyonnesse* a score of times. We landed in July, 1917, to find St. Mary's in a turmoil of excitement. The *Kathlamba,* a cargo boat bound from Australia to England, had been hit just outside the islands but had managed to gain the safety of the Sound and had been beached off Tresco. Doris and I looked at each other, we were careful to be silent about our plans but as soon as lunch was over we rushed to the shore, launched the punt and started to row towards the vessel. Every craft that could float was already in front of us. "She's carrying white flour," one fisherman yelled, "And peach jam," another shouted in reply. Neither of these items had been in the shops for months, besides your true Scillonian is always a wrecker at heart.

It was a fantastic sight. The torpedo had made a hole in the side as big as a large room. The tide was washing in and out, bringing litter from the hold. About thirty islanders with hooks and shrimping nets grabbed these sacks as they floated away or gave an occasional, helpful push to those stuck near the opening. A strong, unpleasant smell of flour rotting in salt water, it was rather worse than sulphur, almost made us sneeze. "What is the use of saving the stuff?" Doris asked a fisherman who had recognized her. "Oh, the outside cakes into a sort of cement but if you scrape it off, the inside is perfectly edible and sweet."

We edged our way cautiously along the steamer and looked up hopefully. An officer saw us and invited us aboard. I followed Doris up the companionway with intense admiration because I should not have had the temerity to suggest the visit myself. It was our first experience of the effects of blast. The paint had been stripped from the woodwork and many doors smashed through the force of the explosion. Fortunately nobody had been much hurt. All the sailors had their stories, one man was sure that he had seen the torpedo, "It was like a porpoise, only flat," others had been flung to the deck in complete surprise. Now and again the officer interrupted his tale to go and roar at the Scillonians. "If those pirates go on hooking away the stuff like that, there'll be nothing left to salvage if we do get into port."

"They're not pirates," we said together in an indignant voice. The islanders were simply exercising their age-old wrecking rights but of course the officer was a foreigner, an Englishman, and he did not know. It would not be correct to lure vessels onto the rocks but with the side stove in and casks floating about, we were fully entitled to whatever gifts the sea brought to our nets. He laughed at our explanations but sent two men forward to prevent the hole from being enlarged.

We rowed cheerfully home and, instead of being scolded as we had expected, we were actually thanked for having brought back some accurate news. Alas, the sequel was not so pleasant. Mr. Banfield was Lloyd's Agent for the islands so while the populace feasted openly upon white bread and peach jam, we stuck sternly to a wartime diet. Rulers seldom get the best of the game. Still at the end of the holidays after they had patched the *Kathlamba* up sufficiently to continue her journey to "foreign parts" or otherwise England, we were all invited to tea on board and Mrs. Banfield was presented with a large and welcome cake.

Few ships were as fortunate. We were often wakened in the middle of the night by sailors shouting in a foreign tongue under our windows. Next morning an unfamiliar lifeboat would be tied to the quay with a group of men in ill-assorted clothing standing near it, waiting for the *Lyonnesse* to take them to the mainland. The little hospital was full of wounded and occasionally a fisherman came into the harbor, towing a spar, all that we should ever know about another loss. The war was often nearer to us there than it was in London.

Those were our barefoot summers. There were six of them, three before and three during the war. Sometimes as I walk round St. Mary's today, I think of that time as some earlier incarnation. We have moved so fast that even a trained historian finds it hard to recollect the peacefulness and unbroken tradition of those turn-of-the-century years. The islanders, cut off from the mainland, spoke the pure English of an isolated folk. There was a sharp division between men who spoke of the harbors of Australia and Africa as if they were merely an extension of our single road and people who had never visited Penzance. There were even "off-islanders" who had never crossed to St. Mary's. We also knew of a handful of women who took to their beds in their fifties and, in obedience to some strange custom whose origin we could not find, never left their houses again until they died. What a rich field it would have offered to the sociologist! It must have gone back to an incredibly early England but naturally nothing of this crossed my mind at the time; all I thought about was how many pints of shrimps each of us would catch and what we should have for dinner.

The "goodness" of the country can be much exaggerated; most of the humane and progressive movements have originated in cities. Only too often, villagers are harsh and intolerant in their views but all the same we have half a million years of dependence upon nature in our blood and only a thin crust of what we please to call civilization over it. To be cut off from the breakers and the rain or the dawn rising on a windy morning is an impoverishment for most of us and if I had not been able to go back to the wilderness for an all too brief month each year, I am sure that I should have died. Even now, although I have traveled from the Khyber to the Arctic, it is Scilly of all places and countries that holds my heart.

We could not leave St. Mary's in wartime except by the *Endeavour,* the launch that took the mails round to the other islands. Its engineer was the first socialist I knew, his round head would pop up through the hatch like an inquiring walrus while he asked us questions as if he were delivering a speech. Today he would be considered a reactionary Tory. We shrimped, using the heavy, wide nets of the professionals, picked blackberries if they ripened in time and bathed on Pellistry beach. I am afraid that I spent a lot of time sitting on the rocks, trying to invent new words. I thought that "ronded" might be a stronger word than "rounded," I dug up "huttering" for "leaves" because they were sometimes like straw rustling in a hutch. We are more perceptive of color today than our ancestors were but we are poor in words to describe either it or movement. (You simply cannot refer to the sky as being shade number 196 in a Color Chart even if such classification does make trade and gardening easier.) There was a pattern in the waves that broke over the sand in the flutes but not the hue of a shell, the ocean swept above the land of Lyonnesse in a tone that was neither gray nor green but a combination of both yet I wanted direct words and not comparisons. (I still do.) Remembering my early love, I noted that the clouds moved like giant pterodactyls and, thinking of the present, scribbled with gritty hands that emotions were the palette of a writer. I even wrote some verses while the others hunted for cowries.

> Oh, why do the great winds
> come whispering to me,
> my heart's aboard a drifter
> that sails the swinging sea.

"What's that?" Doris looked gaily over my shoulder. "*You* on a drifter! You know you'd be so seasick that you'd fall overboard. Besides, you idiot, they don't sail, they steam. Try to make sense." It was only too true. I was always the first one to rush for the side, I had already run the punt ashore and was extremely clumsy over knots.

We were out all day from early Monday until Saturday night. Sunday was different; we wore our best clothes and were recalled to civilization. In the morning we went to church. This was more bearable for me in Scilly than elsewhere because the psalms were read and not sung, I always preferred the sound of words to music. The vicar, very properly as we thought, sometimes left us in the middle of the service to attend to a new litter of puppies. After lunch we had to read until four o'clock; then we were loosed in a wild scramble of energy among the rocks at Peninnis until sunset.

My holiday reading was Henri de Régnier, Walter Pater and Browning. The few contemporary English historical novelists slid too easily into mere sentiment. I did not like the eighteenth century but at least de Régnier took the period seriously and created some atmosphere. I have always remembered the twins bending over their fishing nets in the marshes in *Le Bon plaisir* in spite of the love stories being rather tiresome. His novels seem now curiously old-fashioned but he was more experimental in some of his poetry. The long flowing lines of his invocation to the sea were running through my head when we sat beneath the carn at Porthellick and heard the door bang open and shut in a wreck as the tides came through it, surely the most desolate sound in the world.

Browning I knew well, he was describing the sights and sounds of my childhood and I remember getting a full mouthful of salt water trying to repeat "Cleon," my favorite among his poems, and have a swimming lesson from Doris at the same time. The colors of a summer day in Scilly are the colors of the South and the words seemed so natural, I could imagine sailors bringing the gifts ashore in so many small havens along the Sound.

I regarded Pater as superior Henty. There was not much difference between *A March on London* and *Gaston de Latour.* I knew nothing about his life at the time but we recognize instinctively those people who are in a similar situation to our own and the first three chapters of *Marius,* but only the first three because I had few scruples and was fighting hard, might have been taken as a blueprint of my then mind. Certain writers can only be read subsequently within the compass of their period and I cannot repeat too often that any deviation from Victorian manners was repressed so strongly that we were driven back onto the points of our own intellects instead of being able to go forward. We reacted against the sadistic denials of the age by a heightened consciousness of nature and of art, places where our enemies could not reach us. I could not share Gaston's love of medieval architecture, cathedrals to me were usually gloomy places, but I wanted to meet others of my own age who could write and I read of his ride to meet Ronsard with approval. His "poetry need no longer mask itself in the habit of a bygone day" was precisely what I had been saying to myself, thumping the heather, to an audience of sea gulls. I liked the way that history was allowed to touch the stories without obscuring the individual and his needs. As for the style, I had just emerged from *Euphues* and it seemed plain and sober by comparison. After all, we should be allowed a year's love of adjectives even if we forswear them immediately afterwards.

It was only the name that I read in Pater. I had always been Epicurean. To seek for happiness is the bravest of the philosophies and one, though not all, of the Mysteries. It happens infrequently, once or twice for an instant during the most favored life, and is, if experienced, painful as well as winged but it is the dynamic twin of detachment and looks from the past towards a future that it may yet take us centuries to imagine. We cannot alter tragedy but we could sweep away an immense amount of frustrating and preventible unhappiness. Are the laws just that we impose upon our fellow men or do they come out of vanity or even laziness? It is the question that the wise have been asking ever since their sayings have been preserved.

I was also drawn to Epicurus by his insistence upon friendship. After I left Queenwood I prayed that my destiny might be service to artists and poets. I saw myself as a Gozzoli page, a cupbearer at the feast of minds, following the flight of speculation and dream as eagerly as children chase their colored balls. Alas, for my innocence! Fate granted me my wish in part and turned me into a mixture of nurse and business adviser, without pay, official recognition or an afternoon off to myself. I have sat for hours with people for whom life would be hard in any age, trying to persuade them to try psychoanalysis instead of suicide, I have put alcoholics to bed or struggled with income tax returns for people who seemed even worse at mathematics than myself. I have rushed to the penniless young not with bowls of soup but with typewriters. I have cursed it all, enjoyed it sometimes and my experiences have helped me to believe more deeply in the doctrine that I have chosen but it has not been in the least like the fabulous state that I imagined, aged seventeen. It is impossible to be too careful when bargaining with the gods.

I wish only that people would think for themselves instead of repeating slogans. I was brought up as an only child in extreme isolation yet I have led a practical and extroverted life. My brother who had playmates from his infancy and a conventional training turned into a recluse whom I have not seen for thirty years.

Yet the moments that I remember most of those early Scillonian days were the hours, usually on a Sunday evening, when we sat on the rocks and watched the foam tower, break and fall in swirling, white crescents far below us. Occasionally we saw a distant steamer, even a convoy, but there was nothing otherwise between us and the distant American continent except league after league of sea. The Elizabethan ships and the first colonists had often sighted our islands at the beginning of their voyages and there were still close links between Cornwall and the West. I did not try to imagine a coast line, to me as to many other thousands the "New World" meant precisely what the words said, a place to discard stupid, everyday conventions, the opportunity for development. It was partly an illusion but not entirely so. I found New York when I eventually got there more formal than London but whatever success I may have had came from there rather than from my own country. As I said then to Doris, as I have to write now, "In England you say 'don't' to me always. In America you say 'try.' "

Letters were censored but not to the extent that they were during the second war. A Boston friend of my mother asked if there were anything that she could send me for Christmas and I replied, "America is the hope of the world, please send me the following books." I wanted the Imagist anthologies and some volumes by authors included in them. In this way I read Amy Lowell's poems. I have already written that we respond emotionally in situations resembling our own. I did not know that Amy Lowell was largely confined to her home through illness and that her work reflected the frustrations from which she suffered. I was unable to expand because of the war. It was natural to feel the similarity in the two situations. I wrote her, she answered and was extremely kind to me but by the time that we met the circumstances were different and I could not bear to think of lines that recalled to me the lonely miseries of the first war. This is one of the dangers of contemporary work. The classics are removed in time but the modern book to which we respond at a certain stage in youth may disappear with that phase of our development. I was a disappointment to her eventually but it was inevitable under the circumstances.

"If you must write," my father used to say, "try to be a journalist. They do useful work." He knew a number of newspapermen and, among them, Clement Shorter, the editor of the *Sphere*. Shorter was very kind to me although there again the gap operated, I was a modern unable to read his favorite Victorian books. He did me a great service, however, because he persuaded my father to buy me a set of Dyce's edition of the Elizabethan dramatists. I immersed myself in them to such an extent that I seemed to hear, not voices but lines from the plays, spoken as an Elizabethan would have said them, tapping at the extreme range of sound in my ears. I rejected the tragedies. It was Middleton's comedies that I particularly liked. His London scenes were exactly like photographs. I did not always understand the jokes but I knew his flat-capped apprentices, the watermen and the old women with their herbs and steaming pies, as well as if I passed them every morning in Hyde Park. Destiny is strange, I forgot them for a time after 1918 only to find them looping themselves around me in 1940, as if I had been faithful to their company throughout the intervening years.

I agreed with Clausewitz. I do not think that we have ceased being at war since August, 1914. A population notices its losses more during the shooting phases but, I am speaking of the world and not of a particular nation, we are capable of as much cruelty in peace as in any battle and all trained observers are aware that we are now caught up in some global upheaval that has been going on for more than fifty years. It would be tempting to write of it as a struggle between the barbarians and civilization but this is only a fraction of the truth. One of the causes is overpopulation, there may be some natural balance that we do not yet understand and we are also in an epoch of change but unless we move and alter, we die. A wise historian once said to me, "Whenever you have to estimate a new situation, look at Asia first." It has proved excellent advice. These conclusions, however, belong to a later part of this story, I had not had enough experience to be aware of them in 1917 and I mention them here only as a warning that the fog that enveloped us cleared only partially at the Armistice. All that I felt at the time was that I was trapped in an ever deeper layer of hopelessness from which there was no possibility of escape. Old ladies asked me to join a "save your paper bags" campaign and to pray for the King. In desperation Dorothy Pilley and I tried to join up as land workers but our parents refused to sign the necessary papers. There was no guarantee about accommodation and though they were not worried about our comfort, they were about the "respectability" of the quarters to which we might be assigned. It was a harsh winter and we shivered in the cold. There may have been gaiety for a small section of the population when soldiers came on leave but most of us were frowned at if we dared to smile.

> They are cruel,
> these faces,
> as I pass under the plane trees,
> is it wrong to watch the tufted buds
> bend the black twigs
> even in war?

It may have been a very bad poem but it was an accurate statement of fact. We felt that the populace hated us merely for being alive and what youth was we did not know.

Complete frustration leads to a preoccupation with death. I could think of nothing else. There was plenty of vitality in me but this only made the situation worse. I found a bottle of rat poison in a cupboard and the only thing that prevented me from swallowing it was that I did not want to hurt my parents. For myself, death seemed infinitely preferable to the subexistence that we had to endure. The rat poison became my talisman. I could struggle on as long as I knew that it was mine for the taking. It was not the year that seemed so long, it was the hour, but then time for me had always passed with an almost unendurable slowness. Under such circumstances, I am always amazed now that I survived.

Sometimes the gods toss us a laurel berry to keep us still afloat. Clement Shorter introduced me to A. A. Baumann who was the editor of the then highly respected *Saturday Review*. Most of his staff was in the army so he sent me occasionally a book to notice. The first appropriately was in French and a study of the work of Verhaeren.

I only saw Mr. Baumann a couple of times and he had no time to waste on would-be aspirants to literature but he drilled me hard and I hope that I have remembered his lessons. "Check your facts" was a message frequently written against a rejected review. Yet he once let me write a "middle" on *Tendencies in Modern American Poetry*. It was incoherent with enthusiasm, a note stated stiffly that it represented my views and not those of the paper but I am still inordinately proud that I stated my belief in American literature in the days when few people had heard of it and during the middle of the war.

It was at about this time that I began to write *Development,* at the rate of about a phrase a day, written almost with blood. I had no leisure; everybody told me it was selfish in war to do creative work. Another parcel of books reached me from America. I unknotted the string and wore it round my neck, it had touched American soil. "Wait till the fighting is over and I will send you abroad again," my father said, trying to console me for the difficulties of the time, "I think you would like India." "India," I snorted, seeing not only another country of the past but also a chaperone, "I want to go alone to New York."

It may be a personal reaction although I doubt this but at the height of the blitz I never felt the same undercurrent of horror and fear that was around us in 1918. "Fifteen hundred men are being killed every minute," people said while we stood helplessly watching the ruin of most of Europe. "It takes more than men to stop machines," my father said, "once they are geared to war." I still believe that if the leaders of my generation had not perished, there would have been an orderly progression in England towards a greater freedom and a more universal prosperity than the country knows today.

The weariness was such that people gave up blaming me for being self-absorbed and silent. Yet I could hardly read or think; my one overmastering passion was to be free. There will always be one book among all others that makes us aware of ourselves; for me, it is *Sea Garden* by H. D. I learned it by heart from cover to cover. The rhythms were new, it evoked for me both the Scillies and the South, it touched Mallarmé's vision. I began the morning and ended the day repeating the poems. It was not until some months later that I discovered from Amy Lowell's *Tendencies in Modern American Poetry* that H. D. was a woman and American.

We did not spend that summer in Scilly because Mrs. Banfield was kept at home through illness in the family but as a special favor Doris and I were allowed to go by ourselves to Zennor for a week or two, to run wild on the cliffs. It was then a lonely village with few visitors. Just as I had left London, Mr. Shorter had got H. D.'s address from May Sinclair who was a mutual friend and I discovered to my amazement that she was staying in the neighborhood. I asked permission to call. It must have been a very Victorian note because she told me afterwards that when she was reading it she had supposed me to be an elderly schoolmistress. I was terrified that my knowledge of poetry might not prove sufficient to meet a writer's standards but I hung about waiting for the postman until, in due course, I was invited to tea.

It was July 17, 1918. I had had to abstract myself from my surroundings in order to survive at all. To wish to create was a sin against the consciousness of the time. Yet I wanted things to be real, I did not want to dream. The gorse was out, I was walking across some of the most ancient ground in Cornwall, I could hear the roar of the sea. I reached a cottage with the familiar, yellow covers of a dozen French books piled up against the window sill. I knew then that it must be the right place and knocked.

The door opened and I started in surprise. I had seen the face before, on a Greek statue or in some indefinable territory of the mind. We were meeting again after a long absence but not for the first time. "Won't you come in?" The voice had a birdlike quality that was nearer to song than speech. There was a bowl of wild flowers on the table, another pile of books on a chair. We sat down and looked at each other or, more correctly, I stared. I was waiting for a question to prove my integrity and the extent of my knowledge. All the moments of a long apprenticeship, no more to be counted than the ears of corn, flashed across my brain. "I wonder if you could tell me something," H. D. began, "have you ever seen a puffin and what is it like?"

"They call them sea parrots and there are dozens of them in the Scillies. I go there almost every summer, you must join me next year."

I did not stop to think about the difficulties inherent in the invitation but only that my test had come through the islands and not through books. "The fishing is better in August and we drive everywhere in donkey carts. Say that you will come with me," I pleaded. It was the moment that I had longed for during seven interminable years.

Thirteen

"It's peace," my father said at breakfast, "the Armistice will be announced at eleven o'clock. Go out and watch the people but be careful."

Doris was staying with us and we rushed together across the park where a few rusty leaves were still hanging on the bushes, and started walking along the Brompton Road. The streets were half empty. The years had been so long that it did not seem to me as yet to be real. We wondered if there had been some hitch, everything seemed so quiet. Then the clocks struck eleven, there was a yell, people flooded into the road and complete strangers flung their arms round each other's necks, women cried, boys shouted "Peace . . . peace . . ." and men jumped onto the running boards of any passing vehicle. We watched but to me at least it was strange and like a play, I could feel little emotion.

My father had work to do at one of the Ministries and had been allotted a small amount of petrol for that purpose. The rules were strict that nobody must accompany him. He had once been unable to take my mother on an urgent visit to the doctor, and I, myself, had not seen the inside of our car for two years. On Armistice Day, every regulation could be broken and as he had to deliver some official papers, he said that we might join him that afternoon. We got as far as the access to Trafalgar Square and there with great difficulty turned back. It was one of the most frightening spectacles that I have ever seen. Thousands of people in drab and worn-out clothes stamped, snarled and swayed in a single mass like some unholy beast, their arms locked round each other, ready to kill. Nobody would have had a chance of escape had they turned on him. A few were afraid and had probably been caught into the mass by accident but most of the faces were masks of rage. There is always violence in the air after a catastrophe and during the next forty-eight hours thousands fought, got drunk and yelled away some of their frustration and anger in what our rulers called a disgraceful manner. Yet through it, I believe, we remained a nation. In 1945 when I looked at the white-faced crowds being exhorted by the radio and officials to remain dignified and calm, I turned to a friend and said, "We have lost the peace." It is possible to build after people have expressed a normal anger; it is much more dangerous if it bursts through later in some indirect way that nobody has foreseen.

My father tried to bring us back to the realities of the situation. "The man who holds a similar position to myself in Germany has just committed suicide," he said later that day. "I want you always to remember, Miggy, the war has been a very close thing." I could not listen to him at such a moment, the gate was opening, perhaps to my freedom. Doris and I hurried instead to Piccadilly. It was about four in the afternoon and perhaps fortunately for ourselves we were swept back into a side street at once by the surging crowds. Wounded soldiers in blue convalescent uniforms had clambered over some buses, otherwise all traffic had stopped. The pavements were empty away from the main roads but we could hear a low continuous roar, there was nothing joyful about it, coming from the masses in the park.

We went back somewhat chastened to an extremely quiet evening and a lecture from my father on the economic problems of the peace. "People have lost the habit of thrift, we cannot blame them, but it will be very difficult building up the reserves." I was not a good listener that night, I simply felt bewildered and tired.

No peace is a return to prewar conditions. It simply brings the full realization of all that has been destroyed. A copy is not the same as the original and it is an illusion to suppose that we can repeat the past.

There was a general sense of disaster in 1919. The English casualties had been three times greater than they were in the second war and as people realized their losses, the influenza epidemic struck the world and gave numbers the death that they consciously or unconsciously desired.

In some ways it was an exciting winter for me. I had a friend at last who talked to me about poetry and did not laugh at my meager attempts at writing. (Not that I thought them meager at the time!) It was my first real contact with an artist, and H. D. was the most beautiful figure that I have ever seen in my life, with a face that came directly from a Greek statue and, almost to the end, the body of an athlete. I remember that when she was seventy, the elevator boy in a big New York hotel whispered to me, "What a beautiful lady!"—and until her final illness, there was little change in her expression or the carriage of her head. She read poetry magnificently. She gave me books to read, laughed at my solemn pronouncements, taught me most of what I know about the Greeks. "I'm a Levantine water rat," I used to tell her cheerfully, "hanging about the quaysides for the ships." She would laugh at me again and shake her head: "Further East, a little Assyrian perhaps, always bringing me flowers"—because I had discovered that she liked anemones with their scarlet petals and black hearts.

We could not meet often. She had returned from Cornwall to Buckinghamshire because she was expecting a baby in the spring. I went there to see her a few times and waited for letters. At the beginning of March she moved to London to be near the nursing home where she had booked a room. I did not hear for some days and then she wrote asking me to come and see her, "I have been ill but it is just a cold."

It was a long bus ride on a bitterly cold day through gray streets to Ealing, a part of London that I did not know. I found H. D. in bed and looking feverish, even to my inexperienced eyes. "Tell me about Greece," she said, "it's hard to speak with my cold."

I was so alarmed by her appearance that I could only stumble through an itinerary of places. I have just found you, suppose I lose you, was the thought running through my head. What had green lizards and sunlight to do with this freezing room? "If I could walk to Delphi," H. D. whispered with an intensity that I knew I was seeing for the first time, "I should be healed."

"I will take you to Greece as soon as you are well." I did not stop to think about the practical difficulties, the consent of my family, the lack of trains and steamers at that postwar moment; it was not even consolation, the words seemed to come from somewhere beyond my brain. Yet to the end of her life Hilda never forgot them. Then there was a knock at the door and she roused herself to say, "That is the doctor, would you mind waiting outside a few minutes?"

It seemed much longer and I cannot remember anything but a feeling of helplessness till I went back into the room. "What did he say?" I asked.

"It's rather a nuisance. He says there is a patch of congestion over one lung. But don't let's talk about it. Have you been writing lately?"

In those days before modern antibiotics, pneumonia was the great killer. I heard a step on the stairs and with hardly an excuse I dashed outside and caught the doctor. "It's the lung," he said, "she ought to have a nurse."

"Can you get her one?"

"With this epidemic?" He must have seen the consternation on my face because he added after a moment, "My other patient here is a little better, perhaps her nurse could help." He turned wearily back to inquire.

Two old ladies emerged from the basement and looked at me. "The woman in the next room had pneumonia, that's how she caught it."

"No doubt." Dr. Boyce had told me a lot about germs.

"It will be the end of her, poor thing, and expecting a baby too."

"She looked so ill when she arrived."

"She should have had a fire when the doctor ordered one."

"Why didn't she?" I asked suspiciously.

"The landlady has only got one maid."

"And she's afraid of infection. You know what they are like now. I carried a tray up to your friend myself."

The landlady appeared at that moment. She looked at me with one of the most malevolent expressions that I have ever seen in my life and said, "Do you know the woman? She is going to die. Can you pay the funeral expenses?"

I was so terrified that I could not speak for a moment; then because the battle seemed lost, my inhibitions broke. I swung into action and treated the woman with arrogance, the only thing that she understood.

I saw that the nurse could help until another one could be obtained, I telephoned to someone Hilda knew who promised to arrange for her to be transferred at once to the nursing home, and to send some proper food. I promised to return the next day.

I looked at my watch, I had been trained that I had always to be back by a certain time and it was getting late. The rule so dominated me that I caught the bus back home, it is an action of which I have been ashamed all my life.

Hilda was dangerously ill for several days. The doctor said that the baby could not be born alive but Perdita arrived on the last day of March with the

> daffodils,
> That come before the swallow dares, and take
> The winds of March with beauty

just in time to earn her Shakespearean name.

Thanks to Clement Shorter who was a friend of my parents, Constable published my first book, *Development,* in 1920. They first returned the book to me for a "happy ending," meaning a romantic one, which I indignantly refused to supply. I knew that my family would dislike the volume and I wanted, anyhow, to kick my way up the ladder alone. I therefore chose the name Bryher, partly from a favorite Scillonian island and also because it was a common Cornish surname. I had often seen it up over offices and shops. Some years later I took the name under Deed Poll, and under English law it is incorrect to speak of it as a pseudonym. My passport is issued to me under that name and no legal document is valid that I sign in any other way.

Educational reform was the topic of the moment, *Development* started a controversy in the *Daily Mail,* no other book of mine has been as successful and a second printing was needed within a few weeks. "Old girls" from Queenwood protested bitterly, Miss Chudleigh was furious, Shorter stood by me. My parents were shocked and upset. "How could you write such a dreadful book?" they asked.

"I am sorry if it worries you but it was my duty to protest."

"But you cannot go against everyone else."

"Why not?"

"Because it will set you apart from others to lead a lonely existence."

"It is better to be lonely than to have a stock-size mind."

"We thought if you went to Queenwood you would make friends with girls of your own age."

"I wanted to go to an art school."

"You were so young."

My instinct about writing had been correct. I knew that *Development* was not a book of which Mallarmé would have approved but I really objected to the human wastage of school. My family bowed to the inevitable. I had committed the unpardonable Victorian sin and made myself "conspicuous." (I enjoyed this very much.) I was allowed to join H. D. in a small apartment that she had rented in Kensington, not far from where the Pounds and Mrs. Shakespeare were living and where I tried, without success, to write my second book.

Hilda was extremely patient with me. Once I interrupted her work and she tore up the page that she had just begun. I collected the fragments humbly, pasted them together and never intruded again. When she was not writing, however, she talked to me about the two forms of art: "the wild, Dionysiac, it might be called, and the cold, stately Helios meters."

"I want to be as wild as possible. Not Athenian. I should never have had the citizenship anyhow. I belong to the islands and the East."

"Why be so serious about it?" I learned as much from Hilda's laughter as from anything else.

"Athens is so cold and balanced."

"And you want Scilly and your puffins. Get on with your work."

"That wretched book. I thought you would hate the stuff."

"I admit when I asked you to let me read it, I dreaded the afternoon. It is incomplete, whole pages need to be cut out or changed, but there is a certain sincerity, you love beauty. Remember the mind of an artist ought to be a vase holding epic thoughts."

I knew that *Development* was bad but I seemed unable at that moment to write anything that was better.

"The essential," H. D. continued, "is to know what you want."

"I am interested in educational reform and sometimes I think that I would like to be a book myself so that I am not always punished for having a brain."

"Little frozen being."

"People do not mind if you read but they hate you if you think."

"I shall try to teach you all I know."

Teach, yes, Hilda was as great a teacher as she was a poet. So many letters reached me after she died both from friends and strangers whom she had met perhaps once, all saying "She showed me my way in life." She was an Athenian of the great period, seeing a problem with complete clarity, giving an answer that we might understand only a score of years afterwards and always stressing "You must love. A person, an island, an idea, but it must be completely and with utter dedication."

Hilda's circle did not like me at all. They said that I was an unmannerly cub who stared and never spoke and they advised her to get rid of me as soon as possible. Ezra Pound boasted, however, that if he could see me alone, he could manage me with ease.

I knew nothing about this conversation but one day when H. D. was out, the bell rang and I found him at the door. He strolled in, his velvet jacket a shade darker than his beard, and sat down on the couch. I had already privately christened him the Leopard and did not share the circle's enthusiasm for his poetry. It seemed to me then as it does today to lack originality and to consist rather of often-superb translations. In those London days he reminded me of a jester, strolling round a Crusaders' camp with an old song and the newest gossip on his lips.

Ezra settled himself comfortably against the cushions and remarked, as if he had been a lecturer, "I have just been reading an account, written in the eleventh century, about a fight between Harald the Saxon and a Danish chief on the east coast of England. I cannot trace the exact spot but the place is immaterial."

"Yes," I agreed politely. I needed no instruction from him, however, if he were speaking about King Harald.

"The interest of the story lies in the fact that the Danish chief, whose name I forget, seduced and raped Harald's wife. He carried her off to a log hut in the Lincoln marshes and while they were having intercourse together, Harald and his bowmen began shooting arrows through the door."

"It was the custom of the time."

"Yes. They fought until all the Danes and most of the Saxons were killed, then they set fire to the hut. The only survivor on the Danish side was a boy, half Saxon and half Dane."

"You seem to be interested in early history."

"I had the Middle Ages badly at seventeen and I may say that I was steeped in them for the next ten years. I do not regret this. Modern European thought is not directly founded upon classicism but upon the Middle Ages and the classical Renaissance."

There was a long pause. I wondered if I were being impressed enough but I could not think of anything to say.

"And what can I do to help you?" Ezra finally inquired.

"I want to go to America."

"America! Why America? Why not Arles?"

"Because America is the hope of the world."

"But the women's clubs!"

"Need I come in contact with them?"

"I fear, being European, you do not know the institution. Once a week, the ladies of America meet to obtain culture and discuss their neighbors and their children. They have lectures on eugenics, on Racine and what to do if bitten by a dog presumed insane."

"Should I have to meet them?"

"Why go to America otherwise?"

"Because the poets I admire are American, H. D., Marianne Moore," and remembering hastily to be polite, "yourself."

"Say rather that we are refugees from the West." He got up swiftly and put his arm round my shoulders. It was a most uncomfortable position, an Elizabethan would have screamed or snatched up a dagger but I decided to be wary and calm.

"Nice hair . . . nice hair . . ." he pecked chastely at a cheek. I wondered what in the world I was supposed to do and decided to gaze at him abstractedly and in silence.

We stared at each other for what seemed a very long time. Then he asked, I felt with some solemnity, "Have you no chocolates?"

"I don't think so," I said but it gave me an excuse to break away and look in various cupboards.

"What a child you are," the Leopard remarked, putting on his overcoat. "When the awakening comes you will have a different tale to tell me."

There was another awkward pause. Then he patted my head and walked down the steps with his stick over his shoulder like a sword. I thought "How very odd" and I heard afterwards that his verdict on me was, "Bryher is impossible."

I did make friends. I met Havelock Ellis and nobody could have been kinder to me. He broke the ice the first time that I saw him in his little apartment at Brixton by telling me that he was a sea captain's son who had made two voyages in a sailing ship round the world. I cannot think now why I did not ask him about his experiences in more detail. I suppose that I was jealous of them.

We shared two interests in common, Elizabethan poetry and modern French literature. I still read his book, *From Rousseau to Proust,* with pleasure. I also read his *Studies in the Psychology of Sex* but with one exception we never discussed it. I talked endlessly instead about women's rights. I do not know if it was due to my Eastern experiences or because I had been spared any furtive allusions in childhood but sex to me then was entirely a matter for science and I grasped immediately that birth control was far more important to women than votes. Nobody had the right to force a woman to have a child, I argued, it must be her choice as a matter of moral principle. "You are trying to crowd into a few years what will have to take generations," Ellis scolded gently, a smile on his sun-tanned face. I was furious with him; reform, I said, had to be accomplished *at once.*

I was completely a child of my age. I was one of the first people to be inoculated against influenza and I argued that if we could find some substance to prevent anxiety, we could really do something about changing the globe.

"But fear perhaps is one of the great motive forces of the world," he chided gently, trying to make me see that life was a balance of composite forces. I never agreed, I am amused to think that in 1920 some vague notion of tranquillizers was already turning round in my brain. Now that I am old, it appears to me more and more that we cannot escape the trends of our particular generation, and the twenties, I believe, was an era of discovery.

It was a difficult time for me because I did not want to hurt my parents, I had always loved them, but I knew that I could not remain at home and live. Ellis always tried to help me to keep a balance, to visit them without saying things that would shock them and yet to keep a hardly won independence. H. D. had nicknamed him Chiron after the instructor of Achilles and we ranged in talk over all the subjects of the day. It was a moment when race memory was being much discussed and books on anthropology were popular. "It is possible that some experiences are common to the race," he said one day, "and that the more sensitive inherit a knowledge of emotional states that they have not felt themselves."

It seemed to me that this ruled out imagination but it offered possibilities for use in a novel. "Would this explain why some people belong to a particular historical epoch and not to others?" I inquired.

"Perhaps," he was very cautious, "but we need to know a great deal more about it."

It was part of the time. The war had brought such a complete reversal of values that it was a good climate for the psychological research that was just beginning to be generally known. Ellis and I were interested in color hearing. He did not laugh at me when I explained my sensations but gave me all the scientific papers on the subject. I wrote down my own observations in detail and I think that they were sent to a Canadian doctor who had done the most work on the subject and from whose paper I found that there were also people who "tasted" words. It was long before Michaux and Huxley but I was also invited to "guinea pig" on mescaline. One of the hospitals had planned a test and I accepted with alacrity but the project fell through, I think because they could not get a sufficient quantity of the drug. They had wanted at least twenty people for the experiment.

I felt very much at home in this early atmosphere of the investigation of human states. Ellis gave me the first paper by Freud that I ever read. It would be pleasant to record that I fell on it with enthusiasm. I try to be truthful and actually I read it with interest but some suspicion. It was a saner way to approach psychoanalysis than by a wild uncritical jump. I started to read whatever was available of Freud in translation and became one of the first subscribers to the British *Journal of Psychoanalysis* and it was Ellis who gave me the introduction that enabled me to meet Freud himself in 1927.

In 1920, however, we talked about Remy de Gourmont, the position of women throughout history and whether I heard colors plain or mixed. My answer, consonants modified the vowels. I accepted his help and kindness without question although I can have given him very little in return. He knew me through and through. Asked to help a scheme to aid some German professors who had been reduced to utter poverty through the inflation, he begged me to give a few pounds to a Dr. Deissmann, who was a professor of Tibetan. It recalled the frontier tales that Dr. Boyce had told me as a child. Ellis also sent me to his own typist, Miss Woolford, who put up with recopying my patched and ragged typescripts for forty years. Whenever I reread his letters I am surprised at my arrogance and his patience.

His scientific work seems old-fashioned today but the different world we live in now was partly made possible through his campaign against ignorance. Freud could have told him that a fellow human being can seldom forgive being helped; few of us are able to feel gratitude without an *unconscious* resentment. The pioneers always get the knocks and never the crowns. I had a sharp lesson in human snobbery and neglect when in some studies that appeared about him some years ago, his lifework was dismissed as of no importance and details of his private life were discussed that he had kept private, out of concern for others. Not one of the many thousands whom he had helped had the courage to say a word in his defense.

Dear Havelock, I disliked your rein upon my impatience at the time but among the many people whom I have met during my life, few have been more honest or more noble.

The London of those postwar years was cold and gray. People seemed stunned and I think that it is due to this and not to lack of observation that the people I saw seem now so shadowy to me. I liked Dorothy Pound. I felt that she belonged to the English countryside and the depths of its traditions. It must have been hard and difficult for her to find that her destiny was exile. I sometimes met May Sinclair, I admired her integrity and love of scholarship but again I was a rebel who longed for, admired and swallowed whole the new age that she found wanting in profundity.

The visitor whom I remember the most clearly was W. B. Yeats. The form of his poetry was too traditional for me at the time but his personality filled the room, it seemed to glow. He was enthusiastic, as the others were not, about America. He had just returned from Salt Lake City and spoke to us about the Mormons for an hour. He had the gift of storytelling because I saw the landscape as he described it, it was just what I had imagined it to be, fresh with great skies and clear, pure colors. How often subsequently I have wished that I could remember his actual words. As he was leaving, he turned with great courtesy and asked me if I had written *Development*. I was almost too surprised to reply. He said that he had also felt the educational system to be wrong and hoped that I was working on another book. Very few writers would have been as kind to a mere beginner.

In general, however, it was a world of tired people, trying simply to exist. I knew that I should never be content until I had trodden American soil and eventually and against everyone's advice, I left for New York.

 *Fourteen*

The rebellion of youth is necessary to the survival of mankind. Otherwise the world would stagnate and die because adaptability is essential to life. If the word "progress" is suspect at the present time, remember that without it, fact or illusion though it may be, we should be still helpless in the face of ignorance and starvation. The ambitious young have to leave their neighborhoods and the love-hate conflicts with an older generation to try their luck in some unfamiliar place. For the past two centuries America has been the European dream. It is also the reverse or peaceful side of war. The same qualities that are needed under fire are wanted to construct a home in a foreign land. The dream has created another civilization and in spite of many failures, thousands of people have seen their children, if not themselves, sharing opportunities that they could never have had in Europe. I think that this is part of the hostility that I find in many Europeans towards the United States. Have not the rebels succeeded where the stay-at-homes failed?

My arrival in New York with H. D. and Perdita in September, 1921, was inauspicious. A passenger was found to have some infectious disease just as we were starting to go ashore and so we were held on board for another ten hours, the prey of wild rumors and endless false alarms. Nothing is more exhausting than waiting and when

Amy Lowell and Ada Russell met me as we landed late in the evening I had expected too much and I could not think of a word to say to them.

It was almost as bad the next afternoon when Amy took me for a drive and kept saying to me, "Look at the light under that bridge, what would you call it?" All I could mumble was I didn't know and she was disappointed. I had dinner with her that evening, and Jean Untermeyer who was also there and realized that I was in a state of shock teases me to this day about the frozen silence with which I regarded the party.

American culture was new and exciting but it was totally different from Europe and I needed a guide to explain its differences to me. Most civilians in England had been shut up within a narrow round of duties for five years, my case was normal, not exceptional, but I could not break through its carapace in a moment. I also had to adapt my fantasy of America to its reality. I failed on my first trip and I am sorry but I do not think that it was surprising.

The thing that astonished me most was that the conventions were stronger than in Europe and, apart from ephemeral slang, the language more old-fashioned. Perhaps it is the counterweight to American audacity in invention but manners and words still seem to me to lag twenty years behind Britain. No nations are able to shed their preconceived opinions and I suppose that generations more will go on talking about English formality and American ease.

Due to the drier Mediterranean winters of my childhood, I had always suffered terribly from the English cold. It had been agreed before we left England that we should go to California for part of the winter and after a brief stay in New York I went out to Los Angeles, where I had cousins, with H. D., her mother, whom she had not seen for eight years, and Perdita.

I took one look at California and wanted to return to the East. I had expected a large-scale Cornwall where we could ramble on the cliffs. We moved to Carmel Highlands, it was then an isolated place full of elderly ladies who were seeking the sun, but it was dangerous to leave the trails because we heard rattlesnakes several times. I did not like the oily roll and the kelp beds of the Pacific and the main conversation was about Prohibition that seemed to me to have brought the people dangerously near to civil war.

The hotel was in the center of a group of bungalows where we slept. I was walking over alone to breakfast one morning when a voice yelled, "Stop, we are shooting." Various tales about lawlessness that I had been told but considered childish to believe flashed through my mind. I was a survivor from a war and I was not going to let any brigand frighten me into standing still. I stamped forward, I admit a little uneasily, and a second voice yelled, "We're shooting, stay where you are." I hesitated and a man rushed up to me in a white coat, "Haven't you heard that Mary Pickford is here?"

I thought that I had seen the name on a poster but I had been inside perhaps two cinemas in my life and films barely existed to me. I was directed to another path that led to the hotel and to my amazement, on arrival, the manageress rushed me up to a small, rather plump boy in a flaxen wig and introduced me to him as "our visitor from England." I was almost as puzzled when she explained that he was doubling for Mary Pickford in the danger scenes on a wreck. I was not sure that film people were respectable. Destiny soon punished me for this thought. A few years later I became an interpreter for film stars in Berlin who did not speak German.

We joined a crowd and sat on the edge of a cliff to watch one of the main scenes being filmed. It was in the informal days when much was improvised and all they asked of spectators was to keep out of camera range. It almost ended that morning in disaster as the hero got caught in the kelp on a dive. I saw people standing about with reflectors for the first time, we watched Mary Pickford repeat a sequence, but it seemed remote, rather like a village fair, it never occurred to me that I should ever take movies seriously and I refused a chance as "a visitor from England" to meet the star. H. D. was much more interested, she often went to the cinema.

The winter passed. I found it impossible to write and even difficult to read. Hilda worked at Greek and I found a companion in her mother whom we nicknamed the Beaver. I was glad when the time came, however, to return to New York. It was a moment when I needed people more than landscapes.

We went to see Jack Yeats. He was so like a retired mariner that I expected to see a telescope in the corner. There were several visitors present, they talked of incidents and people whom I did not know and I stared at the bare branches of the trees in Washington Square and marveled that I was with people who wrote or painted or merely talked about art. I do not think that my silence was the shyness of which I was often accused. It was a form of honesty. I knew that I had nothing to contribute as yet and it was natural to feel unsettled and bewildered. The roots of all England had been destroyed in 1914 and it was going to take me several more years to get over the shock.

I have fleeting impressions of many other people, among them Eunice Tietjens and Alfred Kreymborg. Amy Lowell was disappointed in me, but I was gradually moving away from a restricted world and instinctively withdrew from too strong a personality. My most vivid memory is of meeting Marsden Hartley one evening. We hardly spoke to each other but I must have felt unconsciously his devotion to the sea. The guests were talking that night about Dada, the new movement that was then sweeping Europe, and wondering whether it was a serious advance or a momentary whim. Years later, I came face to face with Hartley's painting of an immense but not quite breaking wave in the Museum of Modern Art and relived the evening with its arguments, its "has it a meaning for us" as if all the phrases had been brush strokes in the picture; I think that a sense of search and something of the vast country that I so wanted to discover must have come to me across the chatter of that New York party.

The reward of my first visit was meeting Marianne Moore. H. D. had known her at Bryn Mawr and had helped to get some of her first poems published. She had also told me frequently that if I were interested in modern writing, I must study Marianne's work. I think that "The Fish" was the first poem that I read. It brought the beaches in Scilly vividly into my mind.

Marianne was living with her mother in Greenwich Village at the time and they asked us to tea. "Why, it's a pterodactyl," I thought or rather a resemblance to the heraldic creatures that I imagined them to be, as I watched her come to welcome us with the massive gold that seemed more like a headdress than mortal hair, swaying slightly sidewards above a dark green dress. "How could you bear to leave London?" she and her mother said together, "How we wish that we could revisit England."

"Is it long since you were there?"

"Ten years. We have the memory of it in our hearts, the mists, the green English leaves."

"I wanted to get away from the fogs," I said, remembering the winter days in unheated houses and the blackout.

"Even the war could not spoil London and its traditions. Do they still have muffins?"

"Not since rationing," and they both sighed.

If I had been forty, I could have talked to them for hours about the nineteenth century but as the proverb says, "You can't put an old head on young shoulders" and it was not even development, it was survival that led me to America. It was not my London of shackles and disappointments that Marianne loved but an image built up from books that had been written, in general, a whole century earlier. She could not understand that I had constructed a vision of clarity and freedom in precisely the same way from the poems that she and H. D. had written. Both of us were playing with dreams, both of us were right, but we were too young to explain this to each other at that moment. "Discipline," Mrs. Moore remarked as she filled up the teacups, "is good for the spirit." How could I explain that this word had acquired a totally different meaning for us since 1914?

We liked each other from the beginning but we understood our objectives better a few years later on. The repetition of early patterns in later life has always fascinated me and there is an element in both Marianne and her poetry, a sense of living in an uncrowded land that links her to the mornings when I found ammonites in the chalk pits of the Downs. Her eyes are different from ours, instead of a flashing whole, her mind sees first and they obey its orders in microscopic detail while she seems to lie perched on a rock above a warm and shallow lake, surveying an earlier globe.

The winter was one of the most negative moments of my life and I am ashamed of *West,* a book I tried to write about it. America was all I had dreamed of it and more but I needed a guide. I found one in Norman Pearson a few years afterwards. I had always loved the country from the first day, the sweep of the skies, the coloring that is less misty than my Northern islands and more austere than the South, but I had to be shown my place in it and that was impossible without help. My only excuse is that I should probably have floundered in any new country at that moment, shock is a process of slow obliteration, it cannot be wiped out with a word.

It was time to return to England but my family insisted that I go back to live with them again. I could have coped with the situation if I had been analyzed but in 1922 I had to face it alone and I was desperately afraid of hurting their feelings. I knew equally well that after a period of comparative freedom, I could not adjust to a conventional routine. I admit that I was foolish but I took the course I did in good faith.

I had happened to meet a young American writer, Robert McAlmon, who was full of enthusiasm for modern writing. He wanted to go to Paris to meet Joyce but lacked the passage money. I put my problem before him and suggested that if we married, my family would leave me alone. I would give him part of my allowance, he would join me for occasional visits to my parents, but otherwise we would live strictly separate lives. It must be remembered that I had been brought up on French rather than English lines and that arranged marriages were perfectly familiar to me. It never occurred to me at the time that there was anything irregular in my suggestion.

Later on, I felt some guilt in having exposed Bob to a postwar Europe of which, it must be remembered, I knew nothing. Years afterwards again, I realized that he was a child of the Prohibition age and that the end would have been the same, whether he had remained in New York or gone to France. We neither of us felt the slightest attraction towards each other but remained perfectly friendly. We were divorced in 1927 but could have got an annulment just as easily except that this was a longer and more expensive procedure.

I think now that there were advantages on both sides. Bob had a gift for meeting people and bringing the most incongruous groups together. He introduced me to my lifelong friend, Sylvia Beach, to Joyce, Hemingway, Gertrude Stein, Berenice Abbott, Man Ray, and many others. He brought me the books of E. E. Cummings and Wallace Stevens. He received, in his turn, the freedom of the Paris of the twenties. It should not be forgotten that he used some of his allowance to print *avant-garde* books, among them one by Gertrude Stein and some of the first of Hemingway's stories. I think that his own writing has been unduly neglected by the historians of the period. It is crude and uneven but not more so than other work of the time that has survived. Yet his real contribution was in introducing people to each other, from "that kid" to "old man so and so" who was probably barely middle-aged, and thus helping many to find themselves through talking out their problems.

If it had not been for these circumstances I should have gone to live in Cornwall. As it was, I remembered the Switzerland of my childhood and returned to Territet, at the far end of Lake Geneva. I expected to stay a couple of years but apart from the second war, I have lived in Vaud since May, 1922.

Fifteen

I should like this book to be read as neither mere autobiography nor period piece but as an attempt to show how external events and unconscious drives help or hinder development. History itself is a philosophy. It dies and is continuous. The skeleton survives; the particular circumstances of time and place perish with each generation. The ages move however frantically the nations may resist all changes and although we can trace an outline from our diaries or from records, no memory can give us back the intensity of that first moment of the early twenties when the artist, it seemed, was more influential than the politician.

We were all exiles. We remain so today. It is our destiny. We were the last group to grow up under the formidable discipline of the nineteenth century whose effect, however much we resent it, cannot be entirely eradicated from our systems. All of us had been taught as soon as we could speak that abnegation and hard work would give us security and peace. The battle of the trenches cracked this myth from one end of Europe to the other. The Armistice offered us influenza, inflation and loss. In such a seething epoch of personal tragedy, the only thing left in which we could believe was art. It was to us what religion was to the Middle Ages, discovery to the Renaissance and what science is becoming to the present day. Only art, if it were to fill the hollow left by chaos, must be revolutionary and new. It must find words that were not tainted by nineteenth-century associations, rhythms that fitted the purr of machines rather than the thudding of hooves, different colors and, above all, a sternly truthful approach.

We believed that if we stated facts without comment, moral or otherwise, mankind must see its follies and revise its laws. It was a vain and idle dream and yet, looking back at it after forty years, how much that we created in the way of thought is accepted now as valid and desirable.

We were very young, in part because we tended to go back to what we had wanted to be in 1914. Many of the men had just come out of the army and were still surprised to be alive. A number of the women were young widows; others had emancipated themselves from their families through their war work. There was too much drinking, less promiscuous love-making than is supposed, and plenty of revolutionary talk, but it was always basically a moral revolt. There was a seriousness beneath the wildest escapade that differentiated it from what often seems mere shallowness today.

It is hard to realize now how *new* everything was. A few of us had begun to read Freud, others talked about the Russian Revolution, but we were not "engaged" by either psychology or politics. War that had been attrition made the momentary our concern. We laughed at everybody and no idea was sacred. We really believed that if we could discover why we preferred a particular café or disliked some otherwise acceptable person's face, we should eventually understand the baffling roots of human behavior. It was a form of crude, spontaneous analysis although such a term would have puzzled us in 1920. The mistake that we made was that though we owed our survival to rebellion, we did not realize that it was not the concepts themselves but the way that mankind had used them that was false. Our incessant mockery of loyalty, duty and honor deprived the next generation of its proper roots and they did not have our apprenticeship of danger to steady them. Yet remember that nothing was left to us of the codes to which our youth had been sacrificed and that we gave our century a sense of honesty (England went into the second war without illusions) and an inquisitiveness of mind. We swept away some good together with much evil but always with such exuberance that compared with us the thirties seem a dull and spiritless age.

Our geography was Montparnasse; our capital, the length of pavement outside a café. The group or, in the slang of that day, "the bunch" went first to one place and then, for a reason divined rather than uttered, they moved to another across the street. At the time that I was there, it was usually the Dôme or the Rotonde. It was the moment of glory for the little reviews. Printing was cheap, whoever had fifty dollars or its equivalent started a magazine for himself and one or two carefully selected friends. Funds failed or there was the inevitable quarrel and the paper died. I pulled a pile of them out of a cupboard a few weeks ago. They were full of misprints, the covers were faded, but the contents blazed with vitality. There were the now famous names besides those of whom nothing more was heard. Some of the unsuccessful died, some wrote a single book, others have vanished. I suppose if they remember their one golden summer now they think of it with surprise, even a little shame. At least we never turned out factual reports or tidy little novels. The sublime epitaph, the trick ending, were pulled mercilessly to pieces as the crowds rushed up from the Métro and the buses thundered along the streets. The scornful, however, were in the game as well and when their stories were printed the following week, we took our revenge with no holds barred. If a manuscript was sold to an established publisher, its author was regarded as a black sheep and for his own safety moved to the Right Bank. We boasted, we knew that we were good and to hell with the bourgeoisie including all reviewers, but we did not write with an eye on fame, security or television appearances. We were permitted to appear without loss of prestige in *Contact, Broom, Transition,* the *Transatlantic* and *This Quarter.*

It was a marvelous apprenticeship and I am thankful to have shared in a historic moment that seems so much richer today than when I was in the middle of it but although I realized the exhilaration around me, I was a Puritan in Montparnasse and Paris could not give me the same sense of enchantment that it offered my companions. The very familiarity of the streets made me uneasy and reminded me of the restrictions of childhood. I had to see McAlmon, however, from time to time; he lived there and it was a convenient meeting place. Sometimes I think of the middle part of my life as the wasted years. It is an unfair judgment because some of the experiences were necessary but I had temporarily lost my way. We advance in zigzags while I wanted to rush straight to my goal, and the book that was nearest to me at that time because it seemed to express so many of my ex-asperations was André Gide's *Paludes*. Were we not always preparing ourselves for the great moment that would light our creative fire, and didn't something always go wrong? It never occurred to me that I was getting some of the impressions that I needed, sitting in the cafés that half of me despised.

I was introduced to the "Quarter" at the end of May, 1921. It was at the beginning of an eventful journey that ended in my settling in Switzerland for most of my life. I had read an account of a new serv-ice from London to Paris and had persuaded H. D. to cross over with me by air.

Flying then was an experience. The youngest girl was chosen at Croydon, thrust into a borrowed suit and pushed into the nose. The rest of us were strapped into our seats, handed paper bags, and the door was slammed. There were no hostesses in those days and no frills. The return fare, I am told, was twelve pounds.

I knew nothing about aeroplanes, it was the "being modern" that appealed to me. I remembered the headlines when Blériot crossed the Channel but that had seemed a feat, like riding out a hurricane, far removed from ordinary life. Later on, I must have been about four-teen, I had watched some oxen drag a strange-looking object to the top of the Downs near Alfriston and had laughed as heartily as the rest when it flattened itself on the ground after about a minute in the air. My immediate reaction as we started towards France was sur-prise. In a flash, I understood modern painting. We could not have been very high and the geometric patterns of the fields, the curves of the rivers and the thick lines of sudden, oblong pools explained the canvases that till then had meant so little to me. I have never really lost the excitement of that initial moment. I prefer to see landscapes from the air and I cannot understand people who find such travel boring. I hate the holdups at airports, the customs and the long drives towards the terminal as much as anybody but once we take off I am a different person, it stirs my imagination, I have lived through whole stories in one flight. The clouds form themselves into strange polar patterns, the sun changes, I saw it once bouncing like a scarlet football from peak to peak on an autumn journey from Geneva; besides we look down at a globe instead of across a segment of earth. On land I am a frightened mouse if I have to cross a road, on the sea or in the air I come into my own.

The first trip took about three hours and I was hauled out at Le Bourget, horribly airsick and almost deaf. In spite of this, I was ready to go up again the moment an opportunity occurred.

H. D. had not been airsick but she did not seem to share my enthusiasm. Later in the afternoon we sat down with McAlmon and Dorothy Pound to wait for Ezra and nobody showed the slightest interest in our then unusual exploit.

"Watch the life on the boulevards," my father had said to me once, "it takes an artist to get even a suggestion of it on paper." I thought at that moment that it all seemed rather ordinary, the men were pale as they came out of the offices, the girls who were eating wild strawberries beside us were not so different from the ones that I had seen in 1913. Their skirts were a little shorter, their faces were half covered by their hats and their summer dresses had brighter flowers than would formerly have been considered correct. The real change was in the number of cars, the many taxis with dusty wheel spokes that looked as if they were made out of wire and the heavy lorries that had replaced the horse-drawn carts. Ezra came but I hardly listened to the conversation, I was looking up at the sky. I have been there, I thought, I am sharing in a great discovery, it is new and free. I did not realize how soon the controls would come to force us small adventurers out of the air.

There was only one street in Paris for me, the rue de l'Odéon. It is association, I suppose, but I have always considered it one of the most beautiful streets in the world. It meant naturally Sylvia and Adrienne and the happy hours that I spent in their libraries. Has there ever been another bookshop like Shakespeare and Company? It was not just the crowded shelves, the little bust of Shakespeare nor the many informal photographs of her friends, it was Sylvia herself, standing like a passenger from the *Mayflower* with the wind still blowing through her hair and a thorough command of French slang, waiting to help us and be our guide. She found us printers, translators and rooms, she was busy all those years with the problem of publishing *Ulysses,* yet she never lost her detachment nor identified herself with any particular group. If there could be such a thing, she was the perfect Ambassador and I doubt if a citizen has ever done more to spread knowledge of America abroad. She loved France, she made us feel that it was a privilege to be in Paris, but the common modern mistake never occurred to her, she never tried to identify herself too closely with a foreign land whose childhood myths she had not shared. Great and humble, she mixed us all together instead, the bond between us being that we were artists and discoverers. We changed, the city altered, but after an absence we always found Sylvia waiting for us, her arms full of new books, and often a writer whom we wanted to meet, standing beside her in the corner.

Sylvia had both kindness and understanding. I was living a placid existence among the Swiss mountains but my family expected me to be in Paris with McAlmon. I did not want to worry my mother and so Sylvia posted letters to her from me and forwarded my mail. It may have been wrong but it saved my parents from a lot of anxiety and I cannot think that it did any harm.

Number seven, on the opposite side of the rue de l'Odéon, was also a cave full of treasures. I was shy with Adrienne Monnier at first, my British accent got in my way and I also knew directly I looked at her round forehead and deceptively placid blue eyes that she was a thought reader. It was an instinctive gift and while others of the Quarter spoke of her native Savoyard qualities, I felt rather that she was part of that timeless nucleus that has, as its purpose, the transmission of a wisdom that cannot be written down, even in poetry. At first she merely suggested a few books that I might have missed and then, gradually, and only as she felt that I was ready, she began to talk, saying little, always waiting for me to take the lead but suddenly revealing in a flash another angle or the deeper appreciation of some author whom I might have neglected. Thanks principally to Flint's articles, I had read many of her favorite books but she introduced me to the work of Valéry and Fargue. It is because of her that I have kept consistently in touch with modern French literature for forty years. She sent me regularly parcels of what she considered to be the best books published every season. It was an invaluable service to render to a foreigner, living outside France.

In those early years our meetings blur into two memories, one of her at her shop and the other of her at home. I see Adrienne coming towards me as I open the door of number seven, with her arms full of yellow, paper-covered books. Some people change according to what they wear but Adrienne and her clothes were one. I could never make up my mind whether I preferred her in blue or gray but the fine woolen skirt never seemed either a clerk's robe nor a Savoyard petticoat as some have written, to me she was a French officer in a military cape, trying in 1812 to bring his soldiers back from Moscow. Adrienne hated war in any form and yet I think that this was what she was, a captain with a wholehearted devotion to her company, the young or would-be writers united to her by their devotion to art. She taught us with a humility born from great pride, not in her own gifts though this would have been perfectly legitimate, but because we were all privileged to put vision above ignorance.

In her own home it is the delicious smells that I remember, herbs, a chicken roasting, the polish on the wood, these and the murmur of talk. I met Romains there and Michaux and later, but this belongs to the thirties, Schlumberger, Prévost and Chamson. It was a unique experience, first to eat the dinner because she cooked better than anyone whom I have ever known, and then to listen to the conversation of some of the finest minds in France. I never spoke unless I was spoken to and so they forgot sometimes that I was a foreigner. Sylvia, of course, had been adopted by them all.

We pray for opportunities and when they are given us often fail to use them. I took Adrienne's kindness too much for granted and lost the chance to learn much of what she would willingly have taught me. She knew me inside out. She said once to my intense surprise, I forget the exact French words but this is the substance, "Ah, Bryher, nine tenths of you is all that is practical and balanced, but the other tenth," she shrugged her shoulders and looked at me as if she were curious rather than puzzled, *"est follement romanesque."* I disputed the matter but once when I was sleeping in a tent up in the Arctic, I suspected that she might have been right. She also added on that same occasion, "You will write but late and in the classic style."

When the time came she showed us how to die and hardly a day passes now when I do not miss her.

One sunny afternoon we were walking down one of those obscure streets that were so familiar to me through many French stories. The chimneys hid much of the sky, the gray façades concealed a dozen disenchanted heroes full of scruples, and the road itself was like the connective word in a sentence, necessary but colorless, with nothing in it to disrupt the attention. Suddenly a high, old-fashioned car drew up beside us. Two penetrating eyes in a square, impassive face seemed to be absorbing every detail of my appearance. "Why, Mc-Almon," a puzzled voice remarked, "you did not tell me that you had married an ethical Jewess. It's rather a rare type."

All my ancestors had been English Protestants or German Lutherans but you did not argue with Gertrude Stein. You acquiesced. The Jewish suggestion linked up to the East but I did not care for the ethical, anything that smacked of morals was suspect. Still I was searching (how had she guessed this?) for a form of absolute truth. I took it therefore as a compliment and nodded. She talked a few minutes to McAlmon, invited us both to tea and drove off in her famous Ford, a jolly little dinosaur riding down the sands of time.

Apart from Shakespeare and Company it is the long room in the rue de Fleurus that I remember most from my Paris visits. It was full of paintings but what I noticed, it must have been some trick of the lighting, was that the atmosphere seemed full of gold. There was a table piled with books and beyond this a high chair where Gertrude sat, surrounded by a group of young men. At first there was little general conversation, then she would pick up a phrase and develop it, ranging through a process of continuous association until we seemed to have ascended through the seven Persian heavens and in the process to have turned our personalities inside out. Make no mistake, however, it was not an ego selfishly seizing the stage, it was rhetoric, spare and uncolored by emotion. She offered us the world, took it away again in the following sentence, only to demonstrate in a third that it was something that we could not want because it had never existed. How bitterly I regret that there were no tape recorders then available to preserve her disputations.

Gertrude had no use for me but she did not dislike me. I had nothing to offer her in the way of intellectual stimulus and, unlike her young men, brought her no personal problems. I knew this and so, whenever I could, I slipped away to join Miss Toklas in her corner.

It was never Miss Stein but Gertrude from the first meeting but only very intimate friends called Miss Toklas "Alice." Her dignity subdued the rawest, most boisterous youth. I wondered why she had not been more often painted, under an apparent repose there was such a glowing quality of life. She had subordinated her own gifts to looking after her friend yet they never grew to resemble each other as often happens in such cases. Her own personality was intact. I left the others busy with their speculations while I listened to stories of her childhood in a remote Californian valley that she transformed as she spoke into some Jules Verne island mysteriously drifting among mountains instead of seas. I wish Gertrude had written more about these beginnings in the *Autobiography* but I suppose they did not touch her essentially modern mind.

Occasionally we ventured to slip away into the kitchen to discuss the shops that sold the best vegetable seeds as we were both gardeners or to talk of the hardships of some French servant who had neither parents nor adequate wages to protect her. Once we were sharply reproved by Gertrude for leaving her circle. I am afraid that while I had a profound admiration for Gertrude, it was Miss Toklas whom I loved. She was so kind to me. Perhaps this came from her long practice as Gertrude wrote "of sitting with the wives of geniuses" but it was very pleasant and the rue de Fleurus, if I were not with Adrienne and Sylvia, was the only place in Paris where I felt at home.

I read some of the magazines of the period over again recently and it is Gertrude's work that now seems the most alive. It is not dated. She was a scientist and one of the few among us who had almost entirely freed herself from the past although her "electronic brain" was stocked with knowledge. Her attack on language was necessary and helped us all, even if we did not follow her. Some of her books are both so simple and so profound that we can read them whether we are eighteen or eighty. The rest of her work is experimental, highly technical and should be reserved for specialists. It is a measure of the decline of real learning that some people today have questioned her genius.

It was quite another story at the Boeuf. There I was a dismal failure and I remember Cocteau's expression of horror when he looked at me as we were introduced. He was right. The Boeuf was a place for men and for decorative women. The most arresting was Nancy Cunard. Every head turned to stare at her whenever she entered a room. In an age of creative activity there is often some external reflection of an inner drive and there were a dozen others, almost as beautiful in their way. (Surely the pointed chin and the overlarge eyes, however, in so many illustrations are an exaggeration?) It is very difficult to describe a particular face or form in words, it is partly a question of movement and light and here photography can preserve memory better than a book. It was another flower of the time. I remember most vividly a discussion one evening. Man Ray, Tristan Tzara, Iris Tree and another man whose name I forget were arguing about the future of art. Man Ray said that technique had reached such a level that it deprived an artist of imagination and that he would work in future with a camera instead of a brush. I imagine the others were only half serious but I agreed with enthusiasm. I would still much rather collect photographs than pictures. (There may be a personal reason, even now it is hard to forget how brutally I was torn from my drawing at fifteen.) Anyhow, from that moment I often went to Man Ray's studio to look at his experiments and there I met Berenice Abbott who was working with him temporarily as his assistant and Kiki, the famous model.

Berenice and I liked each other but we were both inarticulate. I tried to break the barrier but we were at such different stages of development that we never got further than smiles and a few words. It was rather different with Kiki.

Man Ray's studio consisted of a huge, bare room furnished with a staircase that led to a narrow gallery at the height of the first floor. He was explaining one of his photographic plates to me one day when a door in the gallery opened and I looked up to find Kiki, literally a "nude descending the staircase," attired in a couple of soap bubbles and a wisp of towel, tied where she did not need it, round her neck. I was firmly in favor of nudity on the beaches but my training in etiquette at Queenwood had hardly prepared me for such an encounter in town. Impassively, I hoped, but heartily, I shook Kiki warmly by the hand and remarked that the weather had favored us, it was a sunny, summerlike day.

The names were there but who at that time had heard of them? A man used to come striding up to the Dôme about seven in the evening, sometimes alone, sometimes with his wife. "He wants to write but is short of funds," McAlmon explained, "so he's coaching a couple of American youngsters." Few of us had much money although we agreed that the painters had the worst of it as paper cost much less than brushes and colors. He talked incessantly about Spain and bulls but nobody took him very seriously until Adrienne said quietly one evening when we were predicting certain success for a writer whose name I do not now remember, "Hemingway will be the best known of you all." She spoke in French and some of the others did not understand her but I had a great respect for her critical judgment and asked her in some surprise why she felt that he was better than we were. "He cares," she said, "for his craft." (I imagine that she used the word *métier*.) I then discovered that after a hard day's work and some equally hard drinking, Hemingway went to a printer's shop in the late evening to learn how to set up type so as to know exactly how his manuscripts, to the last comma, would look on the printed page.

It was true, so many wrote their masterpieces in their heads with the saucers piling up on the zinc-topped table in front of them but it is a very different thing to live a story and to try to bang out something even approaching it on a typewriter. Besides, we know so little about the raw material of art. On a subsequent visit, McAlmon met me full of stories about a week that he had spent in Pamplona. It was to figure in a number of books but when I listened to the tale at the time, it seemed to me simply another tiresome escapade. It became a symbol for a whole generation in *The Sun Also Rises.* Perhaps a small hunk of a particular material is given to every artist and the measure of his success or failure is how he uses it.

McAlmon called me a frightened rabbit who was unable to "take" Paris. It was not strictly true. I had arrived there through intense difficulties that had turned me into an observer. I was utterly in sympathy with the rebellion of the group but their solutions did not solve my particular problem. I suppose McAlmon must have said something of the kind one day because as we left, Hemingway came up to me in great kindness and asked me to fence with him. I looked up at his broad shoulders and knew his reach would be much longer than my own so for once I decided that discretion was the better part of valor and hastily invented an appointment on the other side of Paris.

Then or now, Hemingway has never seemed to me a "tough" writer. Petronius is tough, so is Norman Douglas but Hemingway is rather the last of the great Victorians who still believed in loyalty and honor. He was writing for a completely different audience than the one familiar to his critics. I have often met people on my voyages who have spoken and felt in a Hemingway manner although they had certainly never heard of him and possibly never read a book. A man has just as much right to express their point of view as the contemplative his tests and trials. Let us only beware of calling either "nobler" than the other. He never forgot the command of our generation to put down truth as we saw it and I see no reason now to disagree with Adrienne.

People have sometimes said to me in awe, "Did you really meet Joyce?" I did on several occasions but the strange thing is that although I only saw Yeats once, I can recall his intonation, the way that he moved his head and something of what he told us, but I see the Joyces in a series of slightly out-of-focus snapshots. The first time that we met he was standing with his wife in front of a shop window and commenting upon the changes that the proprietor had made since the previous day. He was a naturalist of cities. Not a thing escaped his observation, not even the fact that a packet of rice was on another shelf or that the delivery boy's cycle had been moved a few yards up the street. But what did he say while we were sitting at lunch? I simply cannot remember. Of course I recognized his greatness but *Ulysses* was about the nineteenth century from which I was trying to escape. I longed passionately for aeroplanes, a new approach, a different world. Yet to be in the same room with our elders for even a short time is of the utmost value to a beginner. Their works take on a different value after we have met them. It is literally a passing on of the tradition, it is continuity, even if at the time we are plunging off ourselves in a different direction.

More than most of us, I was a child of my age. The one mind among the older writers who spoke directly to me and whose books I read passionately was André Gide.

"You must be kind to the boy," my mother admonished when I joined my family for lunch one day. They had come over to Paris for the Easter holidays and found a tutor to speak French with my brother. "Try not to stare at Mr. Allégret," she continued, "it startles people and I had so hoped that after your marriage you would get out of it." I did stare, it was before I had learned that an intonation or the choice of a word could tell me as much about a person as watching them, but I had been trained to silence for so many years that it had become a habit.

I supposed that I should meet the usual tutor who would be occupied with *le verbe* in its grammatical rather than with its philosophical sense. Judge of my surprise when I was introduced to a handsome young diplomat who asked me politely during a pause in the conversation if I happened to have read Cocteau's latest book. I was able to reply to our mutual astonishment that I had been talking to Cocteau himself during the previous evening at the Boeuf. It may have been imagination but I thought that I saw a feeling of relief pass across his face. We were sitting in the dining room of a conventional hotel, we discussed the question of whether my brother should go first to Versailles or Le Jardin des Plantes as if it were a draft for an important treaty and it was not until I was leaving that Marc managed to whisper as if we were fellow conspirators, "And who, writing in France today, do you admire the most?"

"Gide," I said firmly and with enthusiasm.

"Gide! But he is my uncle." He looked at me as if he could hardly believe his ears. "I must arrange for you to meet him at once."

Allégret wanted my father to leave my brother in Paris for his education and I have often wondered whether this would not have turned out better for him in the end. Perhaps not, he hated being out of London. Whatever broadening of the mind he got while I still knew him, came from Marc. I was not thinking about my brother, however, as I waited in the tiny hall of the Left Bank hotel where I was staying; I had no feeling of awe about any of the other writers, most of them were part of the group and we argued and fought as if it were a bigger Queenwood but Gide was different. He was the one elder writer whom I profoundly respected. He was fanatical in his search for truth, he had actually met Mallarmé, and if *Paludes* had been published in 1895 when I was a year old, the sentence *"Il suit des cours de biologie populaire"* was terribly 1920. Actually, although

I only realized this many years later, he was the forerunner of the present scientific age. We were trying then to throw off the barren and terrible years of our education and the trenches. Gide, I felt, asserted the right of all of us to be happy.

The door opened. Marc came towards me followed by a tall figure in a long cloak who transported me instantly to the Channel steamers of my childhood and the decks full of people in black and white cheviot ulsters. I hesitated, fearing the shock of my Anglo-French upon Gide's sensitive ears. I need not have worried. He shook me by the hand and said in one of the clearest, most precise voices that I have ever heard, "Good evening, Mistress McAlmon." Nobody had warned me that he had learned his English directly from Shakespeare.

To judge from the memoirs written after Gide's death, everybody found their first meeting with him difficult. I was terrified and was only able to utter, *"Oui, monsieur"* while Marc, the wretch, stood grinning at us both in the background. I made the usual mistake of the beginner, I tried to tell him how much I admired his books. Now I should have asked him what he, himself, was reading or drawn him on to talk about some incident of the day. It is hard for the apprentice, he (or she) has nothing as yet to show for his efforts and is desperately afraid that his elders may not take him seriously and in his anxiety makes them nervous as well. As it was, the beauty of Gide's spoken French reduced me to silence (little else did!), he gave me a signed copy of *Le Voyage d'Urien,* glanced at Marc for rescue and left. The meeting could have come directly out of *Paludes* but that, at the time, was no consolation.

I was a disappointment again to my mother in Paris. The irony of the situation was that she fitted into "the bunch" immediately and they all liked her. "Bob would take you out every evening," she said wistfully, "but he says you won't go out at night." McAlmon got on with her happily and easily and they became great friends. He took her to see Brancusi. She did not pretend to understand modern art but she loved the sculptor's birds. He could see to the core of people and knew that it was a genuine admiration. He began to talk to us one afternoon about a city where all the girls were beautiful and the young men wise. It was pure William Morris, as if that writer had come back to tell us a new tale about a land beyond the seas. Brancusi ran his fingers over a block of stone as powerful as his head, and continued, "In Kensington Gardens each branch had its own form and it was golden . . . golden . . . there will never be another summer like it." I realized to my astonishment that he was talking about 1914. It had been his most profound experience as a young man and I, not a mile away, had been too unhappy then to notice whether the days were sunny or wet.

About this moment I committed an unforgivable crime. Gradually and then completely, I refused all alcohol. I had been offered wine and water in the French fashion ever since my childhood so drinking had no glamour for me. I said openly that I wanted to leave a sensation or two for my old age but I had the sense to keep the main reason to myself. It was Mallarmé. Drinks and *la poésie pure* did not mix. I am not bigoted, I should fight prohibition as firmly as a drinker, I take wine occasionally in the South if I am uncertain of the water but I have never regretted my early decision although I once saw it lose me a job I particularly wanted and who knows, of course, what I shall do when I am really old? Yet Fate had me in its keeping because the Quarter was not Queenwood but a postwar world where many lived by their wits. There were many dangers that I did not then fully understand and many of my companions, young, desolate and unsure of themselves, were lost. All the same, if any system of ethics or religion has a meaning, we are here to learn and not to walk smugly through life. It is only after we have passed through some of our particular temptations that compassion, the greatest gift of all, is sometimes within our reach.

It has been the custom throughout the ages to encourage an apprentice to leave home for a time as he is coming to maturity. It avoids much conflict with the older generation. The exiles in Paris were there for the same reason. They were throwing off the yoke, not of their country but of the small towns where they had grown up. I did not want to live in England because I knew I shocked my family with my "advanced" ideas, yet I had been abroad so much that the Continental atmosphere was completely familiar to me and it never occurred to me that I was anything but English. It was different for the Americans; the scenes, the speech, the way of life, were completely new. They could write, paint, love and be gay with no recriminations from their elders and whatever they may have said afterwards, most of them were completely happy.

There was one visitor who denounced the States in stronger terms than his fellows. This was William Carlos Williams and his apparent hatred of his native land startled even us. He was not particularly popular but we tried to help him, this was our code, as he went around making inquiries about what he would have to do before he could practice as a doctor in France.

He repaid this help in his *Autobiography* by making a number of inaccurate and derogatory statements about myself and my friends. We invited him in friendship, he did not need to accept our hospitality. He spoke of Adrienne Monnier, who was as near a saint as anyone whom I have known, in appalling terms, and he apparently hated the lot of us. I wished to bring a legal action against him. My lawyers argued that this would only attract publicity to the book. I have always regretted taking their advice. All the survivors from the Quarter should have joined together to refute his charges in open court. There is the danger otherwise that future historians of the period may believe them after we are dead. I can forgive many things but not the person who turns on the people from whom he has both asked and accepted help.

I remember particularly one June evening. We were sitting at the Rotonde and I was thinking about Thessaly. I had never been in that part of Greece but I thought that it must be like the wild hills that rose beyond Corinth covered with speckled shrubs. Sheep flowers, the captain of the boat had called them or was it sleep? Tristan Tzara was sitting at the next table and complained that I was scowling at him. It was unintentional, my thoughts were far away.

"Here's home." Somebody waved, it was a general greeting that included not only ourselves but everybody else in the café. Half a dozen boys tumbled out of a taxi, all in a uniform of heavy white sweaters with polo collars. "See who's around and bring them up," the leader shouted, smiling his famous-in-the-Quarter smile. The biggest, fattest young man dropped into a chair, I wondered that it did not break under his weight, and banged the table with the flat of his arm. "Paper, *garçon,* bring me paper," he roared in his strongly accented foreign English, "I have to write to Oslo. At once." A neighbor translated the order into equally peculiar French. "He's a nice fellow," somebody explained to McAlmon, "but his cash has gone and he thinks an aunt at home may help him out." I gazed round me dismally and wondered why at least I was not in Switzerland.

"If I have been introduced, I do not remember you," a languid glove touched my arm and I wanted to answer, "Don't you know that gloves aren't languid any more?" It was an Englishwoman in a long, gray skirt that was already trailing in a beer puddle under the table. A gray scarf that matched the meditative sky was draped over her shoulders. *"Ah, comme elles sont belles,"* the dark-haired French girl who was looking for a partner for the evening pleaded too obviously with Oslo for carnations. A smudge of charcoal-colored fringe fell over her made-up eyelashes. I could bear this, I thought, if I could draw, if I could rough out this scene in pencil nothing would matter.

"So you have been in Greece?" The gloved woman turned to me, "Is it really true that an asphodel is an anemone?"

"Oh, no! It is a tall plant, bushy and grows on hills. You can recognize it easily from the columns."

"But the Parthenon surely was a disappointment?"

"I have never seen anything so beautiful."

"Curious! One hears such conflicting accounts. I was reading such an interesting article the other day, by that new Frenchman, you know, in that *new* magazine. He, too, seemed to think it was actually quite lovely." She stared vaguely across the street towards the opposite houses and said to one of the boys who had just arrived, "Tell me, darling, is it a particularly warm night? Hang my wrap for me over this chair."

That settles it, I thought, I do not like a woman who calls a stranger "darling." I could not leave, the tables had spread to the very edge of the curb, there was a figure in black and white stripes crossing the dusty street between a design of elbows, wine glasses and discursive heads, she only needed a camera to duplicate a famous advertisement and somewhere a girl's voice rose plaintively, "Not dinner surely? We never went to bed."

"It's eight o'clock." The leader of the group stood up and stretched himself. He looked exactly like a woolly sheep on the Zoo's scenic mountain. Taxis stopped more frequently, people began to drift away, the sky had turned the rose of a withered flower on some woman's shoulder. "Come on! Let's move!" Everybody but Tzara obediently got up. I was wriggling away when McAlmon caught my arm. "No, this evening you are going to come with us, it's time you went the rounds."

I think we started at the famous Jockey but where we went afterwards I do not know. Figures moved through the smoke in the corduroys that they were wearing that year, in fisherman's jerseys or incongruous taffeta. The lights and the drinks were the same colors, the door opened continually to admit more people, there were shouted, excited greetings. "It plain gets on my nerves," a girl grumbled in plump, white brocade as she passed our table, "everything's happened and he still says I'm a little girl."

"What the hell, if I send them a picture and they know I'm his friend, they'll only slap it back at me," the young painter next us drew angry, puzzled lines all over the tablecloth. "You can say what you like, the Dadaists know where they are going."

"Which is more than you do."

"Will anybody lend me fifty francs?" The Norwegian boy stared round hopefully but none of us answered him.

A girl looking like a stiff golden peony in her taffeta bent over the table and patted my arm. "Too bad you won't drink," she murmured.

"I don't want my perceptions blurred," I protested.

"That's where you're wrong, baby," a stranger shouted, "it would clear them."

"Will anybody lend me fifty francs?" The scarves, blond hair and elongated necks differed from the wallpaper only by being perpetually in motion.

"With your figure, I shouldn't think there would be any difficulty about the economic situation."

Men were strange, I reflected, neither the girl nor her body seemed particularly attractive.

"Will anybody lend me *twenty* francs?" Oslo was getting desperate.

The door opened slowly again, the newcomers were lingering on the pavement. "It's Milly!" Almost everyone got up. A matron stepped majestically into the room in a rather shabby black dress. Only the lemon-colored hair distinguished her from any housewife shopping at the market. People began to talk again but respectfully, in lower tones. "It's Milly!" As if they could not believe their luck, the young men in white pullovers persuaded Milly to take an empty seat at their table. She was a mother come to bring her blessing to some sinister, backyard game. " 'Allo, boys!" she had hardly any accent, "I can't stay, really I can't, I see the Île is in." That meant checks had arrived.

The boys started to yell. They were going to make history, they were not going home as long as they could stand or till they had been locked up. Everything they uttered was a picturesque exaggeration because Milly was their license to break all bounds. She had nothing, she explained, but nothing, not even a franc. She turned her worn but expensive handbag upside down but she could get her children (as they muttered when she was not there) whatever it was they wanted. Her boys must not give her a sou, no, not even a drink, well, perhaps just one double brandy, but she couldn't stop, a party was waiting for her, "their first night in Paris," the words came out like a brutal caress. She looked slowly round the room and I felt her small, rather piglike eyes staring at me for a moment, then she said something to one of my companions but he shook his head. No, really not another cognac, she meant it, her other boys were waiting outside and with three quarters of the males following behind her, she left as magnificently as she had arrived.

"She thought you might be lonely," McAlmon said.

"Dear me," the words slipped out of my mouth, "I had no idea these night places were so sentimental."

"Ah," the girl in the peony dress looked at me sharply again, "you do not give yourself easily."

The mood had broken, more and more followed Milly, a girl's head, dark and beautiful, rolled across the painter's shoulder, the strap of her dress had slipped and another boy laughed. "She's had more than she can carry," he said.

"What the hell! We all like her, let her alone."

At that moment, she was the embodiment of the Quarter's code. Be drunk, be reckless, stick together with the bunch. Beyond the figures, almost a medallion, the green face of the proprietor watched the scene with dispassionate calm. The more his clients drank, the louder they shouted, the less they would count their change. It was a good evening as far as he was concerned.

"It's the war," an older man remarked, he was one of the few who were sober. "They have to forget."

"They are exploiting tragedy," I answered hotly, "and it's horrible," but he shrugged his shoulders and did not reply.

"Let's go!" The few men were wondering what they were missing by not being at Milly's party.

"No, not Montmartre, I won't go there, they robbed me of fifty francs."

"Time to move." There was a general paying of bills and I heard as a couple passed me, "He stole a gingerbread lion at a fair."

In twos and threes we moved toward the door. I glanced back at the overturned glasses, at the girl propped up against the wall as if she were a sack and at rapacious fingers slipping notes into apron pockets. We have not struggled all the years for this, I thought, and in a spasm of quite violent revulsion I was sick on the pavement.

The wretches that I had condemned so harshly rushed to me. I must come back and have some brandy on the house, I was not to worry, the doorman assured me, it happened to everyone and I realized that they thought that it was the first time that I had got drunk. I dared not confess that I had had only a glass of mineral water, at such a moment it was far less humiliating to be thought drunk than shocked.

I soon got tough but I rarely went out with McAlmon at night because I found the places that he visited intolerably dull. I remember only one other occasion. It was at some bar and as I looked round the faces seemed to change into masks, most of them staring at me with hatred. The owner of the place came up to me. He had noticed that I did not drink but I had come surely to amuse myself? He had a friend, that young man standing in the corner, should he introduce me? I shook my head. Ah, I preferred a girl? No! Then, he lowered his voice and whispered the words, perhaps I would prefer some hashish. I refused again and he turned and said something to McAlmon. "He thinks you must be very vicious," Bob whispered, a few minutes later, with glee.

The offer of these things did not perturb me. I knew that they were commonplace in that particular *boîte*. Besides, the fellow was right, I had my vices. I longed for danger, to sail around the Horn and to explore the inmost recesses of the human mind. Nobody needed to consider me virtuous. If I had been able to draw, this was the environment that I should have chosen, with the greed, the cruelty and the piteousness of people swaying underneath my eyes.

My Paris episode ended in London but it was the same Montparnasse group that was present. They still continued to rail at houses, to praise the freedom of the bars (yet they all wanted shelter) and to drink. "There's nobody in this town, it gets on my nerves, hell, how can you stand it?" somebody said reproachfully, the whiskey went round again and the make-up ran in smudges down the women's faces. Suddenly I realized to my horror that it was a vicarage garden party in reverse. These rebels were no more free from the conventions that they had fastened upon themselves than a group of old ladies gossiping over their knitting. I had to get clear of it at once. Just then I heard a sleepy murmur as one guest after the other collapsed full length upon the carpet. "Bryher means to be kind but don't let her sit next me. She is a bore . . . a bore . . . a bore . . ." It was like the buzzing of many flies. I looked smugly at the scene, loosened some collars, placed aspirin and glasses of water at strategic points and then withdrew, leaving them to their headaches and nightmares.

Somebody should have smacked me.

 *Sixteen*

He thought that I was Harré. The Harré from *They Went* who had grown up and wanted to get in touch with him again. In those days I was near enough that imp by temperament for the mistake to be a natural one. It was the autumn of 1923 and H. D., her mother, and myself were visiting Florence. I had admired *South Wind* but *They Went* might have been written for me. I loved it, laughed at it, and immediately wrote to Norman Douglas.

What did I say? I know that there was some joke (but why?) about riding up to meet him on an elephant wreathed with marigolds. Yes, it must have been quite a Harré-like note. Douglas suggested that we meet at a café and I was tempted to keep the appointment but it did not seem quite fair. I wrote most sorrowfully to disillusion him, saying that I was condemned to petticoats instead of deerskin breeches but that if he could bear the disappointment, we expected him to lunch.

He came. Cautiously. Saying that he had an early appointment but he stayed quite late and enchanted us all. Was he not the last of the English milords whose coaches had spread a legend across Europe? He was then fifty and at the height still of his powers.

It was time that I was cuffed into shape and I think that only Douglas, of all the people that I have known, could have done it. He brought me up, like a puppy, by hand. His conversation was free, he was both erudite and adventurous, he encouraged me to have a will of my own but as far as external circumstances went, unlike "the bunch" he was stricter with me than my own strict family.

"Did I hear that you walked down the Via Tornabuoni alone at six o'clock yesterday?" he asked me at one of the first of our meetings.

"Why, yes, Miss James asked me out to tea." She was an elderly lady who was staying at our hotel. "Did you think I might get lost? I know the way now perfectly."

"*Never* do it again." Douglas looked at me severely as if I had broken his favorite snuffbox. "No lady goes out alone in Florence after four o'clock. What were you doing in a tearoom anyhow? Poisonous places, full of envy and gossip. And very bad for the liver. If you ever go again, take a cab and remember it must be a closed one, otherwise I shall have to leave whatever I am doing and escort you back myself."

If anybody else had suggested that I needed to be guarded I should have slapped them but, as with Gertrude Stein, there was no arguing with Douglas; you obeyed him reasonably or he did not see you again. He discussed the cost of girls on equal terms, "Prices have gone up," he said, shaking his head, "in 1905 it was a hundred lire. Ah well, I've had eleven hundred virgins in my time but that's all over. Very happy they were too. I gave the lire to the father, a turquoise bracelet to the girl and most of them made excellent marriages. Remember, the secret is, never deal with the girl directly but always with her family. But a virgin isn't much use to you," he glanced at my skirt, "never mind, you'll get over it, have a pinch of snuff." At that point I usually retired amid a gale of sneezes into my handkerchief. It was cool, impersonal and essentially Roman.

We met for lunch almost every day and then wandered about Florence. It must not be forgotten that I had spent the most impressionable moments of my childhood in the South. Our walks, I see now, were a form of primitive analysis because I was reliving scenes that had puzzled me. Douglas taught and explained, he never once said, "You are too young to understand." Instead he gave me

Isabelle Eberhardt to read and English translations of Athenaeus and Theophrastus. The pale blue sky brought out the red of the tiles more than the summer sun because it was easier to look at them, an olive grower or an old woman rushed out of an alley with shouts of welcome and begged the *signore* to sit down over a glass of wine to help them with some problem, I tasted my first wild boar and the cheese that was only sold in the markets during a special week in autumn, and among these throngs Douglas took my education sternly in hand. "Remember, if you are abroad you must know everybody or nobody." It was an invaluable rule when I started to work.

There were always unexpected meetings, however. To my astonishment Douglas once shouted out a greeting in Welsh to an elderly priest. It appeared that the man had belonged to some missionary order and had spent his life in a mining town in Wales. We lunched sometimes next to a retired diplomat who sat in his corner looking lonely and bored until after a few jokes he was chatting to Douglas in French as if they were two young men *en poste*. And then there were the "crocodiles" as we called the dark-haired, mischievous urchins with Renaissance names who ran errands and ate, as reward, plates of pasta like miniature mountains.

Douglas was always strict with me but he was a born teacher. One day he asked me to read him a letter as he had left his glasses in an overcoat pocket. I got tied up with a word. "What's that? No! It can't be shirt in that context," he snatched the paper away and looked at me reprovingly. "Don't you know what the word means?" I shook my head woefully, feeling ashamed because I prided myself on knowing English. He then explained some Anglo-Saxon monosyllables accurately and precisely as if I were learning cuneiform and added, "Every lady must thoroughly understand what they mean but no lady ever uses them."

There was more insistence upon being a lady than I liked but at least I had the sense to know that I was being properly trained.

He was immensely kind. He discovered that I liked marrow bones so once a week after his early morning cup of tea and before he settled to his own work, he went over to the market, prowled along the stalls until he found the bone that he wanted, bargained for it and then took it to the restaurant where we were to meet some four hours later. "Have nothing in front of it, my dear, eat it alone, that is the way to get the flavor," he would say with a smile, watching me anxiously all the same, to see that I ate it seriously and with due appreciation. Afterwards he would tell me stories, mostly about his own youth. Wonderful as his books are, the prose is sober, it lacks the glorious exuberance of his conversations. I never ate many marrow bones afterwards; let them be a memory of the days that will never come again and of his tales.

We may have foreknowledge of the curves that govern each generation but we do not know what will affect our particular destiny. The day that Douglas invited us to watch the fascist parade to commemorate the march on Rome did not seem of particular importance to me. Actually it was to have far-reaching effects.

Douglas was living temporarily at the top of the Hotel Nardini at the time, waiting until an apartment should be empty. It was a warm, sunny November afternoon and we stood on the balcony, together with other of his friends, looking down at the crowded square. Florence is essentially medieval and the masses were cheering just as their ancestors had acclaimed first one duke and then another, whoever happened to be victorious, without a thought of the deeper issues involved. I was not interested in Italian politics, it was not long since we had emerged from five years of war and if I had a thought in my head at that moment it was gratitude that I had not been trapped unsuspectingly among the people on the pavement. The yells increased, a band marched into view, then rank upon rank of Blackshirts followed it across the Piazza, raising their hands at one point in a salute.

An Englishman was standing next to me. He was writing an economic report about Italy for the London *Times* but unhappily I cannot remember his name. He looked down gravely at the cheering populace and seemed to be counting each black shirt. Then he turned to me and said, almost with a pause between each word, "Watch what is happening. *This is the beginning of the next war.* If these fellows keep control, Europe will be struggling within fifteen years, not for victory but for her very existence."

It was 1923. The war came in 1939. He was one year out. (It is often easy to forecast events, what is difficult is to predict the time.)

The words shook my historical instinct out of its hibernation and I asked him why he was so pessimistic? He based his forecast upon the risks inherent in a nation's consumption of productive capital. "After initiative has been destroyed and there is no scapegoat left to plunder, what can the fascists do if they want to keep power but go to war?"

I never met the man again but I think of him now as a messenger from Olympus. The first effect of his warning was to call me back to contemporary history and this was followed during the thirties by a growing awareness of danger so that I was able to take certain steps that may have helped to save a few lives. If this stranger, however, had not spoken to me clearly, I might have drifted with the main stream until it was too late for useful action.

Douglas did not like the fascists either, less because of the future, "Politics are no concern of scholars, my dear," than because they had dismissed a friend of his, an elderly doctor who had spent twenty years fighting the malaria that, as Douglas said and he was most emphatic about the matter, had caused the decay of ancient Greece. This doctor had refused to join the Party, saying that he had more important things to do than to attend meetings. He was replaced by a newly qualified young man who had been a Blackshirt from the beginning and was immediately decorated for his predecessor's work. The old doctor must have thought, we decided, that mosquitoes were gentler than man.

A little while afterwards I read that Mussolini had forbidden women to read history at the universities. It was another sign that the unknown Englishman had been right.

First impressions are usually the most profound. If it had not been for the march on Rome, the Nazis might never have come to power. They took the fascist ideas and developed them with Teutonic ruthlessness. A number of English supported the Blackshirts eagerly because the beggars disappeared and the trains ran on time. Such things, my masters, if you would look beneath the surface, are merely a temporary opiate. They dissemble the barbarian craving for cultural destruction and universal conquest.

Douglas was installed in his own apartment on our next visit to Florence in 1924 and it is the long room facing the Arno, with the shelves full of books and the morning sun falling on his amber Indian hangings that I associate with most of our talks. There was usually a map as well, lying like a scroll on the table and kept flat by a piece of colored marble, "dug up near Naples, my dear." He once gave me its fellow. By now he was N. D. and I was Br, said always with a little growl. I sat there so often, looking at the smudged brown stones under the green arches of the bridges while he carried on a conversation that he had begun with his notebook several hours previously over an early cup of tea, "the only time I ever drink the stuff and it must be pure Darjeeling." There was no lack of variety in the conversation, he ranged from the lizards to be found in southern Europe, he was one of the few people whom I have known who could handle snakes and other reptiles with impunity, to the classic authors or even his books. "I was writing about cold hands this morning," he began one day, "the cold hands of an Alpine salamander. Wonderful little claws but ice cold, like a Hindu's hands. If you want mystery you must go to India, the men and women are perambulating flowers."

"I would rather go to Greece again, we might in the spring."

"This restless modern spirit! It will never get you anywhere. Still, who would work unless they had to?" He regarded the notebook somberly. "Watch the Arno. It is never the same. The color changes and the volume alters. Chrysoprase and celandine, what's that other word for lemon yellow? Find a new word for the Arno every morning and settle sensibly in Florence."

Celandine was thin, chrysoprase to my ears had a thick, milky sound although I knew that it was a hard green stone. Both were excellent words but I could only shake my head. I was a born wanderer and the globe called for exploration.

"Greece?" Douglas looked at me very seriously, he hated the country in spite of his love for the classics. "Do be careful what you eat. I still think powdered rhubarb is the most efficacious and there's no harm in taking a bottle of castor oil along as well, even if it is old-fashioned."

He was right, of course. The more beautiful the island at that time, the worse the sanitation.

"You had better come to Calabria with me instead. You can walk, can't you, and eat cheese? Good. You'll only need a rucksack. I will get you some clothes, suitable for a goatherd, and teach you how to move. It's a girl's knees, as a rule, that give her away. Then I'll show you what made the Greeks write their poetry. Yes, you must come with me to Calabria."

If I had had a grain more courage, I should have accepted the offer. I still wonder if I might have got away with it. With N. D. as guide, it could have been possible. I was so afraid of losing my nerve in the hills and disgracing him that my answer was inevitably "perhaps."

"Or India. We could go to India."

"When I wrote you first, I said that I ought to arrive here on an elephant."

"An elephant! That would be something. I should have to hang the veranda with catmint. Do you suppose the beast would react to it the way cats do? Ha!" He shook with laughter. "I should like to watch it shake down all the rickety shutters in this street. And now, how about a pinch of snuff? They say the Scots introduced it into England."

"A virgin! A virgin!" Another roar of laughter. "Delicious, my dear, and so refreshing, just persevere. What were we talking about before? The classics, yes, you must read Pliny. Much of what he wrote is lost and it is writing I regret but already the Romans had him, they were moralists, you know, whereas Athenaeus was non-moral, he was interested in life purely as it appeared to him."

"But you belong to ancient Rome," I ventured, stifling a second sneeze, I had seen a marble head in a small museum, some general or one of the later emperors, that might have been a portrait of him.

"Oh, at present I am sick of everything Italian."

He wasn't; actually Italy and the Vorarlberg were the only places where he was really at home but I think that Nepenthe called him at that moment. He talked of India and once I lingered too long and it was almost the forbidden hour of dusk when I started to walk back along the Arno. I looked up and there was a mirage in the sky. A Persian city was floating above the surface of the river. The courtyards and minarets were softer than Cairo, gray rather than white, but it drifted, almost touching the hills, for several moments before it disappeared. I thought as I watched it that the centuries were merely the colors that a painter changed at his will and yet time was not as continuous as it sometimes seemed; there would be subtle differences if Douglas ever revisited India and these were, and were not, the streets that I had first seen when I was eight.

People have written and spoken so much about Norman Douglas that it is strange to think that there may be one mystery left that is still unexplained. We used to go for long walks into the countryside and as I have written, we talked mostly about the classics. The angle of a window or the light catching a shutter in a once fine but decaying palace must have stirred some memory in his mind. He began to tell me about an Italian girl whom he had met and intended to marry. "I was engaged to her, my dear, for several years." He spoke of her with the greatest respect in terms that he reserved otherwise only for his sister. There must have been a strong intellectual bond between them. They had met every day, always with a chaperone, "in an icy room, they were as poor as church mice" but her brothers had disapproved of the match and eventually they had parted. She had died shortly afterwards.

What quality did the Florentine girl possess that had held Douglas to those daily meetings for so long? No mutual friends seem ever to have heard the story but he spoke of her so often that I am sure that she must have existed. There was no reason for him to have invented the tale. He spoke freely enough about the girls of his youth, being discovered, and "I had to hop it, my dear, that very evening." I should have been more curious, I suppose, but I liked simply listening to his talk as we wandered among the olive groves and gardens. I have since thought that she might have reminded him unconsciously of his sister. I do not think that he ever told me her name.

I was always ready to experiment with food but I drank no wine. Apart from a joke or two, Douglas never pressed me to take it, "You puzzle me, Br, you say you belong to the North but you have the Southerner's temperance." There was, however, the incident of the Toscana. I did not care for cigarettes, I wanted to have my hands free but I had always liked the smell of a cigar and felt it would be pleasant to smoke one after work was finished. Douglas used to bring me small Dutch ones but he insisted that they were things that he would not give to a boy, what I needed was a Toscana. "Blow your head off, my dear, but you'll get to like it."

One day I felt I must be courageous and tried: I spent a miserable afternoon. It was hard to know whether risking a Toscana or its predictable sequel delighted him more. "Saucy!" he said and brought me a leather case to take two of the little cigars that he despised. I could not smoke them in public so eventually gave them up.

We left soon afterwards for Egypt. It was an expedition that brought much inspiration to Hilda and that she and her mother always remembered but I seemed to have absorbed so much there as a child that, as I have written previously, it was pleasantly familiar but remained completely external. It was March by the time that we landed at Naples again and we went across for a few days to Capri. This was a very different place from the resort that it has now become, almost solitary in parts with rocks rising, high above the sea, that were covered with wild asphodel.

I found a letter from Douglas waiting for me. He was about to return to Capri for the first time since the war. I was at the harbor to meet him when the steamer arrived and let nobody tell me that he was not loved there. The news of his arrival spread from mouth to mouth. I have never seen a political leader enjoy so great a triumph. Men offered him wine, women with babies in their arms rushed up so that he might touch them, the children brought him flowers. I slipped away as he walked slowly through a crowd of several hundred people, shouting jokes in ribald Italian, kissing equally the small boys and girls and patting the babies as if they were kittens. The *signore* had deigned to return to his kingdom and I am sure that they believed that the crops would be abundant and the cisterns full of water as a result.

I left him to his Caprese but next day I got a note inviting me to dinner. I had often had lunch with him but he had always said firmly that his evenings were his own. Seven o'clock came and I waited in the hotel lounge. He was always punctual to the minute and as time passed and there was no sign of him, I wondered if I had mistaken the day. I looked at the date in his beautiful handwriting and finally sent a message to his room asking if there had been a mistake.

He tottered down, looked at me with considerable vagueness and asked, "What time is it?" I should have been warned.

I still lacked experience and produced his note. He slapped me on the shoulder, another action that surprised me as we seldom even shook hands, and growled, "Kept you waiting, did I? Never mind. I'll take you now to a brigand's den where there's been a dozen murders. But Carmelita (was it Carmelita?) is there, my dear, she's the best cook on the island and she was the prettiest girl too, thirty years ago. She still dances the tarantella better than anyone else."

I ought to have run away but all this was fascinating and we set off with Douglas leaning heavily on a stick or sometimes on my shoulder. "Most of these people don't know how to cook. If you want to eat, you should have stopped in Florence. They're a crowd of cutthroats," he flung back his head and pointed at his neck alarmingly, "every inch of the island has been steeped in blood several times over. Proud, you know. We're near Africa. But Carmelita will do us all right."

I was puzzled why we never kept a straight line and why the stairs should be so difficult but eventually after more jokes and greetings we got to a table where an enormous lobster was eventually set down in front of him.

It was *South Wind* again, the bits that he had kept perhaps for a sequel, he began by describing some special lizards that he had found and from them he went on to the human inhabitants, a Capri of straw hats, long skirts and uninhibited passions that had ended even for him soon after 1900. I listened entranced until I noticed with horror that he was beginning to chew the lobster, shell and all. "Tough, my dear, how wise you were to stick to the omelette." Finally Carmelita came to the rescue and I realized that he was wildly, gloriously drunk.

It was a warm evening, I could see the almond flowers even in the darkness and here and there deep gold where a patch of wall-flowers grew out of some stones. All I wanted was to get home but I did not know the way. I had no confidence that Douglas was even leading me in the right direction but I need not have worried. We stumbled along terraces, climbed some steps and went down others until, to my relief, I saw the hotel. It was still early, tourists were strolling up and down, the sounds changed from Italian to English, I tried to slip away but he clung to my arm. "Let's make a night of it, come up Monte Solaro with me." I hoped my three compatriots had not heard him, they seemed to be schoolteachers who were walking briskly without loitering down the path, shocked I was sure to feel nature was so wanton: a moon had now risen above the over-heavy fruit blossom. "Don't be so damned careful, it's a stiff climb but you're young. We'll wait there for the sunrise."

"Another day," I murmured, five steps more and I should be safe.

"Another day! What is the matter with you this evening? How do you know you will live to see it? You may be stabbed or fall off a cliff."

I did not answer. I guided Douglas as gently as I could towards the safety of his room. It was too late. At that very instant he saw the three schoolmistresses. He broke away from my grasp, pranced towards them, taking off his hat, and said courteously but in a voice that could have been heard on the other side of the Piazza, "Well, my dears, and whom are you tucking in with tonight?"

The years passed and it was natural that we should grow, not less friendly, but more distant from each other. Once I had given up Harré's woad and deerskins (though never Harré's heart), our day-to-day companionship was over because I became a part of that turbulent Western world he so disliked. We wrote each other, exchanged books, and it was through H. D. and myself that he met Kenneth Macpherson, the friend who cared for him so wonderfully throughout his old age.

Our last meeting was in London in 1946. It was cold and sad, there was neither sunshine nor wine and he babbled about Italy as if he were in a fever. Still, a few months later he was able to return to Capri and Kenneth's devoted care for six more years.

A tradition has gone with him, his death marked the end of one form of culture. His books will survive but nothing that I can write will make you feel the forces of his love for the visible world. Some power would rise in him until, standing beside him, I have actually seen some bent, old woman whom he had known in his youth turn for a moment into a beautiful and happy girl. It is cold in the places that knew him. I listen for the click of the silver box and the familiar roar, "How about it, Br? Have a pinch of snuff." It has taken me thirty years to realize how much I owe to a chance word flung at me over his shoulder as I struggled behind him up some steep and rocky path. I was only one of hundreds among his friends. What can words do but make him seem a shade? The legend will endure and not all of it will be true but Fate saw that it was correctly knotted, there were Scots and Austrians as well as his Italians with him when he died. Something of what I have become is due to him, especially his advice. Even now I seem to hear him saying at difficult moments, as he said so often with his head almost touching the amber gold curtains in front of the windows of his Arno room, "Never be uninterested, Br, that is what is ruining the race."

Seventeen

"When I want to remember England, I think of your books." This was, I believe, the beginning of the first letter that I wrote to Dorothy Richardson. I had learned in Paris that writers sometimes responded if apprentices wrote to them and her prose had been a part of my life for years. I knew the people in her pages, the girls in *Pointed Roofs* were like my companions at Queenwood, I was passionately interested in the Miss Pernes of this world, I had met families like the Corries and the Orlys, whereas the characters in the novels of Virginia Woolf or Aldous Huxley, the two idols of the time, were in general unknown to me, or persons whom I should have disliked. It was Miriam's determination to win independence at all costs that had gone straight to my heart when I had first read *Backwater* and that I feel as strongly today, almost forty-five years afterwards. She and Colette have been among the few writers whom I have read with equal pleasure from youth to age. I added various rumors that I had heard about her to the letter: that she never went out at night, that she often opened a window to stare at the street outside, that a famous male novelist wrote the stories under her name. (All proved untrue.) I composed my page as carefully as if it were the first chapter of a novel and received, as reward, an invitation to tea. I think it must have been the summer of 1923 because she spent the winters in Cornwall.

Dorothy and her husband, the artist Alan Odle, were then living in a small apartment in St. John's Wood. It was a narrow, drowsy, still almost Victorian street where only the scarlet of a pillar box broke the gray of the pavement and the sky. Miriam (and she was Miriam) was just as I had expected to find her, with a stiff blouse and a mass of gold hair piled on the top of her head. It seemed inevitable that we should meet. A big table, sinking under the weight of Alan's books and drawings, almost filled the room (I was told later that it had once cracked in two), and he sat behind it, smoking and smiling, always ready to rescue Dorothy or turn the conversation if it bothered her, and otherwise watching visitors or the way the light fell on a door, with his brown, draftsman's eyes. A fireplace almost filled the wall behind Dorothy's chair. They had pinned a row of postcards along its top, mostly of gargoyles from Notre Dame, and faded as these had become through smoke and fog, they were so essential a part of the decoration that I have never forgotten them.

I felt no surprise. I wondered only if people who perceived things in a certain way met at a given moment those of a like experience. It was not that we agreed about many matters, I was a generation younger and differently sensitive to my age, but I felt an immense respect for the way that she had fought literally for our liberty. "Nobody has written as you have about London," I began, remembering how her characters had been my friends when I had gone on dreary errands during the war.

Dorothy stopped that conversation at once. "So you have been in New York? I have relatives in America, did you like it there?"

"Yes, but, oddly enough, it seemed more old-fashioned than here."

"And are there some opportunities for seclusion?"

Seclusion was a point about which I did not agree with Miriam. I had been alone for seven years and I needed to be with people. "It's a little more difficult than in London but it's possible."

"Perhaps that is why the young Americans whom I meet seem so anchorless. As if no country nor thought could claim them. Restless, without hold of earth."

That is why I like them, I longed to say, they are not strangled with traditions; but I knew my place, it was not for an apprentice to argue with his master and I wanted to know more about Dorothy herself. "When is your next book coming out?" I asked.

"There are so many distractions," Dorothy shrugged her shoulders, "the cooking, shopping, letters. . . ."

The characteristic sentence plunged me at once into that attic in Tansley Street that she had described so often. The stranger whom she had invited, not from curiosity but kindness, her hope that a postcard or a note might announce the postponement of the visit and leave her to her solitude with Alan, the certainty that one side of her was watching me as a representative of the young while the other was far away with her own thoughts, made me feel that I was in the book myself however much I might disagree with some of its philosophy. "You must hurry your publishers," I urged, "we are waiting so impatiently," and she laughed, with indulgence but also, I think, some pleasure.

We were silent for a time. Only a rudimentary instinct that, if it were prolonged too far, departure would be necessary, impelled any of us to break it. I tried to tell her what *Backwater* had meant to me during the darkest days of the war, "I could grow again, I could grow . . ." and she told me the story of how her first book had been written. I often think of it now when writers complain to me about lack of security and time.

Dorothy had been loaned a cottage in Cornwall and had lived there on ten shillings a week while she wrote *Pointed Roofs*. The purchasing power of ten shillings then was equivalent perhaps to three pounds today but it had to cover fuel, light, food and, as she particularly insisted, paper. She went without meals for two days to save the half crown that was necessary to post the manuscript to a publisher. She had hoped that it might help the mass of underpaid women workers whose life she had shared, she had no idea that she had invented "continuous association" and she was afraid that by being labeled as experimental she had driven away the audience she wanted. It was the deep drive under a bleak youth that had created the modern novel. I do not think that even in her old age she realized her achievement. The philosophical discussions in *Pilgrimage* seem old-fashioned, but never Miriam nor her characters. We meet them in shops, trains and offices and they still use the same phrases. There is no better English social history of the years between 1890 and 1914 than in her books. Perhaps for this reason she has often a higher reputation on the Continent, and strong links with the new French school and writers like Robbe-Grillet and Butor, than in her native land. I think that she will be rediscovered once we dare to look again at our immediate past. Meantime she is "a writer's writer" and I know of many artists who read through *Pilgrimage,* as I do, every few years.

Besides meeting Dorothy and Alan in London and later in Cornwall, I saw them, I think, on their last visit to Oberland. They spent a few days at Montreux one autumn on their journey to Château d'Oex and returned there on their way back in the spring. Dorothy delighted in being on the Continent so much that I was sad that she saw so little of it; a trip to Belgium as a child, her German schooldays, and half a dozen visits to Switzerland were all she ever had. Alan's health kept her from possible holidays in America and Italy. Like so many English, she was a different being abroad. She became the girl that Miriam had been at seventeen, full of vitality and ready for any experiences.

All the same, enough of the later Miriam remained to make her welcome disputations in the evening. She talked in her amazingly resonant voice while Alan and I flung in just enough opposition to make her develop her ideas. I do not know why I copied the following conversation in my notebook soon after it had happened. Perhaps I realized that after a few hours even a good memory is a poor carrier of actual words.

I went one evening to their room and was amused to find that they had transformed the polished wood and neat linen of a Swiss pension into a replica of their London den. The air was full of smoke, there were postcards on the chest of drawers and a pile of papers on almost every chair. "Would you care to glance over this?" Dorothy inquired. "It is Coué's latest book; by the way, what do you think of him?"

"He once lectured here," I ventured cautiously, knowing her distrust of psychology.

"And that finished you?"

"Hasn't that kind of thing been done before?" I did not question his sincerity but I was used to the deeper investigations of men like Havelock Ellis.

Dorothy's eyebrows lifted, literally. "Not *quite* the same, surely?"

"Oh yes, it is a rehash of the pre-Nancy hypnotists."

"Surely Coué has improved upon the old hypnotic method?"

"What I feel is" (I was fresh from the *Psychoanalytic Journal*) "autosuggestion is all right but it simply means a transference of symptoms and the trouble breaks out again afterwards."

"That is what Barbara says," Alan said solemnly in his corner; he was speaking of their friend, Barbara Low, who was one of the first of the English Freudians.

"Yes," Dorothy brushed aside our interruptions, "but what I feel Coué accomplishes is a control. He does not claim his method can cure, he claims only to establish controls. Then he leaves it to you. Of course his dear kind personality is what counts. As it always does. Not the scientific method but the humanity in him, as you used to get the humanity of the old-fashioned general practitioner."

"Do you know many of the London psychoanalysts?" I inquired.

"Only Barbara and one other doctor whose wife, a strong, forceful personality, dragged him into it."

Alan, ever watchful that Dorothy did not get overexcited, stirred in his corner, "What I feel is that the flesh gets between us and art. It is only when the physical health is weak that the brain is strong."

"Maybe now," I protested, "but not in the great creative ages. Look at the Greeks or even at the Renaissance."

"What was Socrates but a worn-out Paul Verlaine." Alan's surprising statement stunned even me to silence.

"And Aristotle." Dorothy peered at us through the cigarette smoke. "Tell me, who in this room knows the personality of Aristotle?"

"Aristotle?" Alan snatched up the challenge, "That funny little man. I know at least he was different enough from the ordinary Greeks of his time to be thoroughly hated."

"The Greeks were unaware," Dorothy continued, "they were rounded, unself-conscious."

"I grant you the sculptors," Alan lit another cigarette, "but that proves what I say. It is the mind that makes for us the body we desire. And the sculptors had to have a good physique to ply their trade. They had to have it. It is a healthy occupation."

"Yes, you repeat my words, we have the body we desire. We make it."

It was useless talking to them about even my slight knowledge of the Greek islands, I was silent, listened and watched.

"All the same," Alan continued, "most artists—look at the Renaissance!—have been tremendously healthy. I think the Greeks had a balance we have lost."

"I should choose rather the Chinese for an illustration. Their marvelous impassivity."

"Yes. A Chinaman would laugh if you cut off his hand. He would hold the stump up and look at it. Simply by the withdrawal of his vitality into other parts of his body. Not like a savage who laughs childishly, not being aware. He would be aware yet he would feel nothing."

"Yes. But my bag, have you seen it? I must have left it downstairs."

"Did you take it with you when you went to play the pe-ah-no?" Alan always pronounced the word with a strong stress on the *ah*, it must have been some private joke.

"Perhaps, or did I leave it downstairs?"

It was pure later Miriam, a disputation in which she only half believed, mingling suddenly into the everyday. We found the handbag under a pile of papers and discarded envelopes but by that time I could see a desire for solitude growing in Dorothy's eyes and knew that it was time to leave.

The great moment came later. They stopped in Paris for a week. I arrived there the day before they left and found them already adopted (as I never was) by Montparnasse. They told me eagerly about a classic "Quarter" fight that they had watched from behind their café table. They knew my friends and the phrases of the hour, and, to crown it all, Dorothy had bought a dress. I believe she kept the box in which it was packed for years. Paris to them was an Edwardian dream that my parents would have recognized. I have always been resentful that Dorothy's lack of success with her later books distracted her from her work. We have no record of this Paris visit nor of her days in Cornwall and both would have been valuable as literature and social history.

We corresponded and I saw them whenever I could on my brief visits to England. My later recollections belong to another portion of this autobiography but we were friends for over thirty years and one of the things that I miss most are her gay, provocative letters and the way she spoke the English language.

I met Freud through flying and not through any serious consideration of the soul!

H. D., Kenneth Macpherson and I happened to be in Venice together for a few days during May, 1927. I saw a flight to Vienna and back, advertised at a moderate price, and smelt adventure. Hilda could not be torn from a city that she had always loved, but Kenneth and I started with six other passengers from an airport on the sandy shore of the Lido. It was the only way, we agreed as we rose into the air, to see the shape of the lagoons and the outlines of the boats. We skimmed so close to the tops of rounded hills that I felt I could see the prints of goat hooves upon the tiny, winding paths. I was still not used to the landscapes of the air, the way the mountain pools turned into emerald solids or the fields into strips of multicolored brocade. It was beautiful, it was exciting, until suddenly, almost as in a legend, we flew into a thunderstorm. I had been up perhaps three times and Kenneth twice, we did not fully realize the danger. The pilot turned. He made a detour that lengthened the journey by almost an hour but we left the storm on one side. We could see the thunderclouds and the lightning flashing miles away as if it were one of the tempests that the eighteenth-century artists were fond of painting in the corner of their landscapes, alarming and yet detached. It remains one of the strangest experiences that I have ever had while flying. Nobody was sorry when we landed to refuel at Klagenfurt and were able to wander for a time in a field full of extraordinarily fragrant meadow flowers.

The excursion allowed us two full days in Vienna. It was almost ten years since the war had ended but the city had not recovered, the window frames needed painting, the buildings were unrepaired. People looked hungry and the streets were desolate. I did not realize then that to cut a great city off from its seaports was one of the greatest mistakes that the peacemakers had made. It had destroyed the balance of southeastern Europe, brought beggary to thousands and was an indirect but powerful cause of the rise of the Nazi state. I only felt embarrassed at the time at having to watch a stranger's misery. I returned to Vienna several times during the nineteen thirties but never felt at my ease there. I had plenty of Austrian friends but, unpopular though I know my choice is, it was the energy and challenge of northern Germany (and perhaps my ancestors) that drew me more than the melancholy South.

I had happened to write to Havelock Ellis about our proposed trip and he had sent me a letter of introduction to Freud, with whom he had corresponded for years, although they had never met. I sent it round by messenger to the Berggasse and we were invited to call the next afternoon. I discovered afterwards that his family rationed Freud to one visitor a day on account of his health but he was interested in hearing about his contemporary, Ellis, and we had been chosen, therefore, from a number of applicants.

We were taken into the famous room with the ancient statuettes and the chow. The dog approved of Kenneth, another element in our favor. Freud sat behind his desk, I recognized him from the photographs but what they and reports about him had lacked was his gaiety. He asked us first several questions about Ellis whose courage as an investigator he admired, but then an amazing life came into his eyes as he questioned us about flying: why had we chosen to come by air, what did it feel like, how high had the pilot taken us, what did a landscape look like from above? We told him about the storm and the strange impression that we had had of seeing lightning sideways and I knew that he wished that he had been with us himself.

Kenneth was able to give the Professor details about the machinery that I did not know. The excitement to me in those days was the absolute newness of what we saw in the patterns on the ground and in the changing colors of the clouds just beyond the wings. I could feel that Freud had grasped our enthusiasm. The sky was as interesting to him at that moment as the mind.

That first visit and one later occasion were the only times that I saw Freud as he really was, gay, kind and curious about everything. Otherwise I met him only with his family. They warned me so often to remember that he was an invalid that our meetings became purely artificial. There is a wide difference between the attitudes of the English and the Europeans towards genius. We do not expect to be invited but, if we are, assume that it will be on a basis of reasonable human give-and-take. Europe stresses the intellectual achievement to the exclusion of everything else. It was not an accident that Freud chose to explore the influence of family life upon development. The older I grow the more profoundly I am aware that the broad lines of my character were established before I was seven. It was simply a matter of contact, of a national attitude if you will, that made it possible for Havelock Ellis and me to talk and joke together, whereas with Freud, apart from the two occasions that I have mentioned, the conversation was confined to general observations. I saw enough, however, to know that Freud in himself was not what his admirers wanted him to be, a silent sage or hermit sitting on a rock and staring at the horizon. He reminded me rather of a doctor of the nineties, full of advice and kindness, who would have gone out in all weathers to help his patients and turned no one away from his door. He had his wish, nobody this last century has helped humanity so much.

Eighteen

In the autumn of 1927, I married Kenneth Macpherson. It was natural that he was passionately interested in films because his ancestors had been professional artists for six generations, his father was a painter and he had himself received a thorough training in art.

We lived at Territet and one day as we were walking beside the lake and Kenneth compared the ripples drifting across the water with an effect that should be tried on the screen, I remembered my Paris training of the early twenties and said, "If you are so interested, why don't you start a magazine?"

So *Close Up* was born on a capital of sixty pounds. We expected it to last three issues and had five hundred copies printed. It was an immediate success and when we ended after the collapse of the silent film, six years later, we had five thousand readers.

I had been born before the cinema age and the only film that I had seen in childhood, and that when I was already about thirteen, was one of an Antarctic expedition. I kept to the business side of the magazine as much as possible and attended to much of the correspondence, but I was pressed into service occasionally to review educational films. I saw the possibilities of the movies but I found the screen restricted my own imagination as a writer and since *Close Up* ceased I have been

perhaps to see one film a year. Yet it was a magnificent training because it taught me speed, not to hang about looking at my characters
in a novel but to get them moving and to try to fix a landscape in a
sentence as if it were a few feet of film.

It was the golden age of what I call "the art that died" because
sound ruined its development. I have written already that we had to
get away from the nineteenth century if we were to survive. The film
was new, it had no earlier associations and it offered occasionally, in
an episode or single shot, some framework for our dreams. We felt we
could state our convictions honorably in this twentieth-century form
of art and it appealed to the popular internationalism of those so few
years because "the silents" offered a single language across Europe.
Switzerland was a perfect place for our headquarters. It was possible
to see French, German, American and English films all in the same
week.

To our utter amazement, the first issue of *Close Up* sold out within
a month and it was enthusiastically reviewed. I wondered if we had
done anything wrong because I was used to the "little magazines" with
half the issues unsold and growing dusty in some corner. We made two
new friends, Robert Herring, a professional film critic of the *Manchester Guardian,* and Oswell Blakeston, a cameraman, with hilarious
stories of his adventures on British sets. Herring had just returned
from Germany and urged us to go to Berlin.

We set off from London in November. It was before the days of
flying and the easiest way was to take an Atlantic liner from Southampton to Hamburg. It cost then five pounds first class and was
much cheaper and pleasanter than the train. I enjoyed my brief taste
of salt air but was startled when I asked a sailor the name of a gray
rock emerging from the mist. He snarled "Helgoland" and turned his
back on me. At that time I felt that the leaders in Germany had been
responsible for the war, but not the people. I was to learn in 1933
that all politicians represent some form of national feeling and that a
citizen is responsible for their views and must share their guilt unless
he either protests or goes to another country.

We spent two days in Hamburg. I knew that my ancestors had left
the city for England about a century before but I had not then discovered that they had been millers at Hitzacker. My aunt had told me
grim stories about a cholera epidemic and how one of the women of

our family had died from it, "So you see, you must never drink un-boiled water abroad." Hamburg was unfamiliar after the places that I knew, my German showed no signs of coming back into my mind and when we went to the cinema and the screen filled suddenly with German soldiers, I felt like some agent charged to transmit a message that I did not understand to somebody I did not know. It was an odd, uneasy sensation that seemed to come out of the air because I do not remember having another such experience again.

We took the train to Berlin the following day, passing through an extraordinary landscape of black and white cows standing among pools of coral-colored leaves. The description sounds strange but there was no other word to describe the color and occasionally, to add a *surréaliste* touch, strips of blue bark hung from the trees. I had only been once before to Germany, at the age of nine. All that I remembered about that visit was a trip to the Wannsee on a sunny afternoon.

I fell in love with Berlin at once to my own amazement. There is a time when if development is to continue, childhood associations must be put temporarily aside and I had known France too long and too well. In the sharp bite of the air of the North I could watch the first patterns evolve of the postwar decade. Russian and Polish refugees sat on benches in the station, clasping bundles done up in old, faded blankets, too weary at first either to look for work or beg for food. We were conscious that we were standing near the center of a volcano, it was raw, dangerous, explosive but I have never encountered before or since so vital a response to experimental art. In Paris, people had used the classic phrases of me, "She doesn't drink, she doesn't make love, what are her vices?" They guessed everything but the right one, it was danger. I was to have rather more of it than I expected during the next ten years.

The first person we met on arrival was Marc Allégret, come like ourselves to see the new German films. We went out together to Neu-Babelsberg. In our innocence, we had supposed this to be the appro-priate name of a studio, it turned out to be a place. A guide led us through pines, startling many tiny rabbits, and stopped at a platform covered with sand. "You cannot hurry documentary films," he said reproachfully although such a thought had never crossed our minds. An ichneumon was sleeping on a corner of the table, an assistant in a white coat lifted a small, wriggling serpent out of a glass jar: both refused to perform for us, the snake coiled up on the sand, the ichneumon took refuge between two boxes. I noticed a bottle labeled "Dangerous. Do not open." Did it contain chemicals or more reptiles? We were asked to look for an insect hanging from a branch like a dead leaf and felt when we could not find it that we were being judged contemptuously as unobservant English. It was very thorough, very German, and we stood about like small children following a learned uncle round a zoo. Yet the documentary was perhaps the true expression of that time. Such films caught the everyday and revealed it as unfamiliar. To photograph a landscape seemed in some way to ensure it against memory's loss and these cameramen approached their subjects as if their work were some royal form of ritual.

A studio today is a fort with its own passwords and sentinels. Oh, we were lucky. We were in at the beginning and wandered freely about the studios as we liked. After all, in England in those days, films were barely respectable. The last time that I was on a movie set, it was regimented and formal, reporters were spectators, herded behind ropes. In the early days everybody was mixed up together in a wild informality and I think this gave life to the episodes. The technical advances have been enormous and imperfections of both lenses and lighting strike the senses if we watch the projection of an early picture but the life has gone from modern films, they are seldom creative, but have become what we prided ourselves should be avoided, photographed theater. They do not "move."

A gigantic crucifix was standing inside the main building against an immense backdrop of sky. There was a crowd in front of it and hundreds of green leaves had been strewn over the grass. There were ledges full of lamps above our heads, wires crossed the floor in what seemed to be a pattern of idly drawn lines, there was a small wooden platform for onlookers. "*Luther*," our guide whispered, "it will all look natural on the screen." We stood still while a shot was taken and then hurried through some plaster columns into the next set, a "dancing" where the air was an Indian temperature under the mercury vapor lamps. A mechanical piano played and stopped, played and stopped, at a whistle's command. We dodged a make-up woman plastering the heroine with powder, paused to watch a cameraman fixing an electric motor, huddled into a corner among more wires while the director shouted, a waiter moved among the dancing couples and the cameras whirred. The whistle blew, all was silence and we walked on, passing an old carpenter pasting strips of wallpaper on frames and a group of weary people sitting on decrepit chairs round an old piano. "White Russians," the guide remarked, "they have no money for real sets and only shoot their scenes twice." Three times was the normal number although there was a rumor that in Hollywood von Stroheim had shot some of the scenes in *Greed* ten times, an exaggeration we could hardly believe.

It was pleasant to get back into the open. We passed a wooden pavillion that had been constructed for the just finished *Waltz Dream* and turned into a wide street that had been built up to one story, mirrors would reflect the additional height required and thus save eighty per cent of the cost. It had already been used twice. There were German names over the shops at one end of the street and Spanish ones at the other. We skirted a trench and rolls of rusty wire, "our battlefield for the second *Weltkrieg* film," came up to Rotwang's house from the newly released *Metropolis,* and wandered further across sandy soil that was like the floor of some newly drained sea. Tiny violets grew among discarded Agfa boxes, the ivory ends of scrapped film and lengths of discarded paper littered the trolley lines for cameras that stretched in every direction. Yet all these objects had gone to make what we should now call tranquillizers for a war-shocked generation whose members had been torn from everything they had been brought up to revere. Perhaps the films were illiterate but they reflected their time and gave a moment's respite to the millions whose lives had been wrenched out of shape. They may have also fulfilled the same purpose in the twenties as the epidemic of dancing is said to have done after the plague and the Crusades. There really are moments when reality is too grim to be faced by the majority if they intend to survive.

Marc stayed on to attend a conference. Kenneth and I walked back to the station and I tried to buy two tickets for Berlin. The official knew no English, I tied myself up in knots. I apologized and explained that I had not spoken any German for fifteen years. He looked at me with hatred and snapped in German, "That is obvious." There were few English people in Germany in 1927 and there was hatred of us everywhere but I responded vigorously to such a challenge.

There was one film that we felt expressed our generation. It was *Die freudlose Gasse (Joyless Street)* directed by G. W. Pabst and starring Greta Garbo for the second time in her career. It seemed to us the first picture to use contemporary material with a sense of intelligence and art. As I have already written, love seemed less important than a sudden act of kindness, and beauty alone was immune to the pestilence of the time. I had come to films too late myself to take any interest in their stars but with one exception I have never seen anyone more beautiful than Garbo was in this film. It was truly Greek.

Almost at the end of our first stay in Berlin, Kenneth returned from another conference with the news that he had actually met Pabst who had invited us both to a party at his house that evening. It proved to be an important moment for me because among the dozen people collected to meet us, there was a quiet, almost Eastern-looking figure sitting in one corner who was afterwards to be my analyst, Dr. Hanns Sachs. He had recently been acting as adviser on the first attempt to make a psychoanalytical film, *Secrets of a Soul*. It was a "lost" film because although it was shown, the producers had decided that the audience could not stand a purely psychoanalytical story and all the interesting portions had been cut.

At first we had ears only for Pabst. His round face was usually a mask of helpless laughter when he was off duty. On the set he ruled the assembly, actors, cameramen and technicians like an officer on a parade ground. His tongue was as sharp as any sword. "Everybody warned me not to take Garbo," he was saying as we entered, "she photographed so badly," we all laughed till the tears ran down our cheeks.

"She wanted to stay in Europe and she waited for a year after *Die freudlose Gasse* was such a success but nobody offered her a chance and I had no suitable part for her in my next film."

"They will ruin her in Hollywood." (They did.)

"And are you pleased with your new film?" somebody asked. "Surely now you can do as you like?"

"As I like!" Pabst exploded again into his characteristic laugh, "The distributors will not want it as it is. There is not a smile in every sequence and nobody dances."

"When will it be released?" Kenneth inquired.

"I will show you my real version. Once the exhibitors get it, they will give the heroine flowers and a happy ending and then they will say that the sets are too dark."

A discussion on lighting began and I found myself talking to the only other nontechnical expert in the room, Dr. Sachs. I told him that I had met Freud and that I was interested in analysis though I was not sure that I could accept it completely; he confessed that he had had a daydream that a desperately neurotic maharaja would invite him to a remote palace in India where, after the daily hour of treatment which he agreed with me could easily take place on the back of an elephant, he could study one of his favorite subjects, the philosophy of the East. It was a strange ending to a fantastic evening. The films had brought us together but an inquiry into the secrets of the mind was nearer to me than the world of the studios. A few months later, after a long correspondence, I began the analysis that I have always felt to be the central point in my life.

I spent several months a year in Berlin from 1928 to 1932 nor was my work interrupted in the intervals because Dr. Sachs spent most of the summer in Switzerland where he continued to take his analysands. I went to him for an hour a day, during the rest of the time I saw films, attended to the business side of *Close Up* and shared in the extraordinary ferment abroad. Sometimes Kenneth was with me, sometimes I was alone. My German came back to me, I relearned it from the captions in the movies.

I had many friends, although looking back at them now the only Berliner was Lotte Reiniger (whose silhouette films have had today the same artistic success in England as they had then in Germany), the others were Austrians like Pabst and Sachs or Hungarian like the film director, Erno Metzner. Most of us made fun of the bourgeoisie but they had their revenge, the Nazis destroyed all forms of expression and drove the artists into exile. We were so full of what we could do with the future that we never perceived the darker motives of our enemies, who were gathering strength to destroy us. We were certain that obedience for obedience' sake had been broken by the war and it was not until 1931 that we realized that the barbarians had broken through our undefended outposts. Sachs saw it early because of his deep understanding of human nature. I could not forget the words of the *Times* correspondent in Florence at the time of the fascist march.

At first, however, Berlin was all excitement and promise. It was a place of violent contrasts, a baby elephant at the Zoo tossed the fallen yellow leaves about its enclosure with the petulant trunk movements of an awkward child. We went to see *Hoppla, wir leben* where shots taken on an actual battlefield were suddenly flashed onto an immense screen behind the actors' heads. The impact of the scene brought many of the audience out of their seats. We sheltered from the cold November winds inside small cafés whose red plush seats and marble-topped tables must have been a legacy of the nineties. There was desperate poverty, life and death seemed to hang upon trifles, a missed bus, an unexpected meeting. I sometimes felt that a collective but unconscious mind had broken through its controls. We went to obscure cinemas to see experimental films, Pabst took us to Neu-Babelsberg again where we followed him to his own set across the lunar landscape of the *Frau im Mond* and met Fritz Lang, its director. On another occasion I was sought out hastily as an interpreter for Harold Lloyd when he was visiting the studios. I myself found Berlin easier and nearer to me than any city where I had lived. It is rare for people to escape their inheritance and I was English with a century-old dash of German. It had always been hard for me to accept a given condition. I had always wanted to alter it or improve it. I never had to translate my feelings in Berlin; in Latin countries I was a wild plant escaped into a formal garden. It is not a question of one being better than the other. I was born and trained to be useful in a special way at a certain place. Remove me and in my uselessness I should become dangerous just as someone like Norman Douglas would have been wasted and unhappy in the North.

Dr. Sachs was then living in a small apartment at number seven, Mommsenstrasse, just behind the Kurfürstendamm. I went back to look at the outside of it in 1960 and it was one of the few houses to have escaped the bombardment. There was a center bed in the courtyard that was usually full of azaleas, guarded by a melancholy black and white cat with a blue bow, and a long, steep staircase up to the fourth floor. I usually went at noon (the hour that Theocritus describes as being the most dangerous), a sleepy, sultry time that was particularly pleasant in summer. Later I was transferred to the first hour in the morning. Dr. Sachs spoke English perfectly and had a number of English analysands, among them Barbara Low.

It is given to many to dream but to few to find their dreaming granted. Up to that moment I had asked questions but had received no answers. The object of my search since I had been a small child was absolute truth. Not to be believed was what I found hardest to bear. Also, as I have written, my vice is danger and there is nothing more perilous than to look at truth, that Gorgon's head. I believe that it can be approached only through a long, slow training of many generations because to accept it fully would be to alter our beliefs and not always in the direction that our contemporary moralists suppose.

I began to understand from the beginning of my first hour. I had always known that my emotions had been stronger when I was six and that the unrelenting social machine had tried to crush them out of me ever since I had left the cradle. I had often thought that good intentions masked evil drives. A classical, Freudian analysis in the right hands is perhaps the sternest discipline in the world, the hardest form of intellectual activity and a great spiritual experience. It offers, as reward, liberty and understanding. There is probably no movement about which more popular misconceptions exist, largely because it threatens the irrational. There are many situations in which both guilt and fear are realities. What psychoanalysis is trying to do is to relieve us from the burdens borne by our prehistoric ancestors so that we can make further discoveries on the seas of the human mind. If you must have a comparison, it is our compass. A lot of us will die as pioneers but sometime, somewhere, we shall solve more of the mysteries that will then become so commonplace that their discoverers will be relegated to a footnote of history, probably with sneers.

Artists say to me continuously that they dare not be analyzed lest they lose their creative powers. The ones that I know who have gone through the discipline found that, on the contrary, it deepened their gifts. My own perceptions were enlarged, it taught me the mystery behind everyday events. Others tell me that they can analyze themselves. It merely shows that they have not grasped the first lesson. We are not dealing with what is conscious in our minds but with what is *unconscious,* and for that two people are needed. We surrender nothing of what we desire, we learn why we want it and occasionally find that it was simply a cover for something that we wanted more.

I admit that I was lucky. I was one of the early group of analysands and it was much less stiff (stuffy, I think, would be a more correct word) than it is today. We were made to feel that we were part of a band of explorers and I was packed off most evenings to lectures not only on anthropology and the theory of analysis but on the common forms of insanity and their symptoms. I grumbled at the time because my German then had not entirely come back to me but I have been immensely grateful since for the privilege. It enabled me to help people during and after the war who had gone temporarily over the border-line. I am not frightened of mental illness and because of this I am able to understand and handle certain cases during the difficult hours between their treatments.

There is one catch. Psychoanalytical work is one of the most trying jobs in the world and analysts prefer to deal with acute cases where there is more chance of making some spectacular discovery. Being a practical Anglo-Saxon, I told Professor Freud that in my opinion they should be rationed to not more than two such people and should devote the rest of their time to analyzing the best-adjusted individuals that they could find and in particular those who had to deal themselves with big groups. Freud laughed and did not altogether reject the idea although he pointed out gently that analysts needed much experience with abnormal states in order to deal with the normal. Dr. Sachs and I agreed that ideally nobody should be allowed to teach who had not been analyzed; but again, Sachs added, they might then want to leave their schools. "Pedagogy as a science, that is as applied psychology, is in its cradle."

As far as I myself was concerned, I enjoyed my own analysis tremendously. It shocked people, they felt I ought to be unhappy at times but I got more benefit out of our work through laughter than by going to the Mommsenstrasse (as some did) with a pocket full of handkerchiefs. Of course there were snags. One afternoon, after what had seemed to be a harmless enough hour, I was careless enough to get severely bitten by a mangabey at the Zoo. Nobody was sympathetic. The doctor at the first-aid post ("We always have a monkey bite a day") rushed off to find a paper upon which he had written down a number of difficult English words and insisted upon my explaining them in detail before he would tie up my finger and my German friends giggled when they met me, "Ah, you have ape bite, yes?" All Dr. Sachs remarked with a sigh the next morning was, "Well, it had to happen."

I could not have burst through the barriers that were holding me up without help. We tried to dig down to the bones of the past and to excavate memories in the process. Sometimes an episode came to light, then there would be dreary weeks when the grains of sand we sifted had no meaning. Even those Sachs found rewarding though they infuriated me. "Try not to butt through the wall with your head," he would admonish, "an indirect approach is more likely to be successful."

"But not so much fun."

I could feel his dark, almost Indian eyes glittering behind me as we plunged on, more often than not, I thought, by the most roundabout and illogical way possible. "I hope you feel you are getting enough out of your hours," he said once a little anxiously; the word "session" had not then come into use.

"Of course, I can grumble as much as ever I like and I needn't feel guilty because I've paid you to listen to me."

There was a roar of laughter that time. I was certainly not an orthodox patient but I was immensely happy. Sachs told me honestly and with infinite precaution that he was obliged to charge his foreign analysands his full fee, it was twenty marks in 1928 or at the then rate of exchange, five dollars an hour. He took his German patients for ten marks or less, according to their circumstances, and yet he was one of the original "Seven" around the Professor. Freud told me later in Vienna that ideally no charge should be made at all but as psychoanalysts had to live the same as anybody else and as their professional training was so long, fees must be asked but should be adapted to each analysand's means. The prices today are linked to an inflated world economy that has raised medical costs everywhere, not to the founder's ideas.

It must have been Fate that led me to Sachs. The matching of analyst and patient is an important factor in a successful analysis and nobody else would have suited me so well. We shared so many interests in common, travel, the classics and the East. The Buddhists, we recalled, had used a technique of remembering for over two thousand years. He himself was preparing a paper upon the conquest of fear in the Roman schools for gladiators. He suspected that they had used something akin to analysis before the men were sent into the arena. He usually took about ten patients a day and they left him little time for his research. I know that he had made notes on the subject, I tried to trace them after his death but they seemed to have disappeared. Perhaps the most arresting of his articles was "The Delay of the Machine Age." It is still applicable to conditions today.

The English commonly discover nicknames for their friends. It is a sign of acceptance. It was not long before Sachs became the Turtle, partly because he often retired behind an impersonal and impenetrable shell and partly because, if a word dropped that seemed to offer a clue to the situation, he responded to it with a sudden, darting movement of the head. There could have been no successful outcome to our work, however, if we had agreed too often. His pacifism was matched against my pugnaciousness, his desire for a scholarly life was in opposition to my wish to go to sea. We fought, we argued, but I think on both sides we enjoyed ourselves though I was a little hurt to hear outside that he regarded me as an easy patient. It would have been so flattering to be difficult! After my analysis was over in a release of great freedom, we corresponded regularly until his death in 1947.

I am a convinced Freudian both because it offers the greatest challenge to the mind and because I know through my own experience that it has given the most lasting help, not to myself only but to friends. Many individual psychologists, Havelock Ellis was one, can smooth out difficulties for a time but without research in depth they usually recur. I have not myself known anyone helped by Jung. His treatment is horizontal and shallow whereas Freud is vertical and deep. Jung's books naturally are easier for the populace to read. I could never feel myself that a myth was the slightest use to me in everyday life whereas the analysis of some small apparently incongruous incident could suddenly, like a miner's headlamp, light up the dark pit of the brain.

Analysis must have no morals, only mirrors, and yet if I have a criticism of it, it is that most analysands become drearily good, adaptable citizens. Afterwards it helped my history because I was able to watch the story of many ancient political and religious movements taking place within a circle that I knew. The gay excitement of the early days died with the founders, the second generation was engaged in obtaining official recognition, they aspired to become part of "the Establishment." They succeeded and yet because in the deepest way they thus betrayed some of their leader's ideas, they tended in compensation to make laws of what Freud had suggested were points worth investigation.

And outside was Berlin. It was the time of the Bauhaus and experiments in modern architecture. The schools were locked in a struggle between light and darkness. I loved the new functional furniture, the horizontal windows and the abolition of what I thought of as messy decoration. I saw the documentary film of a rocket; people laughed, I was interested. I understood very little of what was happening politically in Germany. Berlin was an international city but in any period of great artistic expression, and we had one in the twenties, there are always centers that draw people to them to form a kingdom of their own. "It's got to be new," we chanted because old forms were saturated with the war memories that both former soldiers and civilians wanted to forget. We were too savage, too contemptuous, but would you have had us be prudent? We did not realize at the time that it was not the concepts themselves that were at fault but the way that they had been used. Perhaps because my own unconscious was in the process of release, the unconscious passions of the city struck me with the more force. The war losses had been the same in all countries but there had not been the total upset of all values elsewhere as in Germany and Austria. I saw hunger, brutality and greed but there was also the sudden compassionate gesture, a will to help or the pre-battle awareness of the single rose, the transient beauty of some girl's face.

There were films to see and review because I was the only one of the *Close Up* group to speak much German. Beware, my masters, a knowledge of languages is not always an asset. It adds riches to our reading but I have been put in charge of a group of refugees, had a baby dumped in my lap and had to lead various helpless people round customs all because for very shame I dared not deny some knowledge of French and German. Yes, it has certainly added to the color of life but has not always been helpful to an impatient traveler.

I did not actually see the *Dreigroschenoper* though I met Lotte Lenya later in New York but we all knew the words of it and *Mahagonny* by heart. Nothing else expressed so well the mood of that Berlin with its love-hate dream of America and what can be written about it now? "They say I am too realistic," Pabst grumbled when he was compelled to cut out a scene, "but what am I to do? Real life is so romantic and so ghostly."

It was also the moment when the first Russian films exploded on the screen. The early ones had been made in comparative freedom and expressed the shock of war and its resulting comradeship rather than propaganda. The mass scenes were impressive because although (as at the Armistice) we had formed part of a crowd, standing in ranks we had seen merely the backs of the heads in front of us, and never an individual face. Eisenstein's work, Pudovkin's *Storm Over Asia* and a strange film made by Kuleshov from a story by Jack London are the ones that remain in memory. The Kuleshov picture was a study of loneliness in an Arctic winter that ended in death and judgment. It was said that he had so little negative that he could only shoot each scene once and yet although it is thirty years since I saw it, the sequences still have a terrible clarity whereas the movies made last year with all the resources of a huge studio are forgotten. We reviewed these films in *Close Up* and once at the press showing of a new Russian picture we were sent in ahead of the *Times*. Oh, how our tails swished!

Eisenstein was in Berlin once when we were there but instead of discussing the cinema, I see him leaning back on a rickety chair, helpless with laughter and with tears streaming down his broad cheeks as he watched us ransom two beds and two chairs for our landlady. She had furnished the pension on the hire-purchase system and we had returned to find a moving van outside and everything being carried out of our rooms. We had some trouble in saving our own suitcases. It was commonplace in Berlin and again a legacy from the inflation.

The postwar feeling that we should all be one nation went too fast and too far. It has been replaced by a fiercer nationalism than the Victorian squire with his gospel of empire ever knew. "Engagement" came with the thirties and the depression when political movements replaced even the artists' fellowship. Here my training as a historian prevented me from following many of my friends. I had made a study of the French Revolution and, in particular, Robespierre. A class went up, a class went down, but in fifty years everything was the same. Now for the first time—and it was so exciting that sometimes I felt that I could hardly breathe—psychology was beginning to uncover the true motives of mankind. Once we understood them we should not go round in a circle but truly move forward into a new age. Professor E. R. Dodds has written better than I can of this matter in his *The Greeks and the Irrational*.

The "talkies" were another symbol of the changing times. The silents had been shown from Scandinavia to Spain, they had cost less and the material was richer, they had to suggest rather than state. Now each country made films in its own language. Until this happened my *Close Up* work took me continually into the studios. I was often sent to talk to the English and American stars and found this an ordeal until I discovered a simple solution. All that was needed was a recent copy of the *Financial Times* or *Wall Street Journal.* They were interested in investments and contracts and the movies were a road to money. They were thus very different from the theater people whom I had known who usually possessed some feeling for their art.

My own interest, however, was in education rather than film. I went to congresses, I visited schools. I wrote some articles in 1930 suggesting that the essential lessons should be planned by highly paid specialists and given through films and radio, leaving the local teachers free to supervise and ensuring that the smallest country school should have the same opportunities as those in cities. There was laughter, of course, even anger but now, thirty years later, they are beginning to use machines. I taught several children to typewrite at the age of six and noticed that none of them had any spelling difficulties afterwards. I suggested that this was because it was hard for a small child to trace a letter with his hand and see the whole word in his mind at the same time. People merely said that I wanted to degrade learning. Why? A Viennese friend, Gertrude Weiss, and I produced an easy textbook called *The Lighthearted Student* for visitors to Germany in 1931. It was the most successful book that I have worked on, every copy sold. Again we were attacked for saying that it was better to learn grammar through phrases than repeat unconnected rules by heart. It has now become general practice in language classes.

One day I went over a famous so-called progressive German school with a friend. I disliked the director at once, I felt that he was a bully under his seemingly soft words. I happened to look up at the program of studies. Several hours a day were devoted to gliding and aerodynamics. "Did you see what I saw?" I asked my friend when we left. She shook her head. "We are about to have another war." I wrote an article for *Close Up* warning the English that they would lose their leisure and their little cars unless they stopped German rearmament before it was too late. They called me a warmonger and a hotheaded fool.

In 1923 I went to Berlin for the last time. Sachs surprised me on my arrival by suggesting that we meet privately that evening for a walk. The air was full of the scent of lime flowers and roses, the new houses looked gay, people were strolling peacefully along the quiet streets. He told me that he was leaving for Boston. It was more for him than a judicious move, it meant a severance from the language and literature that formed the core of his life. There was nothing that I could say. I knew that nobody in Europe would lift a finger to arrest the situation.

The magic of Berlin was still about me, I had this last month. Or had I? The schoolgirl daughter of an acquaintance lay for twenty minutes on the pavement near where I was staying while two political groups shot it out over her head. Perdita was with me and Lotte Reiniger took her out to her house at Neu Westend to keep her away from the turmoil. I used to go out on the train to see them among savage faces and clenched fists. The non-German-speaking British tourists in the center of the city saw only the heavily policed main streets.

One night Pabst invited some of us to the private showing of a film in a house near the Wannsee. It was about ten o'clock when we started home and just before we got to the bus stop, we were surrounded by a gang of brown-shirted youths. Who were we? Where were we going? Had we papers? I produced my British passport, it was unsafe to go out without it. Even so, I think there might have been trouble but the bus arrived at that moment and they stood round watching us until we left. It was one of the infamous nights of horror and murders.

A short time later, I had just gone to bed when I smelt smoke and heard the crash of an ax. I crawled along the floor, stiffly because I was terrified, and peeped cautiously round the curtain. The courtyard was full of men in uniform. "It's the revolution," I thought and I wondered how I could get to Perdita, she was several miles away. Somebody pointed, I saw a fireman's head at a window. A fire had broken out in an apartment whose owner was on holiday and they had had to break down the door. Amusing, yes, but not in that tense atmosphere. I found the uncertainty, the never knowing what would happen, as trying as actual war. People were beginning to whisper about each other, Pabst, they warned me, was "uncertain"; on which side did he stand, they asked? Some people would not work for him.

I can understand something of Pabst's conflict. He had been directing a German theater in New York in 1914 when he received a telegram that his mother was dangerously ill in Vienna. He took the first steamer, it had no wireless and he landed in France the day after war had begun. They immediately put him into a civilian prison under the conditions that E. E. Cummings described so well in *The Enormous Room* and he had remained there for almost five years. There was inadequate food and he had also felt cut off from the experiences of his generation. He went to Hollywood during the thirties but returned to Austria in the summer of 1939. It is wrong to judge when we do not know the full circumstances but I did not feel able after the war to see someone who being "outside" had returned to a country that the Nazis controlled.

The station filled with the more fortunate refugees. They were not necessarily the rich but rather those lucky enough to have relatives in the States, South America or England. Not all were Jews; there were many war veterans who wanted to end their days in peace. We all formed the habit of never going out unless we were obliged, while people in England continued to praise German discipline and order.

Since I discovered that my ancestors had come from Hitzacker, my friends teased me; "Why you're from the Lüneburger Heide, it's the cradle of Prussia," they said. There was no time to go there and for the first time I was glad to leave Berlin. It was to be twenty-eight years before I saw the city again.

It became the fashion for the *avant-garde* cinema groups to make films as it had been the custom in Paris to bring out two issues of a magazine. There were societies all over Europe, they corresponded with *Close Up* and subscribed to it. Kenneth hired an attic and began to experiment. He bought a Debrie with six lenses, a professional number at that time. His first documentary, *Monkey's Moon,* starring his pet dourocoulis (tiny owl-faced monkeys from South America), was shown a number of times and greeted with enthusiasm. He became more ambitious, rented a broken-down theater and made a full feature, *Borderline,* for what seemed to me the huge sum of two thousand dollars.

Kenneth wrote the scenario, directed, photographed and cut the picture. H. D. was superb as the heroine with an almost too realistic death scene at the end. Paul Robeson, who was curious about films at that moment, came for a couple of days to play a stranger whose chance arrival started a tragedy in a village but the show was stolen by a retiring gentlewoman from the British colony whom we called Mouse. She was quiet, certain in her movements and unforgettable. I spent my days keeping a register of the shots, helping to change extremely hot and dirty carbons in the lamps and now and then being the keeper of a disreputable lodginghouse with a cigar in my mouth and my eye clamped to a keyhole. "Just be natural, Bryher, and imagine you have heard a dirty bit of gossip about your best friend." Uncle Norman's training with the Toscana came in useful and even Pabst giggled when he saw the sequence. The only paid member of the group was an electrician. Extras had to be dispersed rather than sought, everybody wanted to be in it and every twenty minutes all the lights went out because the tram went by. Yet it was shown in half a dozen countries, Pabst sent all his cameramen to the performance in Berlin and would have given Kenneth a position on his own set if he had been willing to take it. Spain showed it a number of times, the English asked "Whatever is it all about?" and there have been requests for the loan of a copy as late as a couple of years ago, when there have been exhibitions of early *avant-garde* cinema.

It was part of "the art that died" because these small pictures were training the directors and cameramen of the future as the "little reviews" had trained the writers but sound came in, nobody could continue on account of the expense and by 1934 *Close Up* and about sixty of these groups had ceased to exist.

Analysis liberated the past and I remembered my childhood wish to go to Greenland. A permit was needed and I got as far as the Danish Embassy with an introduction from Havelock Ellis. The official I saw was not helpful. "Greenland!" he said in surprise, "But you can go to Paris." I tried to explain that I had dreamed about the North for years but he refused even to look up the regulations.

I ought to have known better but in desperation I persuaded Kenneth and Herring to join me on a cruise to Spitsbergen. I had supposed it would be a large type of cargo boat and was quite unprepared for such scraps of conversation as "I think we are down to play deck tennis together. Isn't it time we did something about it?"

The wildest rumors went round because we refused to join in the community games and perhaps I was a little too sniffy as I walked briskly up and down the deck with a history of Iceland under my arm and listened to the old ladies saying to each other, "My dear, how gray the sea is this morning."

"Well, it's never blue in the North. You have to go to the Mediterranean for that."

"No, you don't. You have to go to the Indian Ocean."

On the whole, the passengers were elderly but they were determined to have fun. It makes such a difference to know the landscape of a poem and I had a perfect day at Thingvellir, wandering over the saga country among dwarf, intensely blue gentians and short grass. Both were an adaptation to the fierce winds. It was a moment that made up for the rest of the trip. We steamed round to Akureyri and from there to North City in Spitsbergen. Of course we were tourists, admiring the huskies in an enclosure outside the post office, but I saw a typical Arctic summer for the first time, with stretches of heather, bog cotton and in one place the short, creamy petals of the reindeer flower, *Dryas octopetala*. I have often found that if I have longed for something very much, the actual experience is more vivid than my picture of it. There was pack ice at Green Bay on our return and I stared into the light of a brilliant evening, wondering if I should ever see Greenland.

In May, 1933, my father was seriously ill for only the second time in his life. The doctors told him he must cut down on work. "How can I, Miggy," he said to me, "we are still in the aftermath of the war and if I retired now, hundreds might lose their jobs." I was not unduly anxious because apart from a few attacks of influenza, I had seldom known him to spend a day in bed. He was worried, however, about my brother who wanted to marry almost the first girl that he had met. My father asked him to wait for a year, travel and then if he was still of the same mind, promised his consent. None of us knew that there were people who were already doing all they could to break my brother completely away from his home.

On July 16th, I woke up at dawn, saw that it was too early to get up and drifted off to sleep again. I dreamed that my father was dying.

I was not particularly startled when I woke up, I thought that it was an anxiety dream because he had been ill. It turned out afterwards, however, that he had had a stroke at that same moment. They telephoned me from Dieppe, where he had been on holiday with my mother, to come at once.

There was no train before the late evening so I rang up Geneva Airport and they offered me a small charter plane. It was a two-seater but the engine had a reasonable amount of power and the pilot had been trained by the Swiss Air Force. It was still the early days of flying and weather reports were meager. We got caught in a hurricane of wind above the Juras that twisted us round and sideways as if our machine were a stray bit of paper until it looked for a moment as if we might crash before we could turn. Somehow the pilot circled, asked me if I were willing to try again, I nodded, he found another route and once over France the turbulence ceased. I believe that we were in extreme danger but due to the circumstances and my ignorance of flying I did not care. We refueled at Paris and flew on towards the sea. It was almost evening and I think that I have never seen a more magnificent sunset in my life. The gold and scarlet seemed to recede from us and I knew at the precise moment when it happened, that my father had died. We had always been so near to one another, and analysis, while freeing me from dependence, in other ways had deepened our relationship.

We landed. I went to the hotel but I did not need to be told. My father was cold beyond any ice that I had ever felt but he looked peaceful and it was fitting that he died in the Normandy that he had always loved.

I could not do much for my mother. She never recovered from the shock but had six long and, I fear, unhappy years before she could join him. "Oh, don't look at me," she begged, "you have his eyes." It was a great love story that endured to the end.

They were kind in France, one of his own ships came to take the body back to England, covered, again fittingly, by an English flag. We were utterly unprepared for the veritable charge of press photographers that met us on land. Death comes to us all and this was a moment that concerned only the family and intimate friends. Reporters lined up in front of the hearse with cameras, they broke through the relatives trying to hold them back and literally charged my mother. I had the great satisfaction myself of kicking one cameraman hard in the stomach. It was the most disgraceful exhibition that I have ever seen because by no stretch of the imagination could it be called news and even strangers wrote to the *Times* in disgust to complain about such an intrusion.

The people who had loved him, those whom my father had helped, came and were welcomed. He was buried at Putney after another tussle with the photographers who tried to interrupt the burial service and turn their cameras on the grave.

I believe now that my father could have become a religious leader as easily as a financier, he had such an extraordinary inner detachment. I could appreciate this the more because I never had it myself. Had he been born half a century later, he would have been interested in pure science. It should not be forgotten that England is enjoying a higher standard of living today because of the efforts of the nineteenth-century industrialists to open up vast tracts for settlement in Canada and Australia and create risk capital. All of us, the entire welfare state, are living upon the riches that they made possible. We are moving now into another type of development but it is one that has emerged from the last hundred years, it is not a new growth. People like my father had a much deeper sense of responsibility about those whom they employed than is found in the huge, amorphous corporations of the present time. Bureaucracy has replaced private enterprise in many fields but it is arbitrary and less sensitive to human needs. The present tendency to scrap men and women after a lifetime of service simply because of some age limit, seems to me far more evil than Victorian initiative.

Sachs came straight to me from his holiday, it was an act of great kindness. My brother disappeared just when my mother needed him most. The will was read, we tried to resume ordinary life, we answered letters that came from people whom my father had befriended during his youth, we cleared up papers.

And then the jackals came.

My mother had always left her jewelry when she went abroad in a safe in my father's office. It was her own property and she was asked to remove it before probate. The safe itself was in a basement and thickly covered with dust. We noticed marks as if it had been recently opened but did not trouble further then about the matter. My mother took out her case and we went away.

My father had told us all on several occasions that he had left a Letter of Directions as well as a Will. Nobody could find it. The lawyers put forward the theory that my father had omitted to write it because of his illness but I happened to remember distinctly that he had mentioned it to me when he was still doing a full day's work at the office. I cannot of course prove that it existed: on the other hand my father never made such statements lightly, so the strong inference is that somebody, at some time, perhaps during the funeral had managed to get at the safe and remove it. Not that it would have affected my mother or myself who were provided for under the terms of the Will. The document in question was rather in the nature of a directive (or so we understood) about the carrying on of the business.

Be that as it may, almost all of my father's trusted associates were demoted or retired within the next few weeks, and as for my brother, he returned for a few hours and said unpardonable things to my mother although she was ill at the time. I remonstrated, he threw a chair at my head and I have never seen him since. He married before my father had been dead a month.

The family split. Aunt Emily and her family clung to us loyally and I shall always be grateful to my cousin, John Todd, he visited my mother or invited her to go out with him regularly until she died. I broke off communications with my other aunt and her connections. I knew what my father would have asked of me, to defend my mother in every possible way, and I did the utmost to carry out his wishes. "You had such patience," my mother wrote to me just before she died.

I had to spend some months in England that year with only occasional visits to Burier and as it was necessary to leave somebody in charge of the house, Elsie Volkart came to me as secretary. At least that is how it started but she now rules us all, as I say, with a rod of iron. We are a complement to each other because her ancestry is out of the mountains and the earth and I am from the sea. She had been the most faithful of companions for thirty years and loyal to such an extreme that when I returned to Switzerland in 1946, I found that she had preserved some pencil stumps and a paint rag that I had forgotten to throw away and had given her own rations to keep my dog, Claudi, alive.

It was 1960 before I visited Germany again but I saw Sachs twice in Boston and I went to the congresses of the Psychoanalytical Society at Luzern in 1934, Marienbad in 1936 and Paris in 1938. There I met friends and made new ones, particularly Walter and Melitta Schmideberg and Christine Olden, all three of whom were analysts.

The Marienbad congress is the one that stands out in my memory. Lotte Reiniger joined us for what I called "our ride to Bohemia." It was the first time that I had realized how landlocked much of Europe was and therefore static and traditional because bound to the fields whereas we at the western edge were seafarers and fluid. It has always made me wary of the idea of a united Europe. There are some chemicals that will not mix.

Marienbad itself was a faded Edwardian portrait under a glass dome, all the stranger because at our meetings we were so ardently alive. There were psychological discoveries to be discussed and, privately, the problems of analysts already wondering whether they ought to leave Vienna or Prague. I met an explorer who had traveled in Swanetia, "a swan land among mountains where the passes are only open three months a year," and afterwards in Pamir. We planned an expedition to the North together but the war prevented us from carrying it out.

One day we drove through woods and waddling geese to Eger. The peasants had made patterns of blue, green and cream bowls among the eggs and bunches of flowers. "Lovely designs," Lotte said, "but how could I carry them home?" I looked at the sloping roofs, the window boxes thick with white petunias below the pigeon loft windows and wondered how much the old market women had changed in their ideas since Wallenstein had been murdered at the end of the square?

We knew although we did not speak of it that we were seeing a doomed countryside for the last time. Yet man's stupidity could be fought, I said, if only the analysts would be less prudent. "You cannot treat the psychoanalytic movement like a boxing match," Sachs admonished me gently, "things have to go slowly."

I believed in speed. "If only they would get a move on," I grumbled, "we could change the world."

Lotte had connections in the town and told me something of the

267

other side of the story. Frustration can explain a lot of history. "They want to make their own stupid experiences," she said but there were no opportunities for the young professional men and the Germans cleverly exploited their discontent. "I am appalled to death," Lotte continued, "at what may happen."

We returned to Switzerland by way of Vienna where I saw Freud for the last time. He was already too ill to do more than talk with us for a few minutes. Yet in spite of Vienna being the birthplace of analysis and of many of my friends, it was too southern for me in atmosphere. I could not help thinking sometimes of my lost city. A moment, a memory, would come back and I could not help murmuring, it was childish but I meant it, "Why, Berlin, must I love you so?" It had gone, I thought, for ever.

 *Nineteen*

It was during the thirties that I began to know America better. I went over several times between 1934 and 1938. My first impression was always of the beauty of the landscape, the width of the sky, clouds sometimes floating like birds across the skyscrapers, a new range of colors. Outside the city it was "Artemis country" and I have always wanted to walk some trail in summer and get closer to America, as I was near to Switzerland because of my Alpine walks.

I usually went straight to Boston on arrival to see Sachs. The worsening situation in Europe had subdued his natural gaiety and, as the years passed, he became more and more anxious about friends who had neglected his advice to emigrate while it was still possible to leave. He had begun to read American history with his usual thoroughness and we walked up and down the Charles River for hours, discussing assimilation. It seemed remote to me at first but rapidly became a problem that has absorbed more and more of my time up to the present day. Forced migrations have almost become the symbol of the twentieth century and it was the ability of America to absorb so many cultures and turn them into a unity that fascinated him. England has not been able to do it in the Commonwealth. The process is unknown in Europe. Unlike Dr. Sachs who favored a sudden plunge, I myself found that a slow, unconscious assimilation was the surer road to success. The native-born is less likely to resent a pleasant stranger with slightly different ways to his own than a man who tries to copy him hastily and badly.

It was not only politics, however, that Sachs and I discussed on our walks. There was language, "I value English for its freedom from grammatical formulas"; my own ideas (always a pleasant subject!), "You cannot change character, in yourself you have been a seaman, in yourself you have died"; and the future of psychoanalysis in America. He favored a slow and careful process of development, I wished to charge all adversaries at sight. He answered other queries in a way that turned the answers into further questions so that the mind soared upwards into space. I wish I could have recorded what he said to me because memory, although less fleeting than some believe, is also less exact than we like to think.

Sometimes we met friends. There was a winter evening when I discussed Freudian theory with Conrad Aiken as a group of us walked back to the hotel, and another night when Merrill Moore enthralled us with a theory that the American habit of following the seasons north and south was possibly a legacy from the Red Indians. It was rich in experiences, whether I was discussing children's literature at the Bookshop for Boys and Girls, exploring the Eastern collections in the Boston Museum or merely watching the stiff, elderly ladies munching a single white peppermint after dinner as they sat chatting in the lounge.

H. D. kept to a strict seclusion while at work but, once this was done, she had a genius for friendship. She clung particularly, as I think we all do, to the friends of her girlhood. I thus met Mary Herr, at first in London but afterwards in America, and I owe so much to her explanations and help. Mary was living temporarily in Chicago in 1934 and took me to the office of *Poetry* to see Harriet Monroe. I had such a feeling of unreality after the long years of my lonely apprenticeship, when I entered the place that had been associated with so many early Imagist poems, that I almost wanted to touch the desks to see if they were solid; but thanks to my analytical training, I was able to combine fact and fantasy after a few moments without any feeling of disappointment. I met Harriet several times subsequently in Europe. She was a true servitor of art but such people are ill rewarded. They do the difficult and tiresome jobs, and afterwards how few remember them?

Modern architecture seemed to fulfill a need in me from the moment that I first saw it. It was open and free and belonged to the present age. I shall never forget the skyscrapers standing in their detached, impersonal beauty beside the dark lake on a winter night. Each century has a style that speaks for its aspirations and I felt the towers were a symbol of the wider life that we wanted to create.

On subsequent visits, Mary invited me to her home at Lancaster and drove me about the Pennsylvania countryside. She took me to Bethlehem where H. D. had been born. Hilda was Greek, it is true, but her training and background came through every word she wrote. Her long residence in Europe merely intensified her love for her native country, and to me she has always been the most American of poets.

Mary was a wonderful guide, she showed me the great Amish barns that reminded me of Switzerland, she drove me to Ephrata and told me stories of the early Moravian settlers. I accepted it all unthinkingly but afterwards when I began to study American history, I had so many memories to clothe the bare bones of a textbook. We wrote to each other regularly for thirty years and now that she is dead I miss the warm, gay comments on events and people that I had come to take for granted. It must have been a rich culture that produced so many gifted people in the last years of the nineteenth century, H. D. and Mary Herr, among them, and the artist, George Plank.

"A lion! There will be a lion. . . ." No wonder that the astonished commuters looked up at us when the rumor passed, as if we were a circus. We were on our way to Hartford to see the first performance of *Four Saints in Three Acts* and, as Kenneth whispered, anyone who counted in the artistic world of New York was on the train. I could not have been prouder if the world's chief newspaper had sent me to report it. My orders were to write at once to Gertrude Stein and Miss Toklas. I smiled at everyone smugly and hoped that I looked *surréaliste* without being conspicuous.

Theater is the matter of an instant. Its immediate impact may be greater than that of a poem or a picture but there is no way of recording the experience on the tape of another art. It was the perfect moment for *Four Saints* to be performed. The depression was gradually ending and many Americans had returned from Paris full of *avant-garde* ideas, and *avant-garde* in those days implied a serious dedication. The evening remains for me one of the most triumphant nights that I ever spent watching a stage. The Negro singers stood stiffly as in an eighteenth-century painting of a courtly festival, there was a plaster lion though he had less to do than I had hoped, but Gertrude's text soared out magnificently and with it her, and our, rebellion against outworn art. We had all been afraid that the words might not have survived the transition from the library to the stage but we had forgotten Gertrude's rhetoric. I do not know much about music but Virgil Thomson seemed to bring out the implications of her ideas. It is sad that her work has been so completely absorbed that today some people question her originality. They have no picture, being devoid of imagination, of the shackles that she broke for us and of how well she led our revolt.

In the middle thirties Negro literature was beginning to emerge and we read the first novels and poems with sympathy and interest. Some of us were invited to a party to celebrate the founding of a new magazine. I have never been able to feel any color distinction. People are people to me, it is character and not appearance that matters. I hate parties but a sense of solidarity with fellow writers pricked my conscience and I agreed to go. "You can be as highbrow as you like," my friends assured me, "they may not have caught up with the latest André Breton but otherwise they will have read as much as yourself."

I do not remember now where the house was, but it was not in Harlem. The proportion of light and dark was evenly mixed and everybody seemed serious. I found myself sitting next to a man with a golden-brown skin who seemed to have arrived recently from Paris. I supposed him to be one of the assistant editors and remembering my instructions began to talk to him about Proust. I decided that this was a middle choice between the classics—he might then have thought me condescending as many of the people present were teachers—and the extreme *avant-garde*. He stared, he said yes and no, I perceived him finally to be making frantic signs. Somebody rescued him and shortly afterwards my friends rescued me. They were silent until we reached the street, then they turned on me furiously. "If you did not want to go, you should have refused but you ought not to have behaved in that outrageous manner. You frightened the poor fellow badly."

"But what did I do?" I asked in genuine surprise, "I thought Proust was such a safe choice."

"Proust!" they snorted, "That was Mistinguett's dancing partner. Didn't you look at his legs?"

It is always the tradition rather than geographical environment that counts and, although a common language is a convenience, if Americans and English had to approach each other with clicks and snorts we should not misunderstand each other nearly so much. Why is American history not taught more often and more thoroughly in English schools and why are American children given so often a picture of King George the Third's England without the corrective of the evolution of Britain during the last hundred years? I shall always remember a well-educated English lady saying to me in about 1935, "Oh, my dear, I believe you have been to New York. Do tell me, what do they do with all their buffalo carcasses? They can't eat them all, and every time I go for a picnic I am terribly afraid I am eating canned hump."

I had the good fortune to find an interpreter. H.D. came with us on one of our trips and returned from a visit to her publisher full of enthusiasm for a new friend whom she had made there who had helped her to wriggle out of some literary interview. It was Norman Pearson and she brought him to see Kenneth and myself a few days afterwards. I am slow as a rule to friendship and at first we regarded each other warily from our separate corners like two suspicious dogs. Yet I should never have gone to Greenland nor written my historical novels if it had not been for Norman. I happened to have begun a short novel at that time, of which a portion had appeared in *Life and Letters To-day*. He astounded me by having noticed a difference in the color of the phrases and discussing less what I had written than what I had wanted to make. Such a creative understanding is rare. Nobody had spoken to me in such a manner in either London, Berlin, or Paris. I suppose it is my function to write, my wish was to see the Arctic; but both of these things are unimportant beside what Norman gave me, some knowledge of the America about which I had dreamed so much that it had really become my youth. It is seldom that a desire of such intensity is ever realized in later life but it was in my case, thanks to him. He was not able to do this before the war, three years of which he spent in London, but from 1947 onwards he has helped me to become what I have most wanted to be, a unit in the bridge between two great civilizations. It has been salted with quarrels naturally, otherwise it would not have been alive.

I was walking down a New York street just before Christmas in 1938. The sky was the curious copper that comes from neon lighting, the pavements were full of shoppers, there was a feeling of snow in the air. By this time my visits had become so regular that they were almost routine. I was about to return to London to see my mother but I had told my friends that I should be out to see them the next fall. Suddenly I looked up and for a piercing and unexpected moment I knew that I should not see the city again for a very long time. I told myself that I was stupid, I tried to shake off the feeling, I laughed but it proved true. It was nine years before I returned, but to the airport and not the harbor. A war, for the second time, completely changed my life.

It is to the postwar days that I date a real knowledge of America and they belong to another volume of this autobiography. I can only repeat here what I used to say, looking at the Atlantic from the rocks in Scilly, "In England you say *don't* to me always, in America you say *try.*"

 *Twenty*

1934-1940, that block of years was Swiss. Part of it was grim because devoted to the refugees but I also studied with some thoroughness the eighteenth-century history of Vaud. My first fugitive from the Nazis arrived actually in 1933 but the flood began during the following year. Do not think that I had a simple task. Try to feel it instead as if it had happened to yourself. Suppose that you were a citizen of good standing with a wife, children and a respected position. Then overnight you were declared an enemy, beaten up, your possessions seized and if you were very, very lucky, allowed to leave with your family and a suitcase apiece for an alien land where your professional qualifications were useless. I had to meet the people to whom such things had happened, some still scarred from the beatings that they had received. Yet it was the intangible things that they mourned rather than their former security; comradeship, childhood memories and above all, their language.

I should not have felt compelled to intervene in some political struggle in a country different from my own but this was another matter. It was the attempt to exterminate a whole section of the population no matter whether their characters were good or bad. Nor was it only the Jews who suffered, many Germans who objected to the regime on moral or religious grounds were equally persecuted. Roughly two thirds of my cases were Jewish but the other third were Christians of purely German descent. I cannot understand how any person anywhere who professed the slightest belief in ethics could stand aside at such a moment.

I warned the English privately and also in print. They called me a warmonger and jeered at me for my pains. It did not help me when I stood among the ruins of blitzed London to know that my forebodings had come true. I remain ashamed of the majority of my fellow citizens and convinced that apathy is the greatest sin in life. If Europe had reacted with horror to the murder of both the Jews and many other honest German citizens in 1933, the regime would have collapsed. An economic boycott and the threat to take up arms unless such persecution ceased would have settled the matter swiftly if it had been done at once. "You could have bribed most of the leaders for a couple of million pounds," a Swiss in a position to know said to me at the time of Dunkirk, "it would have been cheaper for you than a war." Most of us, wherever we live, must share the guilt of having done nothing at all.

The English newspapers, with the honorable exception of the *Manchester Guardian* and an occasional weekly, refused to print the news. I know. I took attested documents and photographs to London but they were rejected as being "not in accord with the Government policy at the moment" or simply as "too hot." A larger number of English than people want to remember were pro-Nazi and the general feeling was "It's not happening to us, why should we care?"

Many of the refugee committees were poorly organized, cumbersome, afraid of "the government" and too slow. Some were extremely dangerous. It was difficult to impose security checks upon large and usually voluntary staffs and there was reason to fear Nazi infiltration in order to get names so that they could round up and torture the relatives of those who had escaped. The Quakers were a magnificent exception. They were efficient and prompt. The very lucky ones got on their lists.

A few of us who had been interested in psychology organized a private group. The leading psychoanalysts had been rescued by their colleagues, we started with students but our lists soon widened to include people from a wide variety of occupations. We pooled our funds. The

Americans among us arranged for affidavits and looked for jobs so that the exiles could get back to work. The English concentrated upon educational courses, these gave their students the chance to wait in England till their visa numbers were reached. I was the receiving station in Switzerland.

It was considered too dangerous for me to enter Germany but I went several times to Vienna and Prague to interview applicants and bring out documents that they needed for their visas. It was a favorite Nazi trick to withhold such papers. I used to smuggle them out in copies of the *Times*. This newspaper was considered so pro-Nazi at that time that its readers were usually unmolested at the frontier.

We were tough. We made loans for travel expenses and retraining on condition that as soon as the borrowers found work, they paid us back even if it were only a small sum each week. In this way our funds were continually employed and as the loans came back we could rescue another person from our long waiting list. We helped a total of a hundred and five. About sixty were Jews and the rest went into exile because of their moral beliefs. I do not now remember all the names because I burnt my notebook in 1940 when we expected the Nazis to invade Switzerland but I am still in touch with about forty of them. Of the hundred and five, ninety-eight became fully integrated into their new countries; two died, one was an elderly and gifted lawyer, the other the writer, Walter Benjamin. Three were troublesome although they eventually settled and we suspected two of being German agents because they returned to Germany just before war broke out. I think that five failures out of a hundred and five was a magnificent record.

The authorities would not allow refugees to remain in Switzerland. This was reasonable because of the policy of neutrality and the geographical position. They were liberal about transit visas so that many of my visitors could rest for a couple of days before going on to take their steamers at the various ports and they allowed a number of students to finish their training at the Swiss universities provided that they left as soon as they had gained their diplomas. I met these exiles at the station, saw that they had some funds and a room, gave them any new information that I had about visas and collected their news in return. Besides this, I looked after a group of medical students studying at Lausanne and had them come to see me whenever they wanted to talk over a problem. I thought one or two would go crazy before their final examination because we all knew that they had no second chance.

Even sympathy had to be rationed. It was impossible to listen continually to their stories without growing a tough hide but it was then that a personal experience of my own came to my help. I had had my individual world taken away from me (and how abruptly) by school and I knew all about the difficulties of adjustment afterwards. At fifteen, however, I had been young and pliable whereas some of my refugees were fifty and one was seventy. I do not think helpers should have to work longer than three years at such a task. It is so distressing that in self-defense names have to turn into ciphers. I had to work six years because we were so few. If I asked my fellow Englishmen for assistance they only said, "Oh, don't be so emotional, there must be something wrong with the people or their fellow citizens wouldn't have turned them out" and if I showed them photographs of the brutalities they answered, "Can't you see, they must be faked." I found that there was nothing to choose between the political parties. The Right said, "Wait and see" and the Left asked, "What about our jobs?"

If I was able to help, it was due to the Protestant training of my childhood. Like the Quakers, I dared not sit idly by while such things happened. Yet if destiny offers us a chance at such a time, Fortune heaps us with riches. I was amply rewarded for any assistance that I could give by some of the best friendships of my life. It sharpened my political sense and there was also adventure because I was occasionally in some danger, it trained me to sift the essential from the less valuable and never to relax my guard. It is one thing to take a holiday abroad and another to be an exile, the bitterest fate according to the Greeks and our Saxon forefathers that could befall a man. I met my people at the station, I saw their faces and I knew. "If a man say he has another country in his heart, it is not true," Ben Jonson once wrote and how should I feel, I wondered, if because of a mark in my passport I could never see the Scillies again nor watch the Falmouth lights?

Dr. Donald Galbreath, the historian, surprised me once by saying, "Remember, whenever general education rises above a certain level, revolutions follow. However much we may regret it, the masses are unable to bear too much knowledge." I hardly believed him at the time but I know now that what he said was largely correct. Jobs were so scarce in postwar Germany that it was commonly said that a boy had to have a university diploma merely to sell potatoes and I am sure that an overbalance of academic learning contributed to the irrational outburst of violence although it was not the only cause. If my refugee experiences have taught me anything it is that survival depends upon fluidity and I believe that the old English doctrine that sport is next to godliness is often true. Any deep division between body and brain is weakening to a nation. Thought and action should balance in the same person as they did in Elizabethan times. Both are needed to create a healthy civilization.

Ironically enough, my refugees were the cream of Germany's citizens. If there were a weakness in them, it was overcivilization. They could not imagine brutality and kept repeating over and over in bewildered voices, "How could we even know that this persecution was possible?"

There had to be relief from such appalling sadness and I found it in research. Dr. Sachs had once said to me, "I think you settled at Burier because of *The Swiss Family Robinson*." I felt that it was equally due to my Alpine excursions with my father but it was a fact that the version of the story that we usually read was written by Madame de Montolieu at Bussigny about thirty miles from my home. My interest was reawakened by an article on her by Henri Perrochon in the *Revue historique vaudois* for 1937 and as a result, I plunged deeply into the history of eighteenth-century Lausanne when the city was spoken of as "the new Athens."

The Swiss Family Robinson is a folk tale of migration and could not have been written anywhere except in Switzerland. Actually the word "family" is a later English interpolation, it is more correct to speak of the book as the Swiss Robinsons. The original tale was written by Johann Wyss, a pastor and native of Bern, to instruct his children. It contained more sermons than adventures and was first published by one of his sons. Most of the subsequent editions, however, have been based upon an adaptation made by Isabelle de Montolieu to amuse a sick grandchild. She herself was the daughter of Antoine de Polier. He was a friend of Voltaire, a contributor to Diderot's *Encyclopédie* and the author of a fragment of autobiography that brings the age vividly to life and has been printed in the *Revue historique vaudois* for 1913. Isabelle omitted many of the sermons and stressed the adventures. There were many interpolations during the nineteenth century. All the early versions end with the return of the whole family to Europe. The present conclusion with the parents remaining at Rock House and two of the sons leaving for the Old World seems to date to about 1841. The English introduced a girl, dressed as a midshipman! They naturally claimed the island. There were always two dogs but the names were seldom the same. The original popularity of the book probably owed much to the fact that as Vaud was governed by Bern and there were no opportunities for its youth to serve in any official capacity, hundreds left every year to seek their fortunes as soldiers or merchants often as far afield as Canada or China, or they became tutors at the Russian or German courts. The emphasis on plants was due to a desperate need to improve agricultural methods at that time to provide food for a rising population.

One October day in 1938 I went with a friend to Bussigny. We found the house where Isabelle had lived and that, to her bitter sorrow, she had been compelled to sell because of poverty in her old age. The owner of the place in 1938 was a white-haired lady who might have come out of one of Isabelle's books. She met us at the door in a stiff black dress and the black buttoned boots that seem a heraldic emblem of the Victorian age. The house had been turned into a school, the salon was a bedroom for some of the girls and the dining room had been altered but the kitchen and the garden had not been touched. A picture of Madame de Montolieu was hanging on the wall together with a cutting from a newspaper of the time advertising the sale of the house. "My pupils never read her any more," the owner said sorrowfully in French, "but I was brought up on her *Châteaux Suisses.*" She took us out to the wooden gallery along the first floor where Isabelle had worked. There was still the view towards Mont Blanc that could sometimes be seen on a clear day and the huge tree that towered above the railing might have been a sapling that she had planted. Her flowers were below her as she wrote about Falcon's Nest. The best description of the house is in a letter by Maria Edgeworth after she had visited her at Bussigny. It was strange to stand in the exact place where Isabelle had worked and know that she had died after a stroke brought on by poverty and overwork while her tale must have earned riches for many strangers during the century after her death. We can only hope that her vision of the island was a little compensation.

Vaud had been full of refugees from the Huguenots to the émigrés at the time of the French Revolution. There had been intrigues and foreign agents. I often felt that I was reliving those old and troubled times with merely a change of names. Once you know that a moment's carelessness may cost a life, you yourself alter in a dozen subtle ways. I learned watchfulness, never to say a word on a telephone that could not safely be overheard or to leave notes where they might be read. I carried the particulars of my refugees in a tiny notebook that I usually wore suspended round my neck and inside my clothes. I had to suspect every stranger and as the years went on it was difficult to remain humane as well as alert.

One day I was told that someone was waiting to see me in the library. A white, anxious face peered round a bookcase from the only dark corner in the room. I asked the usual questions, he evaded the answers. Where had he come from? Vienna, he answered in excellent English. Oh, he was Austrian. He shook his head, he had been studying there for a short time. I waited for him to tell me his nationality. He blinked and said nothing. What was he doing in Lausanne? He had his medical course to finish, he hoped to get his diploma in two years. Had the authorities accepted him? Provisionally, yes. On what quota was he registered? He turned that question by saying that he was low on the list. It flashed across my mind that he was a Nazi spy, some wretched fellow that they had tortured and let go provided that he supplied them with the names of other refugees. It was a difficult moment. If I made a mistake, he might have nowhere to eat or sleep and be driven through need to the very act that I was half accusing him of having committed. Yet the fate of half a dozen other students was in my hands. Suppose that I helped him and he passed my name and address to the Nazis, I should be watched and their safety would be compromised. His hands were shaking, I thought how little the conventional citizen ever knew of the realities of life but I decided for once that the group was more important than the individual and answered sternly that I could not think why he had come to me, it must be a mistake, I was only interested in English students who had come to Vaud to learn French. He looked at me helplessly as if he did not know how to leave and as a final concession I asked almost angrily, "Well, where were you born?"

"That is the trouble," he said, looking more frightened than ever, "all my family come from Riga but I was born in Moscow while my father was there on a business visit."

He was in trouble. The Americans required people to go on the visa lists not according to nationality but according to where they had been born and I did not even know if a Russian quota existed. But Riga! Ever since my childhood I had dreamed about the city with its associations both with Elizabethan venturers and the amber trade. "I have always wanted to go to Riga," I could not help saying and for the first time he smiled. He then pushed a letter of introduction into my hand. It was signed by one of my friends. "Why didn't you give me this at once?" I asked in some exasperation. "I thought you were a Nazi agent."

"And I thought you might be careless about names."

We both had to laugh and agree that it was not safe to be frank at first. The misunderstanding created a friendship between "Riga" and myself. He came to see me regularly during the next two years and brought me more students to help to safety. I christened him "the Marmot" because he hid in the darkest corner even on a warm summer day, on guard and ready to disappear at any hint of strangers.

1938. The year of Munich, appeasement and shame. I was in England in the spring and warned people so continuously that one friend wrote, "The only suitable ally in any campaign you may wish to undertake would be Winston Churchill. I should be delighted to try to arrange a little dinner or lunch with him any time."

Clio deserted me. I refused. I have never understood how I could have been so stupid. It is a sign of how lightly Churchill was taken at that time that such a meeting should even have been proposed. It could have changed my life had we met because I might have been spared six years of complete frustration during the second war but perhaps it was an object lesson. If a historian is stupid he is more obtuse than anybody else. For some reason I was particularly homesick at that moment for Burier but I missed my opportunity and as usually happens, I was never given a second chance.

I had no feeling that war had been prevented that September. It had merely been postponed. We lost the benefit of the well-trained Czech army, the trust of the stable elements in France and we encouraged the Germans to think that we would accept the most shameful conditions rather than fight. The Luftwaffe used every moment of the extra year to perfect its machines. We did not even trouble to prepare an economic program so that the government wasted a nation's savings in panic in 1939. It is perhaps the most disgraceful chapter in our history and we should never forget it for our own safety. Yet, today, how much do the English remember of that terrible year?

We redoubled our efforts to get our people away but lost our first refugee, he was murdered on his way to Palestine. With others, safety was a matter of hours. Visas, birth certificates, journey money, there was not much time left for historical research. People flocked to me whom I had never seen but I was a soldier in Mithra's army, right was right to me, wrong was wrong and it never occurred to me for a moment that I *dared* do anything but help.

The war drew nearer every day and I wanted one thing for myself. I longed to see the Lapps and persuaded Robert Herring to join me at Stockholm for a trip to Finland. The Marmot who had just got both his visa and diploma suggested that we travel together as far as his native city. We went by Holland because it would have been dangerous to cross the German border and when I met him at the airport, after I had visited some Dutch friends, he was carrying a Siamese kitten in a basket.

My mother had despaired of me for years. "I know you are going to get into serious trouble one day and who will get you out of it?" Still, I was a reasonably law-abiding citizen and the last thought that entered my head as we landed was that we were about to be arrested.

It really was most unpleasant. It had nothing to do with my refugee activities nor with smuggling. It was the kitten. The Marmot had inquired if there were any regulations about animals in transit and had been assured that the restrictions applied only to cattle and dogs. He should have been told that there was a strict law that no living animal could be landed on Swedish soil. We were flung into a whitewashed room and left there for hours. Finally they took me out for questioning, it was quite severe, they went through my luggage item by item and sent me into Stockholm by the last bus to leave that night. Dinner was over by the time that I got to the hotel and Herring had gone out, leaving an angry note. He assumed that I had played a trick on him and had given up the expedition. I went hungrily and gloomily to bed.

The telephone rang the following morning. It was the Marmot. "Are you all right?" he asked in a very sad voice, "They kept me at the airport till midnight and took the kitten into quarantine."

"I got no dinner."

"I want you to have breakfast with me. I hate being alone in the morning and I have heard of a wonderful café. . . ."

"No," I said hastily, "I want breakfast here and now."

"Come with me and I will give you sixpence."

I knew that he had a phobia about being alone at meals. I hesitated, grumbled some more and then joined him in the hall where I insisted upon having my sixpence at once. He possessed a student's guide that really did give the names of restaurants where the food was inexpensive and good but we did not know Stockholm and naturally lost our way. We went back to the hotel, they had finished serving breakfast. I was sunk in gloom, it was almost twenty-four hours since I had had anything to eat. Finally about eleven o'clock we found a place where we could get one small cup of coffee and while we were drinking it the Marmot told me dreamily about his first love affair as a boy; it was, I felt, in the best Russian tradition.

Late that evening two policemen marched down to the Riga boat. The Marmot followed with the kitten in a basket and his luggage. Two tall, stiff policemen brought up the rear. To our intense regret, Herring and I were out on an excursion and missed the spectacle that naturally collected a crowd.

We joined the steamer early the following morning and just as we arrived, the captain stamped angrily into the Marmot's cabin, picked up the basket and took it up on deck. The kitten, it appeared, had howled miserably all night. I next heard my cabin companion, a stern, elderly German, complaining to the steward that she could not share her quarters with a degenerate Englishwoman and I must be moved elsewhere. The ship was full and there were no other berths. She slept that night fully clothed, even to her hat, presumably to escape contamination. Her only concession was to take off a pair of black boots and put on bedroom slippers.

Riga was sleepy and delightful, it was exactly like the pictures that I had seen in my book as a child when we wandered along the cobbled streets under the pointed gables. Our only trouble was hospitality. I do not think I have eaten so much otherwise during a day. "To make up for Stockholm," the Marmot teased as he pressed upon me yet another delicious native dish. In the afternoon he took us to the amber beaches. They smelt of pine and salt and I sat on a log and thought of Apollo and the Nine Muses while I let the sand that was full of crushed scraps of bark sift through my hands. There was still some amber to be found there after the autumn gales.

People kept asking if the Marmot and I were twins. We looked alike when we both wore berets. I am short and built like a Balt although I know now that it is rather my Hitzacker inheritance. We took the plane to Tallinn the following day and spoke at parting of a probable meeting in America. Suddenly, in one of those flashes that come to us all at times, I knew as I waved good-by that I should not see the Marmot for a very long time. He escaped almost at the last hour but we lost trace of each other during the war and I have never seen him again. Yet to have seen Riga was a great advantage to my classical studies, particularly when I wrote *Roman Wall*. We do not know whether a trader made the full journey, it would have taken several years, or whether the news of the coast was passed from tribe to tribe but the amber road and its stories were an integral part of the folk material of Greece.

We flew from Tallinn to Finland. This is no place for a travel diary but what was important on this journey was "the thawing of the ice." We crossed the Arctic Circle on a bus and as I watched the reindeer moving between the birches, I knew that, apart from my refugees, I had been following the wrong path. I did not belong to the literary movements nor even to a particularly intellectual group. I was an Elizabethan who needed action and the sea. I should only become a writer when I returned to my proper material and I wondered why I had wasted so much time. As a beginning, I decided that I would learn to fly.

The first news that we read in the papers at Stockholm was the death of Havelock Ellis. He had been desperately ill for some months, he had fretted against his inactivity and it would have been cruel to wish for his life to be prolonged. Freud made the discoveries but it was Ellis who was a friend. He had replied to my letters within twenty-four hours of receiving them, told me about books and advised me about writing for twenty years. A myth has grown up that he was a fussy old man who compiled lists but had no original ideas. It is a false picture of a very great Englishman. All pioneers face a desperate task. They have to fight ignorance and often persecution of themselves and their followers. They stand in the "shield wall" and therefore have to leave theory to the men who will succeed them. Yet the audacity of their propositions seems so obvious to a second generation that the dangers of the early battles are forgotten. Ellis opened new ways and relieved the anxieties of hundreds of uneasy minds. At least we can offer him respect.

I returned home by way of London to see my mother. People were beginning to be anxious and to talk of air-raid shelters. Doris had bought a bulb farm in a beautiful valley near the Lizard and was developing new daffodils. I arranged for my mother to join her if war broke out until I could get back to England. It was late July when I reached Burier and the peace of the Swiss mountains.

Twenty-one

In Switzerland it was a wonderful summer. The air was so full of light that the sunflowers in the cottage gardens turned the color of corn and the Grammont was darker than its own wild cyclamens above a silver lake. A moment had come when our minds could react to warnings no longer and we sank into an enchanted sleep where nothing mattered except the movement of the grasses and the heat of the earth.

I forgot Clio in these last moments of a disappearing epoch in an adventure of my own. The North had unlocked a door and I took flying lessons at Lausanne. Switzerland is a difficult country for a novice on account of its mountains and few civilians wanted to learn. The instructor landed me a dozen times in quick succession. I thought in my innocence that it was a demonstration of the machine, a little Moth. Afterwards he explained that it was to test my nerves as if I had shown the slightest uneasiness it would have been wasteful to continue the course. It had not occurred to me to be nervous; as I have already written, I belong to the sea and the air. To our mutual astonishment, although my age was against me, I was forty-five, I seemed to get the feel of the plane at once. It was not only having the stick in my hands, I seemed to be using all my senses a new way. It was an affirmation that what I had believed was true and that is always deeply satisfying to the mind. There was a dual control on the Moth but as we went in for my first landing, the instructor remarked cheerfully, "You know, if you make a mistake, there is very little that I can do." Of course there were howls of laughter as I bumped her along the ground but I had the feel of it, "It will be slow but you will learn." Even the engine did not trouble me too much. The instruction book was in French and every section was explained so logically and clearly that for the first time I understood some elementary mechanical rules. It is always easier to learn scientific facts in French. The explanations are clear. It is the reverse with German. Complications are added in that language until the essential facts are hidden under pyramids of words.

The course was thirty lessons. I had barely had four when the aerodrome was closed to civilians. Walter and Melitta Schmideberg, whom I had known in psychoanalytical circles, had arrived for a few days but we seemed to have made a pact not to listen to the news. A cable came from the Marmot, he and his wife were on the high seas, bound for New York. Drums sounded, the Swiss mobilized. Women replaced their husbands in the fields. A guard marched up and down the platform of our little local station. We sat round the radio and heard that England was at war but our own minds were numb. "It was the sight of the first dead," Walter exclaimed, remembering 1914. I seemed to be struggling up the lane in the Isle of Wight towards the post office as if the intervening years had been wiped out with some dark sponge. We had all known so well the inevitable end of appeasement that I am sure that there was a break in the continuity of time and we felt again, quite literally, the utter exhaustion of the earlier conflict.

The march to the consulates began. Traveling was impossible until the French mobilization had ended but it was important for names to be entered early on various lists. I was torn between wishing to remain at Burier and my duty to my mother. She cabled me that she had joined Doris at St. Keverne. Nobody had listened to my warnings in England, I had no particular place there and there might still be ways in Switzerland where I could help.

I had barely time to think about the problem. Another wire came to say that my mother was dangerously ill in the hospital at Truro. Curiously enough, all her life she had dreaded going to Cornwall. I had refused several opportunities to travel in the Far East because I did not want to be far away in case I were needed, "I can always get to you in a day from Switzerland," I had often reassured her. More cables came, she rallied, grew worse, and on September 16th she died. It was merciful that it happened so swiftly because she had always said that she could not bear another war.

I used to think that I was more like my father but now I know better; the fire, the adventure in me, came from my mother's side. I have never had my father's detachment though I may have a little of his prescience and initiative, even a rudiment of his prudence. It is now more than twenty years since my mother died but I still get letters from those of her friends who survive, praising her goodness and speaking of the ways in which she had helped them. Both my parents had great courage. I was a disappointment to them once my childhood was over because I could not accept a number of stupid rules that had, after all, almost deprived them of happiness. It was the inevitable conflict of the generations. Their mark is on me although I am also myself: I try to carry on the essential part of their tradition whilst modifying it to meet the changing times and much of any aid that I have been able to give is directly derived from their influence.

We got our ration cards, we waited for permits. One late September morning the Schmidebergs departed for France in their car and shortly afterwards H. D. left by train. She wanted to return to Perdita and her London apartment. I was now free to choose and decided to remain at Burier but our farewells were easy because I already had a visa to go to England to wind up my mother's affairs, as soon as certain necessary documents were signed.

It was dull. We had few letters, the newspapers were censored and to mark Swiss neutrality we had to listen to the communiqués from both sides on the radio. Otherwise nothing happened; it was the "phony war." Many people said, "You wait, everything will arrange itself" but I knew myself that this was impossible. I studied history. I went for walks with the dogs and also had four refugees at Lausanne who were waiting for their visa numbers and terrified of being interned.

Travel in Europe was still surprisingly easy. I left for Paris by train on December 4th with a permit to stay two months outside Switzerland. I spent the night with Sylvia and Adrienne and at their apartment saw Walter Benjamin for the last time. I was even able to fly on to

England where, apart from a strict blackout, there were few signs that the country was at war.

It was a gloomy visit because I had to store or dispose of my mother's possessions. It was the last time that I went inside the London house that then reverted to my brother. I had no idea where he was. The few necessary business arrangements were made through our lawyers. There was a welcome respite when I went to Cornwall for a few days over the New Year but my Swiss re-entry permit was running out and I was not sorry to leave on January 29th, 1940.

London needed no blackout the evening that I left. A fog had stopped both flying and the buses in the streets. Walter took me to the station by underground, begging me wistfully to give his love to the Grammont. I knew that I should regret the weight but I had added a canvas bag to my suitcase, filled with a few new books. The other passengers in the compartment on the way to Southampton were a boy and girl from the Channel Islands, returning home after the holidays. I often wondered what happened to them afterwards. It had begun to snow by the time that we got to the ship and I went to my bunk at once, suspecting that the trip would be hard. It was rolling when the stewardess woke me up next morning. "Are we nearly in?" I asked. "In! It was much too rough to go out last night, we have only just started. You had better stay where you are."

It was a dreadful trip. I had no seasick pills and I spent the next six hours with my head over a bucket. In addition, I knew that I had lost my connections on to Montreux. Being January, it was almost dark when I struggled up on deck in the late afternoon at Le Havre. The scene was extraordinary. About a hundred English girls in uniform were lined up, waiting to disembark. Each carried a large toy, mostly bears but there were also some kangaroos, with blue ribbon bows tied smartly round their plush necks. All that kept beating through my head was "phony war . . . phony war. . . ." The contrast was too great between the situation as I knew it from my refugees and this make-believe world. Either the women should have been treated as soldiers or they should not have been there in khaki. It was another symptom of the lack of urgency at the time.

A Cockney in front of me stamped and swung his arms. It was very cold. He also kept looking at his watch. If time permitted, he explained to a friend in terms that I had not heard used in the wildest moment of the twenties, he expected to visit the house of a certain madam on his way to the Paris train. I did not mind. It seemed more honest than the teddy bears. Our turn came to disembark at last. I could not hurry, the canvas bag of books was getting heavier and heavier. We waited in queues for buses. Some took taxis but I had not much French money on me and I wanted it for Paris. The signs over the cafés, the harbor smells and the narrow houses kept reminding me of trips to France in childhood. How seldom the first strong impressions of life are obliterated.

Most of the passengers went straight into the station restaurant but although I had had nothing all day but a cup of tea, I thought it was more prudent to find a seat on the train. There was an efficient blackout and the platform was very long. I had to put down my two bags every few yards. Suddenly a man picked up my suitcase, it was the little Cockney who had evidently paid a lightning visit to his madam. "We shall never find the train without some light," he said and produced a tiny torch. He helped me climb up the high steps, installed me in a corner seat and left for the restaurant almost before I had had time to thank him. Just as the train was leaving a group of Englishmen belonging to what we should now call the "Establishment" strode into the compartment and tried to throw me out of my place. There were no reserved seats and I stood up for my rights. If I had shown any weakness, I should have been forced to stand in the bitter cold of a drafty corridor for five or six hours. My Cockney had not spent the hour in Havre in a conventional way but he had been kind. I reflected that as we are told in most of the scriptures of the world, there is more charity to be found among the sinners than the saints.

It was the middle of the night before we got to Paris. I was able to spend a few hours with Sylvia and Adrienne the next day and to visit Marc Allégret to tell him the details of my mother's death, he had always been fond of her, before getting a train on to Montreux. There was snow at Kenwin when I returned and a rush both of refugees and English friends to visit me and hear the latest news.

Spring came, a stork arrived in the neighboring meadow, I worked hard on the history of Vaud. Two of my refugees got their visas and left and I saw more of the English colony, particularly Colonel McPherson and his wife. They had spent thirty years in the wilder parts of India and had fascinating stories to tell of their experiences. He was over seventy and furious that they would not give him a war-time job because of his age.

There was an idea that I might do some work for the French Ministry of Information. I did not suppose I could get a visa for Paris but the consul promised to help me provided "you are back in Switzerland by April 15th." I did not realize the significance of his remark at the time.

France was much gayer than Vaud. I was sent for five days to the Midi and found the same characters on the beaches that had amused us so much in 1938, including an elderly gentleman in shorts and a sunbonnet. I heard a shopkeeper propose a beach suit to a lady, *"une blouse d'un rouge géranium exquis, une toute, toute petite ceinture blanche avec des pantalons bleu aériens, pour rendre un hommage délicat aux drapeaux alliés."* Imagine (as I wrote Kenneth) walking about in flags! Half the population of Bath and Torquay seemed to be sitting outside the cafés, grumbling because there were no cakes. It was a respite to be in the sun again but I felt profoundly uneasy nor did there seem any fixed program for the articles that I was supposed to write. I spent two gay hours, however, one afternoon with Norman Douglas who came over from Antibes. In Paris, Adrienne gave a dinner and I saw Jean Prévost for the last time, he joined the Resistance later and was killed. André Chamson was there on leave and Henri Michaux who amused us all by saying that he had become extremely interested in Buddhism in India. He had believed them really to be saints until he happened to say, *"Et les anglais?"* Then, as he said, looking at me sorrowfully, there was more than an explosion.

I was also invited to a dinner with some journalists. They were polite but there was no real interest in my articles. I sat quietly listening to the conversation, because of my English accent they often thought I could not understand although I could follow every word easily, when one of them said to his neighbor,

"I am leaving for my country house next week."

"Yes, it is about time," the other man replied, "and your food?"

"Oh, stocks enough for three years."

He mentioned the name of the village and I found out afterwards that it was in the Unoccupied Zone so that many in Paris must have known the Armistice terms before the campaign began. I did not link it up fully at the time but I had heard enough to make a full report to the English consul on my return. "You know," he said, "and we know here but will London listen to us? I think the war will last five years."

I listened to the fall of France on the radio. Patriotic speeches and the "Marseillaise" were interspersed with messages asking nurses, radio technicians and engineers to report to Bordeaux. In Switzerland we had no illusions. After my experience in Paris I was not intellectually surprised but it was an emotional shock. I suppose I believed that in a moment of danger France would unite. Unhappily individual courage is not enough in our century of vast battles. It is the steady initial preparation that is needed.

We heard full reports about the Belgian surrender but hardly a word about Dunkirk or Churchill's speeches. When that news finally filtered through I sat in the sun on our flat roof and for the first and only time during the war, I felt profoundly sorry for the Germans. If the Elizabethan spirit had come back to us, their ultimate defeat was certain. The Swiss, however, assured me that there would be two wars. First a patched-up peace and afterwards a second conflict.

The Swiss plan was for their army to retire to prepared positions in the mountains and fight from there if their neutrality were violated. Civilians were to stay in their homes, except for a few technicians. Officials measured the rooms at Kenwin and we were ordered to prepare for refugees. There were no rucksacks nor cycles to be had in the shops. Once a day we were asked on the radio, "Have you got your gas mask, swept your attic, and completed your blackout? Do you know where you air-raid shelter is?" The authorities were more helpful than in England. They issued their orders firmly and sensibly and treated us as adult citizens. Everything in London, I found later, was vague.

There came the day when the Swiss radio warned us of imminent invasion. All the population was invited to resist. We were to disregard any further broadcasts, soldiers not with the army were to fulfill orders previously given to them, civilians were to make sure that they were equipped with brassards bearing the Federal Colors and then turn hoses of boiling water on the enemy. Men lined the bridges and the railway lines ready to blow them up at a moment's notice. I was told afterwards that the main bridge at Basel was to have been destroyed after twelve minutes and it went to eight minutes before the order was countermanded.

Elsie and I got out the hose, we had little fuel so we decided to wait until we knew the Germans had reached our district before we heated the water. We also managed to get hold of some dynamite and arranged it at the entrance. Unfortunately neither of us knew how to detonate it. I cursed the hours I had spent learning German grammar instead of having had an elementary course in explosives.

Resistance cracked in France, the German army swung westwards and our orders were changed. Let nobody think, however, that Switzerland was like France. I was there, I knew and felt the temper of the people, they would have resisted to the last child. I was afterwards through much of the London blitz but the fear of that attack was much less than the dread of an invading army marching on Vevey. I do not think the English realize what it means. I suppose it goes back to an archaic fear of the desecration of the home.

Every day during these anxious weeks, Colonel McPherson visited all the Englishwomen who were living alone to encourage them and see that they were not dispirited. He was an elderly man and when I got back to England, I begged that somebody in authority might send him a word of thanks because it would have been easy for the morale of a number of sick and elderly women to crack if it had not been for his help. It would have been possible then to send him such a note but "the Establishment" would not bother. He died, alas, before I returned in 1946.

It was rumored that all foreigners were to be interned. I burned the papers that had to do with the refugees and most of my other letters and documents. Claudi had puppies the day that Paris fell. The first thing that the vet said to me was, "Don't worry, Madame, I will look after your dog and I will try to send you a blanket to your camp."

I was told semiofficially that I was on the German black list because of my work with the refugees and that I had better try to leave Switzerland. It was impossible. The sun was shining, the lake was at its most beautiful, I had sometimes wanted to die but never less than at that particular moment yet I knew that a neutral nation might not be able to resist German pressure to give up enemy citizens and that I should not be able to hold out against torture. I might disclose valuable names. Yet, believe me, it is not easy to contemplate suicide in cold blood. Drowning was slow, I did not know where to get poison, if I had turned on the gas it might have affected others besides myself. It was not the sages who helped me with their wisdom, it was Petronius. I was a follower of Hannibal, not of Rome, but I reflected that Petronius had probably been ready for death but bored that it had to come to him at just that time. There seemed nothing to do except to jump off a mountain or to open my veins.

Elsie offered me her identity card and suggested concealing me in a village but I refused. There were too many differences to be learned in a few days and detection and punishment of my helpers would have been inevitable. I was then told that there was a plane going out to Belgrade if I could be ready in six hours with a suitcase and a hundred pounds in money. Again it is not an easy thing to leave one's home, knowing that it is probable that one will never see it again, and go without friends into the unknown. The marks are still with me, I cannot accept the conventional world, the emphasis upon new curtains, clothes, a set place in life, I know that these are illusions, they do not really exist. I will not say possessions as a whole, there are certain things that are a part of our personality but they have to be things that belong to us, not acquired because "it is done" or for the neighbors. I knew the landscape round me, so different then from what it is now, and the green and white of Vaud, the clouds above the Grammont and the vines, tugged at the mind when I faced having to leave them.

I went to Geneva. I found that I should have been the only woman and the only person with a nondiplomatic passport in the group and that we should have to travel to England via the Cape. The start was delayed. I was sent back to wait for further instructions. We could not take additional funds out of Switzerland and common sense suggested that a hundred pounds would not be sufficient for such a journey. I had not met any of my fellow travelers but I knew "the Establishment." At the first opportunity they would "ditch the old trout" and I might be stranded for months in some country where perhaps I could not even speak the language. I rang up the next day and declined the chance.

The danger persisted and without a qualm of conscience I plunged into the black market for passports. I learned a great deal that I had never suspected and also, I hope, some humility. When people are fighting for their own lives and for those whom they love, the words "law" and "justice" become empty words. I turned down certain papers where I thought detection probable but was about to buy a certain document when help came from an unexpected quarter.

It is seldom the mighty of this world who come to the rescue in a time of crisis. Years before I had done a service not worth mentioning for a Swiss in a travel agency. I had been able to get through Adrienne a textbook that his son wanted for an examination. He now approached me with the news that a coach was being run from Geneva to Barcelona to take out Swiss export men, South Americans and people with United States visas so that they could reach their destinations from Lisbon. He thought that he could get two seats as I wanted to take Grace with me, a young English student who was the daughter of a friend and who had been put in my charge.

The August days slipped away. Elsie had bought a little house near Lausanne and prepared to move there because we could not get enough fuel to heat Kenwin. All but one of the puppies were distributed to different homes. The grapes began to change color and one morning the telephone rang. Grace and I could go out on the next coach.

One cold September morning we assembled soon after six on the quay at Geneva with our permitted baggage, a suitcase apiece and, according to orders, a rucksack with food for three days. We were four in the English group, none of us wanted to leave, it was Cromwell, not Drake, who was driving us home. It was certainly duty and not inclination that had drawn us to this group of forty-four passengers belonging to fifteen different nationalities, to wait for the "road train," two coaches and a trailer for the luggage. The one thing that we could not do was to sit by the radio and listen if England were to be invaded.

"Those gray English skies," somebody said and we shivered in sympathy.

"Ask me to die for England but do not ask me to live in the British climate," I murmured my own slogan mournfully. If only the coach would start! The swans on the jade green water that stretched as far as Burier were being very bad for my morale. Yet lots of the passengers were excited and happy; there was a boy from Bern going on a student exchange to Boston, several businessmen discussing the prospects of the next skiing season, a Jewish family bound joyfully for Uruguay and an American girl from the consulate at Vienna, going home for leave and transfer. Above all, there was "Toulouse."

"Toulouse" was French but married to a Lausannois. She was going out to fetch her brother who had been released because of wounds from a prisoner-of-war camp. She had the magic papers that so many of us envied, a visa that would allow him to return with her to Vaud for a few weeks of convalescence. She was, as she said, very fortunate, her French relatives had lost everything. We slid back to folk tale as people will on such occasions, if she had a permit she was lucky and we were glad when she was put into our coach between an American student and an Irish priest bound for Trinidad. The front row was Canadian, our row was English, and at the back there were Swiss. A Hungarian diplomat and a number of South Africans were in the forward bus. "It's like the old coaching days," one of my neighbors remarked, as we stowed our rucksacks under the seats.

"There is no turning back now," another said and I tried not to look or think while we drove the few miles to the frontier. The days when an official had waved us through on our way to lunch at Bilignan were over. The first sacrifice in war was contact with friends and I did not know whether Gertrude and Alice Toklas were still in France. I could only think of the long, friendly house with Basket running up the path and Alice following him with a basket on her arm, as the French counted our money and examined our papers. Then, as we were on a collective visa, officials sealed up the coach door with great formality. We were not supposed to set foot on French soil.

"Toulouse" was heartbroken. Everything depended upon *"ces messieurs"* but her official had been kind and she knew that she could have got through another kilo of coffee but now, it was evident, it was too late. Coffee would be worth as much as gold where she was going. Ah, there was only one person to blame for the disaster, *"c'est le français moyen."* He had always been so credulous, so easy-going, so sure that everything would arrange itself and look what had happened! He, and he only, must take the blame. The young American tried to soothe her and the priest nodded.

We were following the road to the coast where the previous summer there had been a caterpillar of cars following each other almost in one movement towards the Mediterranean. Now there were neither cars nor trucks and what was strange, no people. Occasionally, far off, an old man or woman was still working in a field but even the villages were empty and once when we saw a face at a window, it was blank with misery and despair. There was no food displayed for sale and no hens pecking among the barns.

We drew up in a side street of Grenoble. The driver walked down the coach announcing that we had an hour for lunch just as if we were holidaymakers on an excursion. Several of us started to reach for our rucksacks but he laughed. A passenger helped him to lift a panel at the side, leaving the sealed door intact. We scrambled out and he led us into a restaurant where tables had been prepared for our arrival. This was certainly an escape de luxe.

The place was full of French, they did not look up at us, they argued. Two young women, I judged that they were teachers from the local school, discussed some problem of the moment in vehement whispers. There were many officers but these were silent. The wall was hung with lists. People were asking for information about missing members of their families. I had often imagined a defeated town when I had been reading history. The reality was different. It was the ordinary routine of a meal combined with helplessness that had to be experienced, as if a clock struck "every day . . . every day . . ." instead of the hour, and time was meaningless.

They gave us melon, a small piece of tough chicken and grapes. There was no bread. We felt guilty about taking it from the inhabitants but the driver insisted that they wanted the money. He beckoned, we got back into our seats and drove away, hoping that Cromwell was right and that there was virtue in duty. Switzerland seemed not a land but an epoch distant. To cheer us up or herself, "Toulouse" began describing a previous holiday in France. It had consisted, it seemed, of eating. There had been an evening when she had had to take three *spécialités* one after the other or hurt the innkeeper's feelings and the lunch when she had only had an omelette, *"c'était un rêve,"* she declared, *"des choses à tomber par terre tellement c'était bon"* although she had had to lie in a chair for two hours afterwards before she could continue her journey.

Suddenly everyone jumped, some from curiosity, others from fear. A patrol of German soldiers in helmets dashed past us on motorcycles. "But this is the Unoccupied Zone," a man behind me declared in a puzzled voice and we all laughed.

"Oh, the victors ride where they like," another passenger answered. It was not a pleasant experience and my morale felt like a ball of lead. We came to a house and a wrecked bridge that the French had blown up themselves during the final days of the fighting but afterwards we drove for hours through a peaceful but deserted landscape until we pulled up about seven between the wall of a Provençal vineyard and a stretch of wild lavender. *"Le pique-nique,"* the driver remarked as he unscrewed the side panel once more and we streamed out to stretch our legs and eat our sandwiches, sheltering behind a small hedge from a sharp, autumn wind. Each of us asked the driver in turn what chance we had of crossing the Spanish frontier. On most trips, somebody was turned back. Sometimes they picked out the English, sometimes the choice seemed haphazard, once they had had to leave a diplomatic courier behind. He shrugged his shoulders and told us to hope.

"Why didn't you go back via Italy?" We stared at the speaker, an American woman with a seagull wing across her hat who had already announced that she had been so absorbed by her studies for a thesis on the Council of Trent that she had neglected warnings to take a steamer in February. We wondered if she were making fun of us. "But we're at war with Italy," one of my English companions gasped.

"Oh, Mussolini is such a kind man. If you had written him, he would have sent you a safe-conduct and you could have sailed from Genoa."

None of us could think of an adequate reply but the driver remarked, he must have felt that his passengers were getting out of hand, that on the previous trip they had had to sleep on the sand, *"et le mistral soufflait."* Today we had made good time and we should all sleep in beds.

We brushed the crumbs from our clothes and I wondered whether I should ever smell wild lavender again. It was growing dark, the lights failed on our coach and it was eleven o'clock before we clattered into a city. I had not known where we were to spend the night but caught the name. "Cette? Is it Cette?" I asked and when someone said yes crossly because we were all very tired, I felt suddenly exhilarated. I, of all people, should have been aware of the power of poetry but I should never have believed, if I had not experienced it, how much the name of Valéry and being in his birthplace could mean at such a lonely and uncertain moment.

They called us at five, we left at six and drove to Narbonne where we had a cup of coffee and a slice of bread sitting outside a crowded café. Somebody remembered that the district was famous for its honey but we told him indignantly not to remind us of food. People were more interested here, they talked to some of the Swiss and "Toulouse" left us to take a train to her native town. "A nice girl," the American student said, waving violently, "she certainly was a nice girl." It then appeared that we had a problem on our hands, a Jewish girl totally without papers except for a permit to join her parents in Palestine. She was green with fright and unable to speak so we wondered what sort of impression she would make upon the officials. I thought of the human misery that I had seen during the preceding years. Peace is as cruel as war but it is easier to dissemble about it.

"What shall we do if we are sent back to France and have no visas?"

Nobody answered, we had been thinking about such a possibility all morning.

"I think we ought to make a plan."

"It is much better not to fuss about it till it happens." It was what I felt myself and I was glad when the driver beckoned us and we started off towards Perpignan. I had never felt at home either in the Riviera or Provence but this stretch of France was new to me and in spite of the ordeal ahead I felt drawn into its atmosphere and its landscape of sandy, aromatic plants. I remembered that Narbonne had been one of the great Roman cities and that the Carthaginians might have passed there on their way from Spain. Suddenly everybody began to stir, we climbed a hill, rounded a curve, and pulled up at Perthuis.

It was eleven when we got out of our friendly Swiss coaches and nine when we left Port Bou on the Spanish side that evening. We spent the intervening hours first in going through the exit formalities in

France, then sitting on the curb to eat a rucksack lunch and finally boarding the buses that were really converted trucks to go to the next frontier. We suspected that our vehicles had been used in the Civil War and the American student looked everywhere for bullet holes. It was up this road that the mass of refugees had struggled during the final days.

The formalities were endless. Papers, money, tickets to our destination to prove that we were not staying in Spain, were checked and rechecked. I was lucky. There was a German standing behind each Spanish official but Grace was both a pretty girl and partly Irish, and Ireland and Spain were traditionally friends. They joked with her for a moment and let her pass together with myself as chaperone.

We sat down, again on the pavement. Now that we were "through" we could wonder about the others. The remaining English presently appeared and to our joy, the Jewish girl joined us, her permit trembling in her hands but safe. For the first time, by some miracle, nobody was stopped although they questioned the American with the seagull hat for almost an hour. They were suspicious of her thesis. "I kept telling them that the Council of Trent had nothing to do with contemporary Spain but they would not believe me," she grumbled, sucking a raw egg that with biscuits was all that she would eat during the journey. She was so indignant that she smashed one egg over her bunch of keys.

We waited in silence as refugees do, trying to be as inconspicuous as possible. The priest and the young American, with much daring, scrambled down to wash in a little stream. Sunset came, a boy with a flock of goats strolled down the hill, it was the essence of the Mediterranean, a ragged herdsman, olives and a little water. Again I wondered if I should ever come back to the South. There were false alarms, orders not to move, and it was dark before we were hustled suddenly into the coaches and driven towards the next village. The drivers got out there for a meal but few of us had any Spanish money and sleep now seemed more important than food. We envied a Swiss who had brought his sleeping bag with him and was curled up on a back seat for *"une petite nuit de dix à douze heures."* Mrs. Seagull of the Council of Trent restored herself to favor by uttering our collective thoughts, "Next time I sit in the middle of Europe in a frontier town, I will do the organization myself." She had had a dream, she continued, of a new passport system, a blanket worn across the back and that could easily be punched with holes at every boundary. We talked to keep ourselves awake and the American girl from the consulate told us that she had tried at first to get away by Petsamo. I could hardly believe that I had seen wild reindeer in its forests during my lifetime as I explained to her that it was not a town but a state.

The moon was full, the houses were dark but at the entrance to every village, electric lights blazed above a police post, and we were stopped while they checked our papers. If only we could sleep and stretch our legs, we muttered, many of us had cramp. It was three in the morning, twenty-one hours after leaving Cette, when we drove into Barcelona.

We had been warned to go out as little as possible so we stayed in the hotel next day except for walking to the agency to check our tickets on to Lisbon. It was in the middle of an immense, deserted avenue. A herd of cows crossed the tram line, as lean as their drivers. We were surprised to see English newspapers only a week old as none had reached us in Switzerland after June. People were sitting crowded against the walls and I wondered at first if it were a feast day. Then we saw to our horror that their faces were literally green, they did not look up as we passed them, they were dying from starvation. I was in some bad raids afterwards but I have seldom seen a more appalling sight. There was nothing that we could do, we had very little money on us, it would have gone nowhere divided among so many, and we felt miserable and helpless.

One of the Swiss who knew the town and spoke some Spanish slipped away and went to see his friends. He would not talk when he returned except to say that conditions were far worse than he had supposed. It seemed strange to be caught up in the results of one war on our way to the middle of another one. I heard two Germans talking in the bedroom next to mine and grabbed my notebook. They were having an ordinary business conversation but it seemed important at that time to write it down. It was stale by the time that I reached England.

We slept a lot, repacked our bags and talked in the courtyard. The staff of the hotel kept trying to do small services for us, we were puzzled at first but then a porter, who spoke a little English, explained. "We are sorry, we know what you are going to." It was the first time that people had spoken to us about the reality of the situation. "They were bombed here as well," I reminded Grace. They were not interested in money as tips but accepted gratefully the remnants of the three-days-old food from our rucksacks.

We assembled at the air terminal the following morning. The place was full of German advertisements and a German remarked politely to us that we had got on the wrong bus. We transferred ourselves hastily to one that seemed even more jerky and battle-scarred as we jolted towards the aerodrome. The road was narrow and dusty and we had to make our way against an incoming stream of mule carts with high wheels, full of clover. There were sunburnt boys sleeping on top of the loads and we suspected that their slumber was due more to weakness from lack of food than to the heat or the monotonous pace of their beasts.

The tiny garden round the airport building was full of dark red oleanders. We went through the customs again as if we were holiday-makers except that we had to exchange any Spanish money that we had over for French notes, apart from ten pesetas each that we were told to keep for lunch. Outside a big plane was just taking off for Las Palmas and Germany. I walked up and down the sandy path remembering with fury the English who had laughed at me in 1936 when I had told them that the Civil War was simply a rehearsal for their own destruction. Prophecy, however, even if fulfilled is cold consolation. Nothing can undo the misery nor bring back the dead.

A German officer at my side chattered gaily to his neighbor about the Western Front and the inadequacy of schoolboy French. His civilian suit was too small for him and he carried his sword tied up in a brown paper parcel. It really looked very odd. His companion remarked that it made him ill with laughter to watch the English filing onto the aircraft. We understood why a few moments later. The line was supposed to be Spanish but it was a German plane with an Italian pilot and of the eight passengers four were English and three Canadian. It was a peculiar war and as I remarked to Grace, we must get over our prejudices. It is useless traveling in wartime if one is narrow-minded.

Our Italian pilot was affable and pointed out the landmarks. I could only think of a porcupine as we looked at the country below us, the rocks stood out like spines in a landscape of black and red speckled granite. In front of Madrid, traces of the fighting and many trenches were plainly visible. It brought back Paris and the discussions that we had had at that time and I wondered where my French friends were now. Scattered, in camps or dead?

We sat at the Madrid Airport for a couple of hours and, as always in Spain, I felt trapped and uneasy. Our lunch appeared to have been cooked in kerosene and when we left we actually had a German pilot. "At least we can say that the Germans flew us home," I whispered but by now we were too absorbed by our own problems to notice much of the countryside. It was sunset and four days after leaving Geneva when we landed at Lisbon Airport. How little did we know that our troubles were not over but about to begin in earnest.

I have never been interested in popular fiction but I have to admit that it is truer to life than philosophical speculation. I myself should not dare to write about the Lisbon I observed in the autumn of 1940, people would say that the incidents were too improbable. Actually they were not, they happened. The first night that we were there our suitcases were searched, I had thought that this might occur so took my papers with me and arranged my things so that I should know if they had been disturbed. The next morning we were told that our reservations to England were canceled. We had only been allowed to bring a limited amount of money out of Switzerland and some had been spent on the journey, we could get no funds from England and so we kicked our heels for days on the Lisbon sands, too poor even to buy a Portuguese newspaper.

If we had been tourists who had disregarded official warnings our fate would have been unpleasant but comprehensible. Most of us had left homes and friends, however, under the mistaken impression that our services might be valuable in England; some were business representatives engaged in the supposedly valuable export trade, others were there at what amounted to a command from the English consuls. We had no help from British sources during the weeks that we were stranded but were treated as if we were criminals. The British Institute had closed for the holidays. This was perfectly normal for an ordinary year but the circumstances in 1940 were somewhat different. We could not even borrow a book to read from its well-stocked shelves. Strangers were put into the same room, dormitory fashion, and then asked three pounds a day at the hotels. We were not allowed to sleep on the beach. I certainly learned the lesson that patriotism and honesty were crimes and I have had much sympathy with lawbreakers ever since. "There was bound to be disorganization," the people said. This was no excuse. A couple of officials could have prepared a comprehensive scheme after Munich and sent directives to each consulate for use when needed.

One of our group was flown back at once because of her health. I cabled to relatives in America and thus obtained a few dollars, these I shared with Grace and the other Englishwoman who had come out with us from Geneva. I first deducted enough to oil the wheels so that we could get our exit permits and then at her suggestion we went to Estoril. The season there was over and we found two rooms in a pension for a third of the price that they were asking in Lisbon. There was a heat wave raging, unprecedented even in Portugal, and as we knew the English climate we had packed our thickest winter clothes in our single suitcases and found life decidedly uncomfortable. I enjoyed the spectacle for about two days of the female missionaries (there were so many of them) having to share tables and rooms with voluble members of the underworld. Then the *surréalisme* of the atmosphere became boring, the reasonably normal are much less fatiguing in a time of crisis. Every other person was an agent of some sort and we soon lost interest as to whether they were spying for Germany, for the Allies or as so often happened, both together. Nobody need ever tell me what a gold-rush town was like. I know and I hope *never* to have to repeat the experience. Yet against this thriller background Lisbon itself was a city of light, there was a beautiful model of a galleon of the time of Henry the Navigator in the Exhibition that we could only afford to visit once and at sunset the sky was a luminous gold dissolving in puffs of cloud above the roofs.

We suffered most from lack of news. I had only dared bring one book with me, Lyall's *Twenty-Five Languages of Europe,* but it was invaluable. We could occasionally pick up a Portuguese newspaper from the beach that somebody had thrown away and, with the help of this book and French, decipher the headlines. Some of the worst bombing seemed to have happened in the area where H. D. lived. What should I find when we got to London?

The apathy that had astonished me among the refugees invaded my own mind. "They" had got me into this, it was not my fault, I had warned people that there was going to be a war, now "they" ought to look after me. It was really a form of paralysis and something that I have never been able to make an ordinary person understand. We become citizens through self-denial and much hard work. If this is no longer recognized, if everything of value is swept away, the result is anarchy. I know that there was a difference between the refugees and myself, I was going home once I got to England, I had my language and they had lost theirs but I do not think that anybody who has had even the mildest of such experiences will ever be the same person again. The majority of the conventions will no longer matter.

I realized that I had to take action at once. We discovered that our chances of getting home depended upon the Clipper being late, the plane that was on the regular line between America and Portugal and that connected at Lisbon with the service to England. If it did not arrive in time, there were places for a few of the refugees. I organized a watch at the air office. We went to Lisbon every afternoon and two of us took it in turn to sit there from four to seven. I was also heartless. One of the clerks admired the girl who had come with us from Geneva. "Flirt with him," I begged, "keep him interested."

We went in day after day for three weeks. One evening the Clipper did not arrive. Our names were low on the waiting list but we were there with our passports, tickets and exit permits. Our friend, emotion in her voice and face, won over the clerk. "Be here tomorrow morning at six," he said and we dashed back to Estoril for our baggage. The lights were shining in the darkness, the warm evening smelled of spices spread on tables in the open air and in one of those moments of prescience that we sometimes have, I knew that it would be years before I saw the South again or really felt the sun.

We boarded the seaplane at dawn and now that we were about to leave, we could admire the harbor once more and the stretch of silver water that we could hear splashing at the take-off against the blacked-out windows. It was dull for an hour or two, then we ran into a storm.

Some idiot had once told me seaplanes were steady. I cursed him for a little but eventually the ability to think or move left me. We were all airsick and there was a serious shortage of paper bags. A message passed that we could not land at the usual airport on account of a raid. None of us cared.

We splashed down in complete darkness at a port in southern England whose name I never discovered. It may have been Poole. They helped us into a hall for interrogation and customs. The navy was running it and the officials were kind, speedy and efficient. Then we were piled into a bus, taken to a hotel and warned not leave it as we were in a restricted area. The pilot joined us and asked if we were now all right. It had been such a bumpy trip that he himself had felt airsick.

We were sent to London by the first train next morning. We stopped several times on the journey, there had been air-raid damage, the censored newspapers might just as well not have been printed.

It was midday when I reached Lowndes Square where H. D. lived. She had gone out to lunch. The last news that she had received from me had been a cryptic telegram on our arrival in Lisbon. "Oh, Bryher is coming over with the invasion barges" had been Osbert Sitwell's comment on the situation.

I sat gloomily on my suitcase outside the front door, trying to realize that I had reached London. It was natural to wonder what was going to happen. I felt resentful and (a sin in English eyes) bitter. "I warned you," I murmured, looking at the blacked-out windows, "I warned you but you would not listen." Here I was, aged forty-six, forced back into the cage and misery of the first war and I had no illusions that the second one would soon be over. I felt a little better when Hilda came up the staircase a few minutes afterwards to look at me in astonishment. She took me immediately to show me the pile of sand kept ready to throw on incendiaries. Many of my friends, I found, were scattered about England but at least I was with the people I loved. Our real wishes emerge in such a moment of peril; let my dedication at need be "the heart to Artemis" because it was only the days among the islands and my first probing of the air that seemed to matter now as the sirens started, the guns began, and we went with our blankets to the shelter downstairs.

Index

313

314

Weiss, Gertrude, 259
West (Bryher), 200
Weston, Jessie L., 135, 136, 137, 139
Whyte-Melville, George John, 54
Williams, William Carlos, 218
Willie (pupil of Bryher's first governess), 41, 46
Woolf, Virginia, 16, 236
Woolford, Miss, 194
Worthing, 8-9, 11, 13

Wyss, Johann David, 279

Yeats, Jack Butler, 198
Yeats, W. B., 194-95, 214
Young Fur Traders, The (Ballantyne), 94

Zennor, 192
Zermatt, 91, 93
Zola, Emile, 14, 16